The Brown Envelope Book

Poetry and prose on experiences
of unemployment, the benefits system,
disability and work capability
assessments

Selected and edited by
Alan Morrison and **Kate Jay-R**

with a Foreword by
John McArdle
of the **Black Triangle Campaign**

Caparison

In collaboration with **Don't Go Breaking Our Arts**

First published in 2021 by
Caparison
imprint of *The Recusant*
www.therecusant.org.uk
in collaboration with
Don't Go Breaking Our Arts Facebook group
and Culture Matters Co-Operative Ltd.
www.culturematters.org.uk

Printed in Consolas font by
Severnprint Ltd
Ashville Industrial Estate
Bristol Road
Gloucester, GL2 5EU

Selected and edited by Alan Morrison and Kate Jay-R
All typesetting, layout and design by Alan Morrison © 2021

ISBN 978-1-8384966-1-6

Contents

Preliminaries

Poems and prose

Acknowledgments

*'One cannot but wonder at this constantly recurring phrase 'getting
something for nothing,' as if it were the peculiar and perverse ambition of
disturbers of society. Except for our animal outfit, practically all we have
is handed to us gratis. Can the most complacent reactionary flatter himself
that he invented the art of writing or the printing press, or discovered
his religious, economic and moral convictions, or any of the devices which
supply him with meat and raiment or any of the sources of such pleasure as
may derive from literature or the fine arts? In short, civilization
is little else than getting something for nothing.'*

— James Harvey Robinson

*'They could not bear to see the unemployed men and their wives and
children starving. In order to prevent hardship, they felt that they had
to provide these people with some means of sustenance. Their principles
told them, nevertheless, that if people were given something for nothing,
it would demoralize their character. ...they were faced with the horrible
choice of (1) letting the unemployed starve, or (2) destroying their
moral character... They decided to give the unemployed families "relief
payments"... (They considered using the English term "dole", but with
their characteristic American penchant for euphemism, they decided on the
less offensive term). To make sure that the unemployed would not take their
unearned payments for granted, however, they decided that the "relief"
was to be accompanied by a moral lesson: to wit: the obtaining of the
assistance would be made so difficult, humiliating, and disagreeable that
there would be no temptation for anyone to go through the process unless
it was absolutely necessary; the moral disapproval of the community would
be turned upon the recipients of the money at all times in such a way that
they would try hard to get "off relief" and "regain their self-respect".
Some even proposed that people on relief be denied the vote, so that the
moral lesson would be more deeply impressed upon them. Others suggested
that their names be published at regular intervals in the newspapers...'*

— S.I. Hayakawa
'The Story of A-town and B-ville: Second Semantic Parable',
Language In Thought And Action (1949)

This book is dedicated to

Erik Zoha
(1 April 1968-15 April 2021)

who sadly passed away during its production.
He was a founding member of the Facebook group
Don't Go Breaking Our Arts
(formerly Nothing4Something)
whose name he helped to create.

Against Moral Anaesthesia

John McArdle
of the Black Triangle Anti-Defamation Campaign

Q&A

John, what first prompted you to start up the Black Triangle Anti Defamation Campaign?

Back in 2010 a virulent campaign against benefit claimants was mounted by the government and the right-wing media in Britain. Disabled claimants were demonised and dehumanised as 'scroungers' and fraudsters. All the while, the DWP's own official figures showed that disability benefit fraud was a mere 0.7% of total claims.

The right-wing propaganda campaign was so successful that, when canvassed, the general public estimated that 34 times more benefit money was claimed fraudulently than official estimates: the public thought that £24 out of every £100 spent on benefits is claimed fraudulently, compared with official estimates of £0.70 per £100.

Meanwhile, as the coalition government sought to scapegoat claimants for the public deficit following the financial crisis of 2010 implementing the most savage and brutal programme of public spending cuts in British history, bankers – who behaved criminally and who caused the crisis – were bailed out with public money and the richest national and multinational corporations were allowed to get away with tax avoidance to the tune of 70 times the annual cost of official benefit fraud estimates. Of course, Europe has seen this sort of thing before in the Great Depression of the 1930s. Disabled people were blamed then too.

Owing to the introduction of the Work Capability Assessment regime – first introduced under New Labour's Gordon Brown and James Purnell – scores of reports started reaching us of the deaths of disabled people as a direct consequence of having had their benefits unlawfully cut off.

We saw that it was imperative to document and publicise what was happening to people and to fight back against the tsunami of falsehood that had swept Britain, poisoning people's minds and enabling these flagrant abuses of the fundamental human rights of disabled people – not least the very right to life itself – to take place with official sanction in plain sight. The mass media ignored it. It was left up to us as disabled people to take the fight to the government ourselves. To have remained silent was to give in to this culture of death and to be complicit.

At first people simply didn't believe it.

Our task was to state the empirical facts. Truth had perished in the public square along with so many of our dead.

Why the Black Triangle?

Black Triangle Campaign's banner reads 'Disabled People Fighting For Our Future: Custodians of Our Past'.

"Remembrance without resolve is a hollow gesture. Awareness without action changes nothing".

We must never allow our memorialisation of the victims of the Holocaust to be merely symbolic. We must not deny our acts of remembrance the power to gift us with the ability to truly honour the lives of all the victims by learning the lessons of its history in order that we may resolve to better recognise and oppose the reemergence of ideas, ideologies and patterns of behaviour that gave rise to that descent into unbridled evil, barbarism and cold blooded murder on a scale that was unprecedented in human history.

We have learned from Holocaust studies that in order for a group, party or government to carry out immoral actions, attacks and murders against another group it is first necessary to 'other' that group and dehumanise them.

This makes it psychologically possible for otherwise 'normal' people to participate in those acts either as 'perpetrators' as enablers or 'bystanders'.

The machinery of the State can then proceed unhindered in crushing the victim group with little or no regard to normative social values. Acts that clearly violate the fundamental human rights of the individuals thus become officially sanctioned and normalised.

The Black Triangle was an assignation given to prisoners in the vast network of concentration camps of the Third Reich. It was a broad category that included homeless people, alcoholics, unemployed people who were labelled 'workshy' ('Arbeitscheu'); conscientious objectors, draft dodgers, pacifists, Roma and Sinti people, and many others who were considered to be 'unproductive' and a drain on the Nazi State's resources.

At the inception of the Holocaust disabled people were branded "useless eaters" and "life unworthy of life" for whom a campaign of euthanasia was the greatest kindness that the state could accord to the victims' 'miserable lives'.

An article published by the UK Holocaust Memorial Trust succinctly summarises what happened during Aktion T-4 [https://www.hmd.org.uk/learn-about-the-holocaust-and-genocides/nazi persecution/disabled-**people**/] and here are the most germane excerpts:

Severely mentally and physically disabled people, as well as those perceived to have disabilities, were targeted because of Nazi beliefs that disabled people were a burden both to society and to the state.

From 1939 to 1941 the Nazis carried out a programme of 'euthanasia', known as the T4 programme. The name T4 is an abbreviation of Tiergartenstrasse 4, the address from which the programme was coordinated.

Propaganda against the mentally disabled: in 1933 the Law for the Prevention of Hereditarily Diseased Offspring was passed, allowing for the forced sterilisation of those regarded as 'unfit'. This included people with conditions such as epilepsy, schizophrenia and alcoholism. Prisons, nursing homes, asylums, care homes for the elderly and special schools were targeted to select people for sterilisation. It has been estimated that between 1933 and 1939, 360,000 individuals were subjected to forced sterilisation.

In 1939 the killing of disabled children and adults began. All children under the age of three who had illnesses or a disability, such as Down's Syndrome, or cerebral palsy, were targeted under the T4 programme. A panel of medical experts were required to give their approval for the 'euthanasia', or supposed 'mercy-killing', of each child...

...Following the outbreak of war in September 1939 the programme was expanded. Adults with disabilities, chronic illnesses, mental health problems and criminals who were not of German origin were included in the programme. Six killing centres were established to speed up the process – the previous methods of killing people by lethal injection or starvation were deemed too slow to cope with large numbers of adults. The first experimental gassings took place... thousands of disabled patients were killed in gas chambers disguised as shower rooms...

It is estimated that close to 250,000 disabled people were murdered under the Nazi regime.

After the cessation of the secret Aktion T4 programme following an outcry by the Catholic Archbishop of Gallen physically and/or mentally impaired 'unproductive' people were simply dispatched to other killing centres and death camps.

But what has the machinery of systematic mass murder got to do with the deaths of disabled people under the UK government's welfare reform programme?

Those of you who have seen the film *Schindler's List* will be familiar with the adage "Whoever destroys a soul it is considered as if he destroyed an entire world. And whoever saves a life it is considered as if he saved an entire world" (Jerusalem Talmud Sanhedrin 4.1 22a).

All lives are infinitely precious and sacred. Propaganda and falsehoods disseminated by government ministers and the right wing media in our country branding sick and disabled people as benefit cheats are an attack on the dignity of the individual and end up costing lives. This is a lesson that humanity should have learned from the holocaust yet we see exactly the same sort of scapegoating today in our own country. This is why we have fought tooth and nail during the past decade to destroy this campaign of defamation with empirical facts and figures exposing the wrong that is being done to us in the name of the electorate. The people of this country.

I think we and our allies have achieved a large degree of success as we see far less of this poisonous rhetoric in the public sphere than we did during the first five years of the Coalition government when it was absolutely wall to wall as a Google search for the term 'scrounger' in our news media for those years will instantly reveal. We have succeeded in changing public perceptions of disabled people but we have not gained the requisite support and influence to change the public policies which we submit have amounted to nothing less than democide.

Democide is when a government causes the death of a person through reckless and wanton disregard for their life. That is what the UK Government has done since they came to power in 2010 and continues to do until such time that they accede to our demand for immediate systemic change to this country's disability assessment regime.

Our campaign's collating and contribution of hard case evidence of the mass immiseration and death of disabled people caused by the UK Government's welfare reforms was instrumental in the fight of disabled people's organisations throughout the UK is gaining international recognition of our plight by the United Nations Human Rights council whose Committee on the Rights of Persons with Disabilities declared in 2017 that the UK was guilty of 'grave and systematic violations' of the fundamental human rights of disabled people. The Chair of the committee singled out the DWP's work capability assessment regime carried out by Atos Healthcare Ltd as a 'human catastrophe' for disabled people in Britain and Northern Ireland.

The UN report managed to make the headlines for a couple of weeks. It was dismissed offhand by the government who, in typically Orwellian style and flying in the face of the overwhelming, irrefutable, damning evidence maintained that they were 'world leaders' in disability rights.

What are the main objectives of the Black Triangle campaign?

'Educate. Agitate. Organise.'
We are first and foremost a human rights campaign.
A primary objective of our campaign is to educate the general public about disability history and what happened to disabled people during the Holocaust so that society will be able to resist propaganda campaigns based on falsehoods that endanger the lives of disabled people. On a broader level we campaign for the day when the UN Convention of the Rights of Persons with Disabilities will be

incorporated into domestic law so that it will be fully enforceable by the courts. The Scottish Government has already set a course to do this though its 'legal competence' to do so is being challenged by the UK Government who assert that it is constitutionally ultra vires or beyond its authority under the current constitutional settlement.

We are fighting for a just, fair and inclusive society where each and every life is treasured and treated as infinitely precious and sacred, independently of market values.

Without education, people are ill-equipped to see through false narratives and political spin. Educated, independent, questioning minds are vital in a healthy, functioning democracy.

We hope and we believe that the majority of human beings, in spite of their many political, religious, economic and social differences agree that certain kinds of behaviour are wrong and must be eliminated in a free, democratic and civilised society.

We believe that, when put into possession of the empirical facts, most people - not all - and there exists a large number of those who will believe extremist propaganda and who will perpetuate oppression regardless - are fair-minded and compassionate. They have the ability to see wrongdoing and to oppose it.

Agitate.

Positive social change and progress does not emerge out of a vacuum.

It requires concerted effort, resolve and above all persistence. It requires working together throughout civil society in solidarity for change.

First, to objectify and highlight the injustices suffered and taking place before our eyes.

Second, to demand justice from those in power. Power concedes nothing without a demand. These are our rights, not 'privileges' and as such they are non-negotiable.

Agitation literally means 'to shake things up': we join together to protest and argue our case in every public forum of struggle, be that in the streets, at Parliament, DWP outsourced assessment centres, the mass print and broadcast media, in every national and international forum such as the UN in order to achieve the change we so desperately need.

Organise.

When faced with seemingly insurmountable injustice it is too easy to throw one's hands in the air and say "I give up!". Giving up is simply not an option because people's lives are at stake. This is when we come together to empower each other through organising.

Have you anything you wish to say about *The Brown Envelope Book* and how you came to be its patron?

To almost every disabled person living in Britain today a brown envelope landing on their doormat hangs over them like the legendary Sword of Damocles – a sword that was suspended over the head of the obsequious courtier Damocles by a single horse hair by a king in order to teach him a lesson about the precariousness of happiness.

A Sword of Damocles is a thing or situation which causes a prolonged psychological mindset of impending doom. A harbinger of catastrophic misfortune, destitution and even death.

This is no hyperbole: it has been validated by the findings published in a recent academic paper entitled 'Violent Bureaucracy: a critical analysis of the British public employment service' (Jamie Redman and Del Fletcher, Critical Social Policy, Jan 2021, (http://shura.shu.ac.uk/28060/)

The main gist of this paper, according to an article published on *Disability New Service* (John Pring, 1 April 2021, https://www.disabilitynewsservice.com/dwp-staff-admit-inflicting-psychological-harm-on-claimants-during-coalition-years/), is that

Department for Work and Pensions (DWP) staff and managers deliberately inflicted psychological harm on benefit claimants, engaged in unofficial sanctioning targets, and pushed disabled people into work despite the risk to their health, shocking new testimony has revealed.

The evidence comes from new interviews with 10 civil servants who worked for the Department for Work and Pensions (DWP) and its contractors under the coalition government between 2010 and 2015.

They spoke – on the condition of strict anonymity – to academics from Sheffield Hallam University, who have now shown how the introduction of a more punitive social security system, with harsher benefit sanctions and conditionality, inflicted years of "institutional violence" on claimants between 2010 and 2015.

The authors, Dr Jamie Redman and Professor Del Roy Fletcher, believe it is the first time that research has explained how DWP workers have been able to commit such harmful acts on benefit claimants in vulnerable and precarious situations.

The two academics built on the work of the Polish sociologist Zygmunt Bauman, who described how modern bureaucracies can produce psycho-social factors that enable ordinary people to carry out harmful practices.

They describe how a change in DWP policy through the new Conservative Liberal Democrat coalition government elected in May 2010 pressured DWP staff to refer more claimants to have their benefits sanctioned.

The policy changes also saw the performance of jobcentre staff measured by "off-benefit flows" – the number of claimants who stopped receiving an out-of-work benefit – even if those people had not secured a job.

This helped lead to a huge increase in sanctioning rates between 2010 and 2013 – reaching more than one million sanctions in 2013 and rising about

345 per cent above their 2001-08 average level.

For their research, Redman and Fletcher interviewed a JobcentrePlus (JCP) manager; three JCP front-line staff members; one Work Programme front line worker who had previously worked for JCP; one DWP decision-maker; and four Work Programme front-line staff.

They were told how "top-down" pressure on staff – through sanctioning tables and off-flow targets that were "legitimised" by the government – acted as a "moral anaesthetic" which "made invisible the needs and interests" of the claimants they were sanctioning.

This allowed workers to view their caseloads with what Bauman called "ethical indifference".

One JCP worker described how staff would often treat claimants with "disrespect" and use psychological harm as a technique to reduce the number of people claiming benefits, "pushing them until they either just cleared off because they couldn't take the pressure or they got sanctioned".

An executive officer in another JobcentrePlus office also said that some staff tried to antagonise claimants in the hope that they would drop their claims...

One manager tried to persuade staff to sanction more claimants by telling them: "It's your money! It's your taxes that they're living off! You know, you should be sanctioning them!"

One of those interviewed said that this kind of "stigmatising" language became increasingly common in formal meetings.

But these tactics were not restricted to JCP offices.

Those who worked for outsourced Work Programme providers, who were under financial pressure to find job "outcomes" for claimants, described how managers pressured them to "push" disabled people into work.

One former Work Programme adviser told the research team: "[I had] a lovely guy who I really felt for who had mental health issues and the day after I had to reluctantly mandate him to something – he attempted suicide. "I also had another lady who we pushed into work and it made her that ill she had a fit in her new job and was admitted to hospital." Another Work Programme adviser said that some colleagues seemed to thrive on their ability to inflict harm and "enjoyed the stick".

In their paper, 'Violent Bureaucracy', published last week in *Critical Social Policy*, Redman and Fletcher describe how the government and media had created and promoted a "hostile" environment for claimants, with the help of frequent "scrounger rhetoric" designed to blame claimants for austerity. This laid the groundwork for the introduction of a more punitive welfare-to-work system, with harsher sanctions and conditionality, and allowed the institutional violence of the DWP regime to thrive. Their research, they write, "seeks to explain how ordinary people carrying out their daily duties in employment service offices were able to implement cruel and inhumane social security reforms"...

The Brown Envelope Book illustrates the trials of claimants with stories of individuals who have been subjected to this cold-hearted barbarism in graphic and heart-rending detail.

'Be a light in the darkness' is the theme of this year's Holocaust Memorial Day in the UK.

The Brown Envelope Book will serve as such a light.

It will enlighten all who read it as to the ongoing injustices being perpetrated upon ordinary people by other ordinary people working as bureaucrats in our country.

The question of how this is still possible must be the one that must be addressed.

Nobody with a normal conscience who reads these stories – indeed, this evidence – contained herein can fail to be moved. Only the psychopaths among us will remain anything other than filled with visceral anger and outrage. It is to be hoped that this will prompt the reader to act.

In the UK today, disabled activists and their allies must continue on with their struggle against the harsh backdrop of power. Our 'first-past-the-post' electoral system continues to deliver majorities in parliament for the governing party based upon a minority of the popular vote.

In the 2019 general election the Conservative Party received a landslide majority of 80 seats - a net gain of 48 seats based upon 43.6% of the popular vote - the highest percentage by any party since 1979.

Tory gains were made in long-held Labour Leave-voting seats dubbed the 'red wall' some of which had not had a Tory MP in decades if ever but which had a strong majority for Brexit in the 2016 in/out referendum. The Labour Party won 202 seats, its lowest number and proportion of seats since 1935.

It therefore seems that we must continue on with our struggle without the help of our natural allies in the UK Parliament, of whom former shadow chancellor John McDonnell and Labour leader Jeremy Corbyn were at the forefront.

The future post-Covid

At the time of publication, according to the Office for National Statistics (ONS) UK Government borrowing as a result of the Coronavirus pandemic stands at £303.1bn on top of a deficit of £57bn for the previous financial year.

Public spending cuts and continued austerity are written into the Conservative Party's DNA.

The future of our struggle for inclusion and justice lies in a two pronged approach.

Firstly, we must continue our campaigning for an end to the brutal Work Capability Assessment regime and it's equally unjust and lethal Personal Independence Payment assessment regime.

We must continue to educate our fellow citizens as to the mass immiseration that further years of cuts and austerity will inflict upon our society. Not just sick and/or disabled people but every single family in the country barring the very wealthy. People need to know the real price that such a policy demands that each one of us pays.

We need the richest people and corporations to pay the price for this next economic crisis. We must look again at how banking and finance can be reformed so as to serve society rather than suck the lifeblood out of it like some deadly parasite. It does not have to be this way as excellent campaigns such as Positive Money have shown.

The UK now has a net debt of £2.14trn - the highest proportion of GDP since the 1960s.

We must ensure that there is no repeat of the past ten years of cuts and austerity.

As I write this the UK is slowly emerging from the long state of emergency created by the Covid 19 pandemic.

Arguably, the pandemic has been as much of a catastrophe for disabled people as the last ten years of cuts and austerity.

Fully 6 out of 10 deaths from Covid have been those of disabled people.

The TUC Disabled Workers Conference this year had rightly pointed out that 'The Shadow of Eugenics' hangs over our country's response to the pandemic. Yet again our lives were deemed less valuable than those of the able bodied as DNR 'Do Not Resuscitate' orders were slapped on those whose lives were deemed too clinically 'vulnerable' to be worth the effort of saving.

As ever, disabled people again have been the hardest hit.

Truly. Our campaigning work never ends.

The second prong of our activism must be to volunteer in our communities to support people in desperate need of help and advice.

Perhaps the most effective campaigning activity the Black Triangle undertook over the past decade was our 'Substantial Risk' campaign that made known to a very wide audience of sick and disabled people and their advocates legal regulations that stated that a person must not be found to be 'fit for work' or 'work-related activity' if there exists a 'substantial risk' to the health of that person or other people. It has been said that as a result of this campaign tens of thousands of people were saved from destitution or an even worse fate, perhaps even death in extreme instances. We regard this as our biggest achievement.

Sick and/or disabled people tend to feel loneliness and often an overwhelming sense of powerlessness when faced with the hostile machinery of the State.

If just a few of those reading this book would volunteer to train to help others in their communities to deal with DWP bureaucracy it would be utterly transformative. Day in and day out ordinary people, for example our friends and volunteers at

Edinburgh Coalition Against Poverty do this work and they are seldom unsuccessful.

The way forward now is for all of us to unite in our own communities in a spirit of mutual aid and solidarity. To continue to call out human rights abuses from the rooftops. To assert the fundamental dignity of our lives and never to give in to bullying and official tyranny.

"It is not incumbent upon you to finish the work; but neither are you entitled to refrain from it."

Pirkei Avot 2:16:

If we save just one life is as if we have saved a whole world. Let us join together in achieving this goal and surely many others besides, while we have breath.

Our lives are meaningful.

Our lives are worth living.

I am deeply moved, honoured and privileged to have been asked to be patron of this book on behalf of our Black Triangle Campaign.

Let us be strong and strengthen one another!

Solidarity, always.

John McArdle
Co-founder
Black Triangle Anti-Defamation Campaign
blacktrianglecampaign.org

A Beginner's Guide to Scroungerology

Alan Morrison

As I sit writing this, ex-Chancellor George Osborne, architect of the devastating austerity cuts of 2010-16 that offloaded onto the poorest in our society responsibility for repaying a 'deficit' which came about by propping up the crashed banking sector for its own rapacious malfeasance, has just been appointed partner at investment bank Robey Warshaw. George '9 Jobs' Osborne already has one position as an adviser to fund manager Black Rock which pays him the princely sum of £65,000 for one day a week. ONE DAY. What crowning irony that the Chancellor of a Thousand Cuts, who made it his mission to pay back the 'deficit' after the banking crash of 2008, is now to become an investment banker himself.

In gorging his cupidity still more from having sold his soul to Mammon many times over, and in addition to his gratuitous inherited wealth and baronetcy, Osborne might content himself that he has attained the ultimate status of personifying one of the most Unacceptable Faces of Capitalism of our time. He has also finally confirmed his status as moral anathema to all recognised fair, compassionate and rational measures of basic decency. He and his equally unscrupulous cohorts, ex-PM David Cameron and the accursed former DWP Secretary and architect of the universally discredited Universal Credit, 'Sir' Iain Duncan Smith, have left behind them a Foodbank Britain beset by Victorian levels of abject poverty, starved children, epidemic street homelessness and general immiseration; a broken-souled society of 'poor doors' and 'homeless spikes'.

It was specifically in response to Osborne's egregious Emergency Budget of 2010 that I first mustered my energies to gather together as many fellow poets and writers as I could towards a protest anthology which started life as an e-book and was promptly emailed directly to all then-sitting MPs. Donations towards a print publication of the anthology, most notably and generously from Michael Rosen, followed, and *Emergency Verse — Poets in Defence of the Welfare State* was eventually published and launched to a packed Poetry Library at the Southbank Centre in January the following year. In 2012, a second, even vaster tome, *The Robin Hood Book - Verse Versus Austerity*, was published. The two unknowingly trend-setting anthologies comprised over 200 poets and writers from the well established to the relatively unknown. Criticised in some quarters at the time for angrily catastrophising, pretty much everything predicted in both anthologies' polemical projections came to pass.

A hitherto mostly apolitical poetry scene was resuscitated into verse-activism in the ensuing months and years: the *Morning*

Star's poetry column exploded with political poems; other anthological initiatives sprang up nationwide, such as *Fit for Work: Poets Against Atos*; and journals and webzines such as *Prole, Proletarian Poetry, Poetry Republic,* and *Lumpen - A Journal of Poor and Working Class writing,* struck chords. In 2015 an ebook to coincide with the Labour leadership contest, *Poets for Corbyn,* appeared, and in 2016, the memorable *Poems for Jeremy Corbyn* was published by Shoetsring Press (ed. Merryn Williams). That same year, the release of Ken Loach's film-polemic on the benefits cuts, *I, Daniel Blake,* discomfited cinema-goers with a new kitchen-sink realism for Foodbank Britain (it is also timely that the same month *The Brown Envelope Book* has been made available as an ebook, the BFI is releasing *Play for Today Volume Two* which includes Jim Allen and Roland Joffé's groundbreaking *The Spongers,* a harrowing dramatic depiction of the devastating effects of disability cuts and anti-claimant rhetoric in the late Seventies, recommended viewing for seeing how little has changed in these regards over 40 years on).

Beyond 2012, as writer, and editor of *The Recusant* (of which Caparison is the occasional imprint), I started a new polemical poetry forum, *Militant Thistles,* to continue in the spirit of the two Caparison anthologies, while my own verse-activism continued in individual form in a collection formed around the horrors of Tory welfare 'reform', *Tan Raptures* (Smokestack, 2017).

There was also a polemical mushrooming of books mostly from the radical imprints such as Verso, Zero, Zed Books and Pluto Press. Among the most interesting, Owen Hatherley's *The Ministry of Nostalgia,* which tackled government austerity narratives, and David Frayne's *The Refusal of Work: The Theory and Practice of Resistance to Work.* The latter, a deconstruction of today's punishing work ethic, is a theme on which this writer has polemicised for some years – specifically in relation to the veneration of paid employment (as opposed to authentic 'occupation'), and its prescriptive, even proscriptive, control and suppression of authentic personality. There has also been *Cash Not Care: the planned demolition of the UK welfare state* by Mo Stewart (also author of the important paper 'Preventable Harm and the Work Capability Assessment' https://www.centreforwelfarereform.org/library/preventable-harm-and-the-wca.html), and, more recently, *Crippled: Austerity and the Demonization of Disabled People* by Frances Ryan, and the informative and compendious *Scroungers: Moral Panics and Media Myths* by my brother, James Morrison, who contributed a piece entitled 'Farewell Welfare?' to the last anthology, and has added another apposite contribution for this one.

It was and remains an enormous challenge to counter the still-toxic 'welfare' narrative in wider culture, to fight against the best efforts of mainstream politicians and newspapers, government ministers and right-wing tabloids, to keep up the specious narrative of 'strivers vs skivers'. This scrounger rhetoric, or 'Scroungerology' as I call it, has gripped the national psyche to such an extent that the welfare state has mutated into a national hate-object - a Scapegoat State - nowhere more so than among those most in need of it. It has been reframed as a scrounger-hatching state Behemoth that had to be put back in its altruistic place and poked with sharp stigmatising sticks until it regressed again to the more judgemental, begrudging, nudging entity originally envisaged by Beveridge.

It's little known that the so often hagiographised Beveridge had eugenics leanings, as did many intellectuals of his time, both on the Left and Right of politics, and that such ideas influenced aspects of his eponymous 'Report'. One example of this was the grading of child allowances so that, counterintuitively, better off parents were paid at a higher rate to poorer parents, thus encouraging the former whilst discouraging the latter from reproducing. This was in keeping with eugenicist principles that 'undesirable' traits believed to be inheritable behaviours, such as, bizarrely, poverty, and, most disturbingly, perceived genetic defects as manifest in physical and mental disability, could actually be 'bred out' of the human gene pool. In our own recent history, the Tories were much less covert and infinitely less 'well meaning' than Beveridge when bringing in the brazenly Malthusian two child benefit cap in 2017.

All that said, current calls for a new 'Beveridge Report' to address the mass immiseration caused by the pandemic are welcome – provided, of course, this leads to a rehumanisation of the welfare state and a restitution of more compassionate social security. It is a dire indictment of ten years of Tory rule that something of such a fundament and scale is now, once again in our history, necessitated; but then the past decade has seen such a remorseless full scale attempt by the succession of Tory-led governments to dismantle our welfare state that this can hardly be surprising.

Today, the DWP might as well stand for the Department for War on the Poor. So feared are the auspices of the DWP that their ubiquitous and unmistakably brutalist brown envelopes - or 'Caxton tans' - have become themselves paper symbols of state malice towards its claimants; agents of malignant governmental origami. It can only be a matter of time before Brown Envelope Phobia is included in the *Diagnostic and Statistical Manual of Mental Disorders* (DSM). Indeed, one of this anthology's endorsers, the University of Birmingham's Dr Kayleigh Garthwaite, authored an important academic paper titled 'Fear of the Brown Envelope', in which she focused on how these vicious missives can induce phobic reactions in their recipients. Hence, of course, the title of this anthology.

So notorious has the weapon of the brown envelope become that, according to current speculation among Facebook users and others, the DWP is apparently planning on replacing it with a white one –

perhaps to help it camouflage better in our future post. Nonetheless, the symbolic resonance of the brown envelope is indelible in the national claimant psyche; and, since the coercive content of such envelopes will remain the same, the change to white paper will sadly not signal a truce but merely give more element of surprise for the ambushers. A similarly empty gesture of cosmetic change occurred recently with a tonal switch on the interminable DWP automated phone line: its once notorious loop of 'Spring' from *The Four Seasons* brought a whole new meaning to David Mercer's titular phrase, *Let's Murder Vivaldi*.

This matter is given witty shrift in this anthology with Kate Jay-R's 'How the DWP Ruined Vivaldi For Me'. The DWP apparently decided Vivaldi was too 'anxiety-inducing' for callers – quite possibly it was (that powdered-wig music can be grating at the best of times!), but changing the record isn't going to suddenly neutralise the anxiety of claimants, even if one public petition asking for the DWP to change the Vivaldi loop did hilariously state: 'Anyone who rings the DWP with a query has to listen to Vivaldi's Spring on repeat for 45 minutes. If being unemployed or disabled was a choice, people would get jobs just so that they don't have to listen to it'. According to a *Guardian* piece of 2 Feb 2020, 'a 20-minute mix of eight unnamed musical tracks that according to the DWP aims to reduce anxiety' and invoke 'a steady neutral pace and reducing the issue of repetition' has replaced the interminable Vivaldi loop. It would seem the DWP are now disc jokeys.

Not only the DWP phone line but society as a whole has been in something of a loop. After a lost decade, we had, in 2020, a very literal lost year: the catastrophic Covid-19 pandemic, which in the UK has cost more than 150,000 lives, not only among the over-80s, care home residents, and those with underlying conditions or comorbidities, but also too many of the long-term sick and disabled who have been just as disproportionately affected by the virus as they have been disproportionately persecuted by Tory governments for the past decade. This has been a bitter sting in the tail indeed. According to recent estimates, people with disabilities accounted for six in every 10 deaths from Covid during 2020.

Through Boris Johnson's initial and fatal dithering over introducing tough measures to try to stop the spread of the virus in the UK and his flirting at first with 'herd immunity' theories, we have effectively seen another form of covert Malthusianism, this time by inaction. Whereas the fiscal Malthusianism of the twenty teens – was in plain sight, during the first wave of Covid, care homes were apparently left completely at the mercy of the virus, with criminally inadequate protections and/or complete lack of PPE.

Just as the past decade has seen the Tories countenance the open rhetorical and financial persecution of those in society they deem economically unproductive - the unemployed, the sick and the disabled - it seemed they were now turning a blind eye to the defencelessness of elderly care home residents. Not only that, but Mencap recently exposed the fact that 'Do Not Resuscitate' orders have apparently been put on the hospital files of Covid patients with learning disabilities. Indeed, this Malthusian pattern runs through everything the Conservative Government has done since scraping back into power in 2010, and everything it will no doubt continue to do.

There is much use of the term 'existential threat' today, yet it's not one which has yet been applied to the disabled population - in spite of our having been under a swingeing sword of Damocles since, at the very least, 2010, and with no signs of this threat retreating any time soon. That the sick and disabled, inclusive of the mentally afflicted, are almost always kept out of such narratives is debatably discriminatory in itself, and symbolic of a tacit ableism permeating wider culture. The same ableism at heart of government which seemed to think the Bedroom Tax was a perfectly reasonable policy to impose even on disabled families needing spare rooms to store special equipment or have as recuperative spaces for their various needs. It is only recently that the climate of fear in which the sick and disabled claimant population have had to exist for the past decade has been recognised as another 'hostile environment' deliberately augmented by government (see 'DWP deliberately conspired with Tory media to build a "hostile environment" against benefit claimants', *Welfare Journal* welfarejournal.com 3 April 2021).

And since the long-standing, scandalous 'No DSS' clause has permeated the private rental sector for decades, massively restricting choice for millions of renters simply for being in receipt of a state benefit or local housing allowance, this has also in turn covertly discriminated against the disabled who in most cases have to be in receipt of certain benefits such as DLA, PIP and ESA, in order to be able to live remotely normal lives. This clause might as well say 'No DiSSabled'. In spite of court judgments obtained by Shelter on 2 July and 8 September 2020 which ruled that "No DSS' policies are unlawful under the Equality Act 2010' as 'rejecting tenancy applications just because someone is in receipt of benefits is unlawful indirect discrimination on the grounds of sex and disability' as 'women and disabled people are more likely to receive housing benefit', countless private landlords and letting agents continue to discriminate.

But undoubtedly the most horrendous aspect to the 'hostile environment' against the sick and disabled has been the notorious work capability assessment regimen, which was originally brought in by New Labour as a result of the now infamous 'Freud Report' by (Lord) David Freud, which he entitled 'Reducing dependency, increasing opportunity: options for the future of welfare to work'.

From this scabrous undertaking was spawned the conveyor belt of medically illegitimate WCAs which have been and remain the scourge of the sick and disabled in the UK.

One can trace a latter-day, decades-long political-psychiatric-pharmaceutical conspiracy to redefine 'disability' and 'sickness' for economic purposes, and the corruption of occupational therapeutic ethics in the process, towards the Kafkaesque 'work cure' and 'fitness note' culture which afflicts us today. This covert campaign originated in 2001 at a psychosocial conference in Oxfordshire, menacingly titled 'Malingering and illness deception', linked to a US insurance company called UnumProvident, which led to the 2005 'Waddell and Aylward Report', the actual title of which was The Scientific and Conceptual Basis of Incapacity Benefit.

From this came Freud's stigmatising 2007 report, which directly led to the introduction of work capability assessments. The WCAs were, in turn, outsourced to profit-driven, bounty-incentivised private companies such as Atos (now calling itself Independent Assessment Services), Capita and Maximus. Post-2010 this despicable regime was given a turbocharge by an incoming Tory-led Coalition in its mission to demonise tens of thousands of disabled claimants not merely out of their state entitlements (and only incomes) but, in many cases, out of existence altogether. A very real existential threat, and to the most defenceless in society. The trope 'Fit for work' has now passed into the lexicon of Doublespeak, as has the lexical flip which insidiously allowed 'fit notes' to replace sick notes.

With an arrogance and sanctimony all the more unpalatable for the grave moral misjudgement and dogmatic insouciance with which it inflicted misery and destitution on the most vulnerable claimants, Iain Duncan Smith resuscitated his flagging political career as failed Tory leader by ensuring his political posterity as one of the most hated politicians in British history. But while he was rhetorical architect of the mythical "something for nothing" culture, it was Osborne who branded in the public mind such indelible memes as "blinds shut during the day", in an open call to provoke widespread resentment among the early-rising working population towards those supposedly "sleeping off a life on benefits" - one of the most spiteful and malicious episodes of political scapegoating in our history.

This was an active governmental stigmatisation, even persecution, of a disadvantaged and vulnerable section of the population, as sure as if they'd placed stickers on claimants' windows reading SCROUNGERS. The hyperbolised phenomenon of some allegedly claiming benefits while working and not declaring their extra income, or so-called 'benefit fraud', led to government calls on the public to effectively spy on neighbours they suspected of such behaviours.

All of these rhetorical assaults, in turn, led to a shocking rise in disability hate crime - that is, verbal and even physical abuse against the visibly disabled. The Big 'Stick' Society had become the Pick on the Little Guy Society, with not gambling bankers, big capitalists or the tax-dodging super-rich but the poorest and most incapacitated now framed as the culprits for all of society's economic ills, and the right-wing red top press more than happy to be its supplemental police.

Through this mass-dehumanisation, a vulnerable section of society was deemed economically unproductive and by extension, subhuman. It was a process of dehumanisation judged necessary in order to persuade the public to accept the mass immiseration of tens of thousands of sick and disabled claimants. Historical analogies were graphically clear to any who endured these years unlucky enough to be unemployed and incapacitated. Small wonder that such brutally punishing times prompted such responses as the Spartacus Report, Calum's List and the Black Triangle Anti-Defamation Campaign. For over a decade now eugenics-inflected rhetoric and lexicon - e.g. 'scroungers', 'workshy', 'parasites' - indistinguishable from that used by the Nazis in the 1920s and 30s to dehumanise certain groups in society - e.g. the disabled, mentally ill, mentally handicapped, unemployed, Roma, gypsies, Jews et al - has been normalised by government ministers and their mouthpieces in the right-wing red top press (most prolifically and reprehensibly of all in the *Daily Express*).

Even now, in the thick of a pandemic, the Tories continue to push this odious latter mantra: the latest successor to IDS, Thérèse Coffey, recently batted back a suggestion of paying all claimants a one-off £500 Covid payment not because it offered a poor substitute for the ongoing 'uplift' of Universal Credit demanded by many charities and campaigners but on the spurious grounds that this would serve as a disincentive for them to look for work. Leaving aside the scrounger-mongering cynicism implicit in this suggestion, what work, exactly, were people supposed to look for, with unemployment rising due to the ongoing economic paralysis caused by continued lockdowns and almost no jobs considered safe enough to perform due to infection risks? (And didn't some Tories actually suggest the unemployed pick fruit during the summer of 2020?).

The dire situation currently faced by many people is that they are forced to keep working even though they are in unsafe, potentially deadly environments - with infected care home workers, devoid of adequate sick pay, given no choice but to carry on shift-working in order to avoid being plunged into poverty or evicted from their homes. (Whatever happened to Health and Safety? Gone the way of all life-preserving 'red tape'...). Indeed, it is grimly ironic that so many workers are risking death in order to live; what a perverse incentive to be presented with in a supposedly civilised society.

Coffey also mooted in a recent interview that part of the reason for the UK having the highest death rate from Covid in Europe was due to its high obesity rate – adding that obesity was known to affect the lower income part of the population the most due to poorer diets and consumption of cheap fast food. As ever, then, the implication is that, as with unemployment and reliance on state benefits, being obese (and, potentially, dying from Covid due to obesity) is fundamentally the fault of the poor. And so grinds on the endless cycle of victim-blaming. The nation's ever-rising death rate is not the fault of the Tories, an incompetent government or a shambolic prime minister – it's the poor's fault. Just as, apparently, it was the fault of the poor, the unemployed and the disabled that the banks gambled our economy away back in 2008.

As it was put in a *Guardian* editorial of 9 February 2021 at the prospect of the Government potentially ending the £20 per week pandemic uplift for Universal Credit claimants:

The Department for Work and Pensions already has a bad reputation. Last month, it and its private contractor, Capita, were strongly criticised by a coroner for errors contributing to the death of Philippa Day, who killed herself in desperation after her benefits were taken away. If ever there was a moment for ministers to back away from the punitive rhetoric on benefits that has debased British politics in recent years, this pandemic winter must surely be it.

We will find out soon... But, if opinion polls are anything to go by, it seems the British public can forgive the Tories their gradualist phasing out of the rights and lives of the most vulnerable in society, as long as it doesn't affect the acquisitive, 'economically productive' majority. Those deemed 'economically *un*productive' have long been reduced to mere acronyms: WRAG (Work-Related Activity Group), NEET (Not in Employment, Education or Training), and the somewhat inarticulate LTB (Long-Term Benefits), allegedly subverted by some jobcentreplus managers to stand for 'Lying Thieving Bastards'.

Unemployment, disability and, indeed, mental illness, seem to be three areas still deemed fair game for stigmatising and discrimination. As for the long-standing and archane acronym DSS, ubiquitous in the private renting sector with the prefix NO, recent court cases finally found this discriminatory and in breach of equality laws. Yet with no vocal recognition of such by the sitting government, and nothing new in legislation to back it up, one wonders whether this judgment will make any real difference for the unemployed or those left underemployed and reliant on local housing allowance to top up their meagre incomes until now treated as social lepers by letting agents and landlords alike.

It is testament to the efficacy of Tory anti-welfare rhetoric that, even today in 2021, after a year during which millions of workers were almost continuously furloughed, a recent social attitudes survey by academics at King's College London, entitled *Unequal Britain*, revealed that nearly half of British people (47%) believe those who lost their jobs during the pandemic were ultimately responsible for their own unemployment. The incessant Tory coda of 'personal responsibility' has reached such a level of social acceptance over recent decades that the involuntarily unemployed can be unblinkingly dismissed as irresponsible - and/or previously 'underperforming' - pandemic opportunists. Perish the thought that such moral judgments should be directed at the numerous private companies (or 'chumpanies') to whom Government ministers have been siphoning off lucrative contracts to produce PPE and other Covid-associated products. Cue cupiditous ex-PM David Cameron 'lobbying'/messaging Chancellor Rishi Sunak to bend rules to allow Greensill Capital to receive an emergency loan from the government in response to the COVID-19 pandemic, all so he could get his 'windfall' of tens of millions of pounds in company shares. Yes, this is the same hereditary multi-millionaire Cameron who presided over the biggest 'benefit scrounger'-scapegoating government in British political history, who has now been caught out on the 'scrounge' for public money, most heinously, vital funds relating to the Government's Covid-19 response. This is greed on a humungous scale; greed of the grubbiest and most pathological kind.

Another example of anti-welfare rhetorical efficacy came from such recent research into Leave voting motives as reported in a *Guardian* article of 19 April 2021 entitled 'Half of Brexit supporters were not 'left behind' red wall voters':

Their views on immigration were more nuanced than the leave narrative suggests and were "most scathing" about British people on benefits who refused to do the jobs migrants would do.

'"The English are feral, and they were fed for years and years off, if you stubbed your toe you got disability living allowance for the rest of your life … The English need to be retrained that, to feed your family, if you have to go and scrub toilets … that's what you do," said one female from the west Midlands.

"Poverty was often linked to narratives of 'scrounging' and 'laziness', of poor role models and a 'something-for-nothing' culture," says the report...

The trope about DLA for stubbed toes is textbook mythmaking, a most egregious example of 'scrounger'-mongering. Welfare stigmatisation is now something so feared by many that it has even impacted on how many - or as the case may be, how few - people made claims for Universal Credit during the pandemic, as Patrick Butler reported recently in a *Guardian* article on 20 April 2021:

Fear of being seen as a "scrounger" meant those entitled didn't sign on during the early stage of the pandemic.

... The perceived stigma around benefits - with some people feeling, for example, that they were for "dole scroungers" and "freeloaders" - meant many refused state help...

Even more didn't lodge a claim because they said they ... thought the online-only benefit was too confusing or too much hassle, or because they believed - wrongly - that they would not be eligible.

Overall, about 500,000 people in the UK chose not to claim universal credit, even though they most likely would have been entitled to it...

Nearly half of those who refused to claim benefits reported severe financial strain, leading them to miss rent payments or skip meals. They were also more likely to suffer stress or poor mental health.

Non-take-up of benefits, said the authors of the Welfare at a Social Distance project, was in danger of becoming "an invisible problem". They urged ministers to reduce stigma around social security and encourage those eligible to claim benefits.

... The data showed that 55,000 did not apply for the scheme because they were worried about the perception of people who are on benefits.

Ben Baumberg Geiger, lead author of the report and a senior lecturer at the University of Kent, said: "Some of these people say they don't need benefits - but others don't claim because they don't understand that they are eligible, hope that things will get better soon, or are put off by the perceived 'hassle' or stigma of claiming." ...

All of this rhetoric aligns seamlessly with the Government's emphasis on public responsibility for maintaining social distancing and mask-wearing as key to suppressing the virus. Even as I write this, Johnson has reportedly boasted to his MPs that it is not mass altruism - or the collective mass efforts and sacrifices of doctors, nurses, carers and community volunteers - but, counterintuitively, "greed" and "capitalism" that has ensured the efficacy of the UK's vaccination programme (readers will appreciate the irony here in light of Greensill et al). If the Tories' raison d'etre is privatising everything in sight, and outsourcing PPE production and vaccination programmes to their 'chums', then Boris Johnson's favourite job is nationalising blame.

Claimants are treated as subhuman, put through punishing, impersonal and deeply humiliating protocols and assessments by often callous and automaton-like assessors, with recent revelations showing that many benefit claims are decided not on the basis of documented medical evidence but on algorithms. All eyes will be on the long-delayed Health & Disability Green Paper, though Zacchaeus 2000 Trust's survey report *People Before Process - The state of disability benefit assessments and the urgent need for reform* (https://www.z2k.org/wp-content/uploads/2021/05/FINAL.pdf) shows, not surprisingly, very low expectations among disabled claimants that WCAs will be meaningfully reformed to a fairer and more compassionate model.

It has also been shameful to witness the spineless compliance of the mental health and psychiatric sectors with such atomistic government-driven paradigms as 'the work cure', 'psycho-compulsion' and the one-size-fits-all abuse of cognitive behavioural therapy towards pushing the mentally ill into unsuitable employment. It is a sobering fact that, a decade on from the turbocharging of the WCA regime under the Coalition, estimated benefit-related deaths of sick and disabled people are thought to number more than 100,000 souls. This figure, tragically, includes all those driven by the DWP and/or WCA providers to take their own lives; 'at least 69 suicides ... related to the department's handling of benefit claims' according to internal DWP documentation but a National Audit Office (NAO) report published in 2020 said the true figure was 'likely to be much higher' [https://www.theguardian.com/society/2020/feb/07/dwp-benefit-related-suicide-numbers-not-true-figure-says-watchdog-nao].

Another reason for the absence of any Caparison anthologies during the past few years was mainly because with Jeremy Corbyn as Leader of the Labour Party this nation actually had a true socialist Opposition for the first time since the early 1980s; and one which was particularly effective in speaking up for the poorest in society. No political leader until Corbyn had managed to change the rhetoric of the welfare debate from its warped discourse of 'scroungers' and 'skivers' implausibly blamed for the nation's speculation-caused bankruptcy, to one of compassion and respect for the poorest and most vulnerable in society:

'We have helped change the debate on welfare … no frontbench politician is now using disgraceful, divisive terms like 'scrounger', 'shirker' or 'skiver'. They have been shamed by the reality of life … for millions of our people in left-behind Britain. …The injustices that scar society today are not those of 1945… Want, Squalor, Idleness, Disease and Ignorance …they have changed since I first entered Parliament in 1983… Today what is holding people back above all are … Inequality … Neglect … Insecurity … Prejudice … and Discrimination…'

[Jeremy Corbyn, 2016]

Arguably Corbyn's greatest achievement as Leader of the Opposition was to drag the toxic debate around welfare kicking and screaming onto centre-left ground, thereby neutralising the worst excesses of Tory rhetoric and prompting a markedly more compassionate discussion on the issue. In this regard, Corbyn provided a robust and courageous parliamentary opposition and was a true voice for the voiceless and most vulnerable in society, most passionate when speaking up for the poor, the homeless, refugees, the disabled, the working poor and the unemployed. This was the sort of moral leadership many on the Left had been waiting for for decades.

Militantly anti-austerity, Corbyn, assisted by the equally compassionate and principled Shadow Chancellor John McDonnell, as much symbolically as politically, took up the baton in Parliament for the cause which so many activist groups had hitherto been fighting without mainstream political representation - from The People's Assembly and Left Unity to the Black Triangle Campaign, Calum's List, the Spartacus Network and Disabled People Against the Cuts et al to our own Poets in Defence of the Welfare State. (The one other honorable political exception, of course, has been Caroline Lucas of the Greens, who, back in 2010, was patron of *Emergency Verse*).

Labour under Corbyn and McDonnell gave us that representation. And, predictably, no doubt inevitably, the Establishment and its mouthpieces, the right-wing red top newspapers - specifically the *Daily Mail, Express, Sun, Telegraph* and *Times* - with all the specious rhetoric and smears in their armouries, brought down that representation, and thereby cheated a generation of its one precious chance of social, economic and political emancipation. The resistible rise of Corbynism was remorselessly resisted right up until its untimely end in December 2019. Had we had a Corbyn-led Labour Government, we would have seen the abolition of both WCAs and UC, as well as the restitution of Legal Aid for claimants. But it was not to be.

It remains to be seen whether a post-Corbyn Labour will demonstrate anything like the same passion and commitment to protecting the most vulnerable in society. Early signs are not at all encouraging as what seems to be the ideological vaccuum of 'Starmerism' moots overtures to the party's past ill-fated flirtations with patriotism - flag, family and other tropes that are more traditionally associated with the Tories. Four and a half years of proper Opposition was all we were allowed and now, depressingly, it's back to business as usual - and an invertebrate Labour Party, frightened of its own shadow and desperate to appeal to points of view it should actually be disuading voters from holding.

So, with a Covid-driven recession (if not depression) under way - and amid talk already of a 'new austerity', just as tens of thousands are likely to have to claim disability benefits due to 'Long Covid' and/or the psychological effects of the pandemic - the plight of those at the bottom of the heap, the poorest in society, is only likely to worsen. With so many people beholden to an increasingly callous and punishing welfare system ever intent on further immiserating its claimants by way of perverse 'incentive' to drive the numbers towards poorly paid, inappropriate or even unpaid 'work'; as unemployment surges back towards 3 million, accompanied by an unconscionable cut in the £20-a-week uplift to Universal Credit; now seems the right time to produce this, the belated third Caparison anti-austerity anthology - themed around the DWP envelope and everything it represents, and threatens.

In addition to all this, while redrafting this Introduction, it has been revealed via a freedom of information request that, in spite of the best efforts of Labour MP and activist Debbie Abrahams, and campaigns such as the Black Triangle and Disabled People Against Cuts, the Equality and Human Rights Commission (EHRC) has indicated *if* it conducts a full statutory investigation into "systemic barriers" facing disabled claimants in the benefits system, it is highly unlikely it will address links between the Department for Work and Pensions (DWP) and the deaths of disabled benefit claimants [https://www.disabilitynewsservice.com/anger-after-watchdog-appears-to-back-away-from-inquiry-into-dwp-deaths/]. All the more reason, then, for the continued necessity of books such as this.

[Though there is some hope in a growing call for a public inquiry into DWP-related deaths gaining momentum just at the point of this book's completion in mid-May, prompted by BBC journalist Alex Homer's 'exposé... on the deaths of over 150 social security claimants, mostly since 2010', which reported that the family of Philippa Day are to sue the DWP and Capita for compensation which will include 'a claim under the Human Rights Act for violation of the right to life over their handling of the case'. The assistant coroner 'issued a so-called Prevention of Future Death (PFD) report to the DWP and private contractor Capita, requiring them to explain what action they might take to improve' how they deal with vulnerable and mentally ill claimants ['Deaths of people on benefits prompt inquiry call', *BBC News* https://www.bbc.co.uk/news/uk-56819727]. This recent and rare burst of coverage also prompted Debbie Abrahams to pen an article renewing her call for an independent public inquiry into the deaths of vulnerable claimants, which also reminded of the shocking fact that 'In an answer to a written question in 2019 by Madeleine Moon, the former MP for Bridgend, figures suggested that over 130 working age people a month were dying soon after being found ineligible for PIP by the government contractors Atos and Capita' [https://debbieabrahams.org.uk/social-security-claimants-need-government-to-wise-up/]].

We must be on our guard against a possible resurgence of 'Scroungerology' which might well be whipped up in the right-wing press once again if another wave of austerity looms. Already the Tory Government is beginning to persecute the gypsy and traveller community again, the default anti-Ziganism of a propertied party that can't tolerate alternative lifestyles, particularly those that deviate from the rapaciousness of the property ladder. So how long before we're back in the 'scroungermongering' quagmire of the previous decade? The fact that the Government is currently clamping down on our right to protest does not bode at all well either. All that said, we might find some consolation in the fact that we're much more experienced and better equipped a decade on to resist (and polemically oppose) any oncoming draconian cuts and associated rhetorics.

So here we are again, a decade of austerity on, entering the 2020s with the third Caparison anti-austerity anthology, in the monstrous shadow of an 80-seat Tory majority.

It was timely that Colin Hambrook of *Disability Arts OnLine* put me in touch with Kate Jay-R (my co-editor) who had for a number of years been publishing poems written by perpetually work capability-assessed PIP claimants, under the punning banner Don't Go Breaking Our Arts – her emphasis throughout being on disability and benefits. Kate is also a veteran novelist, and must be one of the few writers to have fictionalised 'brown envelope phobia' so prominently in a work of fiction, *The Other Side of Carrie Cornish* (2018). A sizeable excerpt from her comprehensive *Diary of an Armchair Campaigner*, a valuable and timely piece of work, is excerpted herein.

The group was looking to publish in some form, and, as I had tentatively planned *The Brown Envelope Book* in the back of mind for some years, I thought why not combine forces. This was the chance liaison, then, that prompted me to finally launch the project and call for submissions. Funds to cover the first print run of the book came in the form of one extremely generous and substantial donation. The icing on the cake has been to get John McArdle of the Black Triangle Campaign on board as patron: his anti-defamation campaign group has been pivotal this last decade in its stand against Tory persecution of the unemployed and disabled.

The sheer diversity of voices and backgrounds in this anthology is immensely gratifying. Of the 107 contributors, 50 are women. Most poet contributors identify themselves as having some form of disability and past or current experience of the punishing benefits system, particularly in relation to Personal Independence Payment and Employment and Support Allowance (though it is testament to the hostile environment that some claimant contributors have felt compelled to use pseudonyms rather than their real names for fear of repercussions from the DWP!). There are herein poems and prose pieces – even a couple of mini-plays – that take many forms and perspectives on their themes, from direct polemics through touchingly personal experiences to satire and surrealism. Among them are poems depicting the despair of dole queues, and of course, the never-ending dread of brown envelopes.

One poem hopes for a returning Christ to turn out the decision-makers from Caxton House, while another juxtaposes the intrusive and denegrating 'voices' (auditory hallucinations) of a female survivor of sexual abuse with the curt and clinical interlocutions of an Atos assessor. On affirming that she self-harms, the assessor insensitively instructs her to roll up her sleeve to reveal the scars, and, on refusing to do so, she knows that she will lose points as a penalty and likely be refused support. Subsequently, before heading home, she contemplates suicide by jumping off a bridge near the assessment centre. This makes us ask, What type of system interrogates and belittles vulnerable people who are already interrogated and belittled on a daily basis by their own traumatised minds? A government's invisible violence meted out to those with invisible illnesses. What kind of society seeks to further afflict the afflicted? One which values money above human beings i.e. capitalism is, of course, the answer to that, a brutal regime happy to administer material and psychological punishments to its embattled claimants.

The thematic concerns of the book have also been incorporated into its design and format. The layout and typesetting is meant to mimic typical DWP letters with their trademark vertical barcodes on the left-hand side; the typeface is not an exact match, but was chosen for its clinical, utilitarian functionality.

All contributions are powerful, moving and occasionally witty tributes to human endurance in the face of brutalising Kafkaesque bureaucracy, of humiliating assessments and soul-crushing protocols. Every single contributor to this anthology has contributed to challenging received narratives of disability and incapacity, as well as battling the stigma of unemployment.

Certainly most of us here, as poets and writers, more than appreciate the potentially transformative notion of a universal basic income, since this would allow many poets and artists to continue pursuing their callings with a guaranteed level of subsistance to keep them going during the - often long - periods when there is no remuneration for their work.

But more broadly, we also support current notions for something post-Covid of the scale and scope of the 'Beveridge Report'; a reformation, if you like, of the welfare state: a new-style Attlee settlement for the nation, and a return to a more compassionate, human-centred social security system. We might, for a start, petition for it to include the following:

An abolition of the work capability assessments and a judge-led independent public inquiry into deaths and suicides linked to the DWP and WCAs
An abolition of Universal Credit and replacement with compassionate social security
A restitution of private rent controls
An uplift of local housing allowance in line with rental market rates of every district
An abolition of the benefit cap
An abolition of 'two child' benefit limits
An abolition of the bedroom tax
A Universal Basic Income (UBI)
A four-day week
A restitution of Legal Aid for those most in need
A governmentally legislated outlawing of 'No DSS' discrimination...

from Diary of an Armchair Campaigner

Kate Jay-R

I began writing a diary of events in 2012 and called it *Diary Of An Armchair Campaigner*. I wasn't sure whether I was going to do anything with it or just for my own personal record of events in relation to Welfare Reform. Horrors were happening so thick and fast I needed to capture it: people dying, poetry, thoughts, Facebook posts, injustices, latest outrages, snippets from articles, replies and counter-replies from my MP and blog posts. I have revisited it from time to time but not in its entirety, until now. Only now, since we decided to do this anthology, have I been able to use it as a map and timeline, to set in context many of the poems that follow.

What prompted me to start writing it was the death of Karen Sherlock.

On June 11th 2012 here is an excerpt of what I wrote:

I have kept thinking about starting it but the campaigning - mainly against the Welfare Reform Bill online - takes it out of you. Means there's little time left for reflection... eats away at your energy reserves.

But I decided to make a start today, every day is, in fact, filled with startling new revelations relating to this government, but yesterday the deaths associated with the Work Capability Assessment, otherwise known as WCA, was brought nearer to home when I heard one of our online community died a few days ago. Her name was Karen... I knew her by name and remember once or twice chatting to her about her predicament... she was put through unavoidable suffering by being placed in the Work-Related Activity Group (WRAG) of the Employment and Support Allowance (ESA). I heard she was eventually put in the Support Group. This is the group where it is said you have to be practically dying before you can get into it, though clearly our friend was, and still had to fight.

Later that day I popped into Sue Marsh's blog *Diary Of A Benefit Scrounger*. The blog that day read: RIP Karen Sherlock. Here is her Twitter profile: 'Chronic Spoonie, lots wrong. ESA stopped by this inhumane government. Preparing for dialysis. Each day is tough.' Sue continued: 'Karen embodied our fight in almost every way. She was desperately ill. Her kidneys were failing, putting a huge strain on her body. Ultimately it seems she died of a cardiac arrest. An operation had recently been cancelled at the last minute, though I have no idea why or if it is relevant to her death.'

I was shocked and saddened, by each new depth that this Coalition government stooped to, and it brought it home even more as it was one of our 'online community'. It was no longer something that you could try and kid yourself wasn't so widespread. This was happening in our country in 2012. The sick and disabled, dying, because of years of slow drip drip propaganda and vilification of the disabled by a heartless government hell-bent on ideological cuts and demolition of the welfare state.

The media had upped the ante against benefit claimants, softening up the public for the all-out assault on Social Security or welfare as it was now being called. In the same month that Karen Sherlock died, David Cameron aligned himself on the side of workers 'rather than those making a living on benefits'. It was a poorly known fact that a single unemployed person aged over 25 years got around £71 per week to live on (excluding housing and council tax benefits.) How then was this 'making a living'? But Cameron knew exactly what he was doing. He was playing to the gallery in the form of the *Daily Mail* baying mob who'd already been indoctrinated to think that benefit recipients got too much because they had all seen the screeching headlines about benefit caps of 26K. 26K? Most people on benefits got under 10K at this point. In the few thousand cases where claimants got 26K, the families didn't see this – it went in rent to profiteering landlords, but Dave and his tricksters would rather have blamed the claimant than the landlords and the rising rents they failed to regulate. It suited the ConDems' ideological agenda if the masses believed benefits claimants all got 26K. But Cameron stated he wanted to 'end the culture of entitlement'.

Meanwhile, a prominent disability campaigner on Facebook posted about his tribunal result. His appeal had been disallowed. He received nil points at his two Atos assessments despite having cerebral palsy and the hospital confirming with x rays that his CP was arthritic: 'The Atos doctor deliberately misled the tribunal with the evidence she supplied. The tribunal was also a farce. The judge totally ignored everything I'd said with respect to what my limitations were. There were even surreal moments. The Atos doctor in the second assessment stated that I was 'smartly dressed'. The jacket I wore to that assessment is creased, faded and frayed in several places. I wore the same jacket to the tribunal and asked the judge how on earth could anyone say this jacket is smart. The judge replied it could be seen as smart. I laughed and said if I wore this to an interview the only job I'd get is as a road sweeper. Then, even more stupidly the doctor at the tribunal said I could be smart compared to someone wearing a ripped t- shirt!!'

In July 2012, after hearing a speech David Cameron delivered on Welfare on June 25th in Bluewater, Kent, I drafted a response which was taken up by the Spartacus community, slightly re-jigged and sent to the PM.

It was a very long, detailed letter refuting all the inflammatory generalisations with facts. Here is just a small excerpt:

You talk about it becoming "acceptable for many people to choose a life on benefits"... But do people really sit down and think this, ignoring all the careers advice and ambitions they've ever had? Tell me, Mr Cameron, do you think work is a good thing? From the way you talk it would seem so. That's why we are struggling with this flaw in your argument: if work is a good and desirable thing, then why would people choose a life on benefits? Because from the way you're talking it sounds as if you think a life on benefits is a better choice than the one of work...

We agree that working-age welfare should be about providing a safety net. However, this is not happening. People are becoming homeless; the biggest of all threats to safety is to lose your home and this is a direct result of government policy to restrict and reduce housing benefits…How can somebody think about a job when they are having to survive? Food and shelter are basic human needs. People are going hungry, hence the huge increase in food banks around the country...

You then go on to say that "we've got to recognise that in the end, the only thing that really beats poverty, long-term, is work". If by work you mean a person who is able, and of his or her own free choice, uses their time constructively, including pursuits which often do not pay, eg voluntary work, the arts, education, caring for children, caring for the sick etc, then nobody would disagree with you. What people do object to is the stick approach, the bullying, the compulsion, being drafted onto community service mandatory labour (which is the work usually reserved for criminals – so what sort of message are you giving there?).

So yes, let's have a sensible and intelligent debate about work. Work is not always good for you. Some people have their health ruined through work. Research has shown the right sort of work at the right sort of pay is right for some of the people, some of the time. But you are trying to prescribe a one-size-fits-all solution, instead of celebrating diversity, and it is doomed to failure...

You then mention that you have "yet to introduce a system whereby after a certain period on benefits, everyone who was physically able to would be expected to do some form of full-time work helping the community, like tidying up the local park."

We take great exception to this statement. Firstly, the discrimination that people with mental health problems face is evident in your statement by referring to "physical ability'. Secondly, why do you think it is a "perfectly reasonable thing to expect" to punish people on benefits in the same way as criminals on community service, by compelling them to do full-time work, especially when in many cases it is a direct result of Coalition policies that people have ended up on the dole? Thirdly, if there are full time jobs to be done in the community, then why not offer them as full salaried jobs instead of 'punishments'? We fear that these will be jobs that have been slashed as part of the public sector cuts, only to be taken up by private providers who pocket a tidy sum while the unemployed are doing compulsory labour in direct contravention of article 4 of the European Convention of Human Rights…

You talk about contribution, and "recognising and rewarding those who have paid into the system for years"... So then, perhaps you could explain to us why people are now losing their Incapacity Benefit for good if they are migrated to ESA-WRAG and their partner earns more than £7,500. Yes, we did say that - £7,500 - just in case, with all these high benefit amounts you keep quoting, you forget about those at the pitifully low end.

People like Karen Sherlock. You may have heard her name. She was diabetic. Her symptoms included chronic kidney failure, partial blindness, a heart condition, and unpredictable bouts of severe vomiting. But the Department for Work and Pensions (DWP) essentially told her to get back to work. She lost her contributions-based Employment and Support Allowance and recently died of heart failure, scared and abandoned by a government that should have been caring for her. Ironically, she was placed in the Support Group only a couple of weeks before she died... it is too late for Karen and her family. Your words that "this is very simply about backing those who work hard and do the right thing" begs the question - whatever did someone as sick as Karen do wrong?...'

In July 2012, the government was nevertheless finding the appeals against Atos assessments were costing millions and there was gridlock with the hearing of appeals. But instead of making the Work Capability Assessment (WCA) fairer, so there were fewer appeals, the government proposed making appeals harder to access from April 2013 because so many people were having their original decisions overturned on appeal. They proposed that appeals would only be allowed once the DWP had considered a revision of your claim. The government indicated that there would be no time limit by which the DWP must complete a revision request, nor would there be provision for Employment and Support Allowance to be paid pending the outcome of the revision. This meant that a claimant who had wrongly been put onto JobSeekers Allowance could be parked there for months or longer, being hassled into applying for jobs, being subject to sanctions, before having their appeal heard. This extra hoop to jump through was now known as Mandatory Reconsideration - ManCon or simply MR for short.

On July 24th 2012, my sister got a letter. A white envelope. The message on the back read 'this is not a circular, please do not throw away'. It said 'Atos' on the envelope. My sister thought it might be for me, as she had already had an assessment within the previous twelve months. She had just four weeks to return it. Under the Equality Act 2010, employers and services are supposed to make reasonable adjustments for disabled people - that would include filling in forms you would think. But no. They made unreasonable adjustments from six to four weeks. My sister has suffered with anxiety and agoraphobia all her adult life (similar to me, but takes different forms in each of us, although there are huge overlaps). Initially she was placed in the WRAG (Work Related Activity Group) which meant that she'd been awarded enough points to pass the Work Capability Assessment (in other words, had been found unfit for work). This group was described as the bullying group where claimants could be 'mandated' onto the highly controversial Work Programme. For some poor hapless souls in the WRAG, they were to be pressured and sanctioned like people on Job Seeker's Allowance. My sister's case went to appeal which was scheduled for March 2012. She couldn't go but a friend from our local Welfare Rights Union represented her. The hearing was adjourned pending receipt of all her medical notes. The new appeal was scheduled for June 2012 and again my sister's representative went on her behalf and she won her appeal and was put in the Support Group. This was common practice i.e. when someone had just won their appeal Atos would send out a letter a few weeks later beginning the revolving door of pressure once again. Unnecessary torture for the most sick and vulnerable in society. I had to see my sister's tears and distress. Her fear. I knew what that felt like. I lived in fear too, as did thousands of others. I still do. They were/are punishing people. It was/is morally wrong. The government knew it was going on. The government were the architects of it. We are still left with the legacy today.

Many of us in Facebook groups and elsewhere in social media were now sitting ducks for trolls and DWP snoops, riled up in a climate that was ripe for abuse against long term sick and disabled benefit claimants. Of course nobody had to declare their benefits status or otherwise in public, but some of us had decided to be high profile in order to support or advise others in their struggle e.g. what they should write on a form to increase their success etc. It was safer to create a second identity on Facebook. Even so, it astounded me that some fellow disability campaigners didn't quite 'get' the need for having a pseudonym or campaigning account, even though it was well known that Atos assessors and DWP employees regularly snooped in Facebook groups. People with mental health problems or trust issues are also naturally very guarded and suspicious. My friends knew I had a campaigning account but then former 'friends' can fall out and turn on you on Facebook. I have learned it's better to keep your guard up in so toxic an environment. The government had succeeded in creating an atmosphere of suspicion and mistrust.

In July, two programmes were aired on national television. Channel 4's *Dispatches* saw former GP, Stephen Bick, going undercover to train as an Atos health professional. He was told that the DWP had given Atos targets and if more than 12% of claimants were put in the Support Group then the Atos health professional would possibly have to go back and change some of the information. The woman who was 'training' undercover reporter Mr Bick explained that with physical assessments, e.g. problems with arms, that the disability had to be bilateral (i.e. in both arms) to score points. So that if someone only had the use of one arm they would score no points. The woman said that all they needed was the use of one finger which proved they could press a button. The woman herself thought it was tough but these were the guidelines. Then there was the new rule about mobilization - that even if someone couldn't mobilize but could with a wheelchair they would be treated as if they had a wheelchair.

Immediately afterwards, airing on BBC2 was *Panorama* with the unfortunately titled *Disabled Or Faking It?* Many of us were dreading it as the BBC had been very pro-government or at least not anti it in their coverage of such issues. However, it was generally felt that the BBC programme was better in that it covered a lot more. For instance, they mentioned mental health problems, not just physical ones. They even mentioned fibromyalgia.

Meanwhile on a fibromyalgia forum, old chestnuts were being bandied about. Our 'own community' spewing out well-trodden lines about the 'genuine disabled' (i.e. us) and all those who were 'milking the system' (them). Of course, they had been fed this line so much over the years. It was that little word 'genuine' implying as it did that there were loads of 'ungenuine' or 'fraudulent' people out there, rather than a tiny number and there were and always have been people who specialize in DWP fraud anyway.

But benefit fraud was extremely low: 0.7% for disability benefit. Nothing has ever been 100% fraud-free but this was about as low as it got. Far more worrying was the number of ill people being denied benefits and dying because of it. Far more worrying too was the widespread fraud by the rich in the form of tax evasion and avoidance. But it was in the government's interest to have the poor fighting amongst themselves in classic divide and rule tactics.

In August 2012, I began the Nothing4Something group on Facebook. This was a coming together of how I and others felt as artists with disabilities and/or long term health problems. The original group description has changed little:

We are sick. Sick of the 'something for nothing' rhetoric when we are in fact people who receive nothing for something. That is, we give something and expect nothing or very little in return. This is a group to celebrate the creative diversity and art forms of the long term sick and disabled, and those with long term health problems be they mental, physical or both, visible or invisible, fluctuating or chronic. We create not only for the health and benefit of ourselves but for the wider community. Our expression is through our writing, our art, music, satire, film, photography, video, radio, poetry, crafts, embroidery, quilting, song, novels, blogs, diverse thought...

If we make any money at all, it is not enough to live on. Successive governments don't value the arts unless they are economically productive. They only value us as economic units, hence all the talk of 'something for nothing'. We are all nothing to them unless we are economically self-reliant... They talk about us as idle and that they cannot afford our art. When they refer to hard-working people, when did you last hear this in relation to artists? ...In an aggressive Capitalist society, we are dispensable if we can't be self-reliant, even though our health problems prevent us from being self-reliant. The arts is precarious, our health is precarious - we are thus doubly affected. They talk about the creative industries and the creative talent of our society but they are withdrawing tax credits for self-employed disabled people - even though self-employment is the only viable option for many disabled people...

The Big Society is alive and kicking on the internet. People give and share their creative endeavours for free or for little remuneration. A government that really cared about the creative talent of its people would invest in its artists, and would subsidise those unable to be economically self-sufficient. They would encourage the long term sick and disabled who spend their time creatively and beneficially, instead of seeing them as only economic units to be beaten, bullied, controlled, disempowered and erased.

We resist.

We won't have our arts broken.

August 2012. Our former MP was one of those who spoke about her own experiences of post-natal depression and panic attacks in a mental health debate in the House of Commons on June 14th. She made the error of saying the route out of it was work. That may well be the case for some people, but not all, and it was dangerous to try and have a one-size-fits-all response. My sister and I wrote to her persistently as the Welfare Reform Bill was going through parliament but she always trotted out the party line.

The generalizations and assumptions that were being made by the government were damaging i.e. assuming everyone could return to work in spite of their mental health problems. In fact, it's a mistake to conflate anxiety with depression - many people suffering from depression need to be working; many people with anxiety get worse by working.

Choice and control are always key.

Around this time draconian measures were brought in for the under 35s who were now expected to share accommodation, and would only receive the 'Shared Accommodation Rate' of Housing Allowance should they fail to do so. My mother wrote to the minister about this and the letter she got in reply was signed by that strangely named fellow who signed all such letters to the DWP - Goff Daft, and he must have thought we were. Daft, that is.

But this was the sentence for me that really stuck in the craw:

The Government wants work to be people's first choice and so are limiting Housing Benefit for those slightly older working-age individuals who have recourse to public funds.

I was so incensed I wrote in my diary: 'First choice? Try telling that to the thousands of unemployed people who have no choice and can find no work, because five people are chasing every job vacancy and obviously in some parts of the country it is much higher...'.

It's long since been obvious to me that it isn't work people are afraid of, if they are able to do some, it's the idea of being forced. Let's substitute work for sex, for a moment. Sex is supposed to be something freely given, an expression of love or lust between two people. For others, perhaps those who've been in a relationship a long time, the spark may have disappeared and partners may feel it a bit of a tedious duty, like others feel about having been in their job for too long, but nevertheless, they go through the motions, for other benefits. Those benefits in a marriage could be for security, safety, companionship. The same could be said of work; the job may be stale, but there are benefits such as security, companionship, and of course, there may be financial benefits. Maybe there aren't, maybe the money isn't worth it, just as in the relationship, maybe it is dead and time to move on.

But none of these cross a line. But forced work, is no difference to forced sex. Forced sex has a name. If a person doesn't consent to have sex, then it is rape. The raped person will feel abused, worthless, guilty, shamed, devalued, angry, powerless. Long term effects may include anxiety attacks, panic attacks, agoraphobia, depression, suicidal thoughts and attempts. This is what happens when people lose control of their autonomy, their right to say who they sleep with and when. It is now agreed that in a civilised society that this should be a person's right, it affords dignity, self-worth and self-respect. Shouldn't this also apply to work? Shouldn't work also be a choice: something that affords dignity, self-worth and self-respect? We've all heard the government rhetoric but on the sly they are using compulsion and force. They aren't the stereotype rapists who jump at you and overpower you in a dark alley. They are much too clever. They use subtle language, blackmail, power and authority to get you into bed against your will. The results are the same and they are devastating. They take away your autonomy, your ability to act freely, your capacity for choice, your capacity for creativity, your capacity to make a simple decision. They incapacitate you, in fact.

I decided to create a blog called Mog's Blog (later changed to Paw Lore) and posted along the lines of the above under the title 'Forced Work'. It was reposted by our friend and fellow campaigner, Asterick Jones. In an ensuing conversation:

Asterick: A4E - 50 Shades of Workfare! Work is no different in MY morality, but the mainstream view is that life itself is like a form of conscription, you must go to school, then vocational subjects (Uni), then have a career and "put something back" and then try not to cost the state too much in old age, the population is just there to serve the economy not the need to be individual and positive creative people.

In August that year, my sister, who got into the Support Group on appeal, had a new ESA form sent out less than a month after the appeal decision. This was commonplace. Claimants hassled in an endless revolving door of assessments, appeals, tribunals and reassessments, costing the tax payer millions. It wasn't ignorance or stupidity on the part of the government, it was by design. Designed to hassle, humiliate, grind down and eventually kill people.

My sister and I decided to start a 38 Degrees campaign as nobody had done a campaign on the scandal of cuts and the number of deaths as a result of welfare reform. We included a link to Calum's List and Peter's List, both of which were recording the deaths of people who had tragically died as a result of the reforms. We called it 'Stop The Welfare Death Scandal' and mentioned the flawed Work Capability Assessment causing 32 unnecessary deaths a week by forcing the long term sick and disabled into work or work-related activity. We managed to get to about 6000 signatures all told but it took a long time and we abandoned it since you needed 150,000 signatures before securing a debate.

In August, IDS was backing up his reform with propaganda with statements such as "Some people on sickness benefit have not been checked for ten years even though their condition has improved. They are used to getting their money with no requirement to get a job and have an 'I don't have to work if I don't want to' attitude." Duncan Smith claimed that the government's rigorous new checks on people on benefits were succeeding, and announced tougher measures were to come. He added: "All the chasing of inactive people into work is having a big effect. The figures for work experience for young people – that the Left hate and call slave labour - show around 50 per cent are coming off benefits and getting into work."

August saw another tragic and untimely death – that of Cecilia Burns, aged 51, from Tyrone. She had her benefits stopped in February, in spite of having breast cancer, and was awarded zero points by Atos. Cecelia was declared fit for work and she lost about £30 a week. Not only did she have to endure the medical treatment for her cancer but she had to endure the financial stress and indignity of it all too. She'd been working since the age of seventeen, paid her stamps, and only stopped work when she was pregnant, before her illness. She began her campaign in February to get the Atos decision overturned, and she did eventually, but she died just a few weeks after having her benefits reinstated.

Meanwhile protestors gathered outside Atos headquarters in London to coincide with the Paralympics. It was a supreme irony that Atos were sponsoring the Paralympics while stripping people of their disability benefits behind the scenes...

In September, something in the ESA manual on incontinence caught my eye:

46

The descriptors cover an assessment of continence while the customer is awake. Incontinence which occurs only while asleep (enuresis) is not regarded as incontinence in terms of the legislation as, with the appropriate personal hygiene, this will not affect the person's functioning whilst awake e.g. at work.

I found this staggering. Somebody with incontinence at night would feel embarrassment and shame. They would have the time-consuming practicalities of changing and washing soiled sheets, and it would have an impact on their social life and relationships, but work came above all that, so desperate was this government to shoe-horn everyone into work, regardless.

At this time, the onslaught on benefit claimants was coming in thick and fast, so there was little time to breathe, let alone protest. Disabled people were wearing themselves out. I think the onslaught was deliberate, it disorientated people so that they didn't know what to focus on and it wasn't only massive cuts to welfare budgets, it was to all public services, so energy for campaigns was dissipated as people tried to focus on specific campaigns. At this time details of a leaked document appeared on social media suggesting that the government was thinking about docking £71 a week (that is 70% of ESA WRAG benefits) for people in that group who failed to do enough to prepare for work, including going on the Work Programme, without good reason. It was outrageous enough and beggared belief that they were thinking of sanctioning sick and disabled people up to £28 (ie the disability component of their ESA) but to take away most of their income was despicable in the extreme. I wondered at the time what would constitute not being a good reason.

Not only that, they could dock it for increasing lengths of time until the claimant had 're-engaged' with the process.

The problem with leaked documents was that whatever was leaked always came to pass sooner or later.

In the same month, I wrote to my MP about the proposed increased sanctions in the ESA WRAG and her response included the following:

'The system aims not to be discriminatory but does aim to install sanctions on those who continue to refuse to take up offers of employment. If someone is too sick to work they will be protected and supported by the state, however if someone can work, then they will be made to work. Without sanctions there will be no way of ensuring these policies are fully implemented.'

This demonstrated a new hardness, and not even a pretense at caring. The fact that they were happy for ill people to live on £28 per week showed a new depth to which they had sunk.

The onslaught and the political rhetoric was stepped up in October with George Osborne speaking at the Tory Conference: "...

then you get the commuter getting up at 6 am and looking up at his neighbour's window with the blind still down and sleeping off a life on benefits". I posted this on Facebook and here are some of the responses from those people supposedly "sleeping off a life on benefits".

AC: Love to see them survive with some of our illnesses on benefits, and they'd soon shut their big tory traps.

RL: or even the commuter who looks at the place with the blinds shut... of the bedroom of someone who has in fact killed themselves due to the severity of their illnesses and has been treated in the most inhumane way by this government. or the person with blinds shut, who has had no care is isolated and alone and has died alone, with out a shred of compassion. despicable evil, and heartless...they disgust me.

SS: Maybe the neighbour works nights and has just gone to bed! Ie a PC who has spent the night protecting the neighbourhood...

In October, my sister received yet another ESA50 which sent her into a spin and a meltdown. She had already been sent one a few weeks previously after winning her appeal and getting into the support group. It seemed Atos were harassing her before she'd even heard back from the last ESA50 she'd been sent.

Meanwhile the Tories were becoming so bold that Lord Bichard talked about OAPs being conscripted into Workfare in order to receive their pensions. I wrote a satire about this in my book *Lost The Plot* because I never dreamed it would ever be talked about seriously. The sinister thing is that ideas first mooted as outrageous have a nasty habit of coming to pass. In my diary I wrote, 'They are so arrogant, because nothing is stopping them, they are on a roll, like mad axemen running amok, and if they can get away with it they will.'

In November, I posted another blog to my Mog's Blog called 'The Genuine Word' after Jane Moore of *The Sun* talked about 'helping the genuinely vulnerable and disabled' on *Question Time*. Coming from one of *The Sun*'s mouthpieces, it was a small step forward that the vulnerable in society even got a mention but she immediately killed it dead with that one word 'genuinely'. That one word spoke volumes and we were hearing it more and more. By inserting that word before the 'sick and disabled' (where it was usually inserted) these media and government spokespeople were causing untold damage. They knew exactly what they were doing, of course. They didn't have to spell it out because the inference was deafening: there were a whole lot of ungenuine sick and disabled people out there who were, in more popular parlance, 'faking it' or 'scrounging off the state'. Such use of language is dangerous and brutal. The rise in disability hate crime coincided with this vile propaganda.

In November 2012, failed banker Lord Freud (or 'Lord Fraud' as he was dubbed) claimed that the poor should take more risks because they had nothing to lose. How could someone with with such eminent lineage in the field of psychoanalysis not understand basic psychology? The poor had everything to lose: their house, their food, their warmth. In that situation, people don't take risks. Risk-taking comes with security and confidence and a cushion to fall back on if all fails.

On December 3 2012, International Day for the Disabled, a National Day of Remembrance was observed for all those who died as as a result of the Welfare Reform Bill and people observed a two minute silence at 11 am in memory of all those who died. Unbelievably, on that very same day, the government increased sanctions for disabled people in the ESA WRAG Group. You just couldn't make it up. This prompted our comrade, Paula Peters to write her poem: Lest We Forget.

The Independent stated:

'Today happens to be the United Nation's International Day of Disabled People, a day to focus on removing barriers to creating an inclusive and accessible society. It would appear that the ConDem Government is marking this occasion by starting to allow private companies and jobcentres to force more than 300,000 disabled welfare claimants into unpaid work experience for an unspecified length of time. Furthermore if they aren't up for a bit of legalised slave labour, they can be stripped of up to 70% of their benefits and forced to live on a mere £28.15 a week...'

On December 5th, my sister, when out, happened to come across the funeral of a man in his forties who died on the streets of our town on one of the coldest nights. She said there were lots there in the Civic Square. Our then Tory MP had supported the cuts making housing unaffordable for many. She voted along with her party for cuts to the disabled, the poor, the vulnerable, many of whom have been clobbered with extra housing benefits to pay and she supported the bedroom tax.

Still in December, I wrote in my campaign diary something which I used for another of 'Mog's Blog', entitled: 'That someone up the road... could be you.'

This arose from that overworked trope seen in benefits forums and threads: 'There's someone up the road from me claiming all s/he can... s/he's a money-grabbing skiver and knows how to get all s/he can out of the system...' It struck me as odd how people always knew 'somebody up the road' who was 'scamming the system' because of course, they were really going to pour out their personal health problems to their sworn enemies. Private and intimate health matters are exactly that – so how come these 'nosey-parkers' knew so much about someone else's private and intimate health conditions and what they were claiming?

The answer was simple. These were people you presumed were

your friends, maybe they were neighbours who you stopped and chatted with. Maybe you let slip a few personal details because they were neighbours and you assumed they were genuinely interested in your health when in reality they were gleaning the facts from you; gathering information so they could pass judgement on what little amount of information you'd volunteered. Maybe you'd confided in them about your depression or your fibromyalgia and the fact that you were getting DLA. Maybe they saw you on a good day, out and about, and naturally thought you must be faking it. They wouldn't pass judgment to your face - that would give the game away, surely - no, they preferred to spatter it all over public forums.

The moral of the blog was that your health was nobody else's business other than your own and your GP's. They weren't doctors, they didn't know your medical history and why would you tell them? Even closest family members and friends may not be privy to this information, so best not give these snoopers ammunition to use it - most likely wrongly - against you.

While the welfare reforms were being enacted, the right wing tabloids were having a field day with their headlines. My sister and I decided to fight back with a bit of direct action. Once when we were in *Morrisons* and were greeted by the latest screeching headlines on the front page of the *Daily Express* - something along the lines of Labour being the party of shirkers because they voted against freezing benefits to one per cent for three years, along with a handful of LibDems who voted against the government - we got hold of a wodge of *Express*es and turned them and their lying headlines over. This was something we started doing from time to time. Failing that we would actually shame buyers who were perusing the newsstands. "Don't buy the *Mail* or the *Express*," we'd say, "they're full of Tory lies." Or if we happened to be in a waiting room where some unsuspecting person had their nose in one of the offending papers we would make loud protests along the lines of "Eeek, a *Daily Heil* - I can't bear to be in the same room as it."

On January 23rd 2013 there was a post in one of the Facebook benefits groups I help run:

Matt P: Hi everyone, if you had to choose, which would you go for: drinking bleach or jumping off Beachy Head? I haven't quite decided what I'm going to do, but the likelihood is I will have to choose before the summer.

Of course there were many comments offering him support and urging him not to. Matt P thanked everyone for their kind words and thoughts.

But I assure you that I may have no other option. A friend of mine took his own life almost a year ago now by jumping off Beachy Head - trust me, it is 100% effective.

Luckily by the end of the thread he had felt sufficiently listened to and his life cared about by people who barely knew him. Many people may threaten to do this when they have no other option and sadly a few will actually go ahead and do it.

In January 2013, Michael Meacher's wrote a blog: 'The nasty party does its dirty work on the Welfare State'. In it he stated:

The power of the right-wing media... has again been put on show by its persistent fusillade of vilifying propaganda against the jobless and low-paid to assist their Tory government allies in pinning the blame and the burden for deficit reduction on the most vulnerable families in society. The one argument used by Tory MPs to shore up the unalloyed nastiness of Tuesday's Benefits Bill – the first to cut benefits in real terms for nearly a century – was that it was wrong for benefits for the unemployed to have risen by 20% since the financial crash while wages for those in work have only risen by 10%. But people don't buy things in shops with percentages; they buy them with money. And in money terms 20% of the £71 a week JSA is £14, whilst even for the lowest-paid in work 10% of the national minimum wage is £23 a week. So actually even those with the lowest wages are £9 a week better off than those on benefit... This bill has nothing to do with deficit reduction... It is intended to demonise the jobless as shirkers, even though there are today only enough job vacancies for 1 in 8 of those chasing them, and to tarnish Labour as a friend of 'scroungers'... it is intended to vilify Labour, in rightly voting against the bill...

On Feb 7th 2013 a brown envelope from the DWP arrived for me. I'd been waiting for it and dreading it so it wasn't unexpected. Friends asked me how I felt having finally received the dreaded brown envelope. I told them that I was less panicky than I thought I would be because I knew my enemy. I felt like I'd been revising for an exam and now the exam had come and so I was prepared. I knew those spare ESA50s that Atos kept harassing my sister with would come in useful. I could use one as a dummy and pencil in my answers with the help from the Benefits&Work guidelines as well as the ones on My Legal (a blog written by the local Welfare Rights Adviser at the local CAB who had helped us in the past).

Also in February 2013, lawyers for Cait Reilly and Jamie Wilson who forced a Judicial Review over the Work Programme won their appeal as the Work Programme was said to be legally flawed. In *The Guardian* Zoe Williams stated that it was 'a punch in the face for this government, the Work Programme generally, and workfare in particular. Even the profile of these two cases significantly damages the reputation of this policy, whose raison d'etre is that long-term unemployment is the result of people getting out of the habit of work.'

People who who had their JSA stopped on similar grounds to Reilly or Wilson's could now claim the money back, they were told.

Williams pointed out that 'People on unpaid schemes, were being counted as employed to massage the government's figures...'.

But if we thought that was the beginning of the end of the Work Programme, we were sadly mistaken. The DWP were defiant. IDS tried to get the law changed retrospectively to avoid repaying any money. The DWP vowed to press on with the Work Programme. "We want to increase the use of mandatory activity and sanctions for the unemployed as the schemes work", a senior government source said. "The short, sharp shock is usually enough to get the work-shy back into employment so the plan is to extend the practice, not retreat in the wake of this odd court decision."

The response was truly shocking - a disgusting, arrogant and inflammatory response to people who weren't "work-shy" but just wanted a decent wage for a decent day's work.

Lord Bach in the House of Lords spoke out on cuts to legal aid coinciding as they did with radical welfare reform. "... it must be a deliberate government policy to bring in radical and damaging welfare reforms at the same time as making it impossible for the vast majority to appeal against the decisions that affect their daily lives... it is a disgrace and a scandal... not only is there the blow for people of losing benefits... they have the added blow of not being able to go and get simple, quality and cheap legal advice to advise them...".

In March I wrote a blog 'Fibromyalgia - Warning DWP Malingering' because I'd unearthed some worrying information. Fibromyalgia (along with ME) is one of those conditions that UNUM Provident (parent company of Atos and advisers to the government over welfare reform) tried to discredit in the United States so that they didn't have to pay out insurance claims. The same model was being used over here and I read their PDF on the matter entitled 'Fibromyalgia - Guidelines For The Disability Analyst'. Under Section 9 of the pdf was the statement:

9.6.1 Malingering

Although apparent inconsistencies between the clinical findings and the claimed degree of disability are an intrinsic feature of these disorders, we must be alert for any areas where such inconsistencies are so unusual or conflicting as to suggest that the claimant is making an intentional attempt to simulate disability in the pursuit of gain. The use of 'malingering' and other pejorative terms should be avoided but it is possible to describe outstanding contradictions in a way that is fair, overt and yet non-judgemental.

So there it was in black and white. This is what Disability Analysts thought about people with fibromyalgia (consistent with the disability denial that swept the States and resulting in UNUM Provident being sued and banned in many states there).

Meanwhile, Michael Meacher reported on his blog something that was unprecedented in his forty years of Parliament:

...the work capability assessments carried out by Atos Healthcare, has been a top-line matter on the political agenda for many months now. I had therefore written to Iain Duncan Smith on 31 January asking him to receive a delegation from some of the key campaigning and analytical groups ... I heard nothing for more than 5 weeks and therefore put down a Parliamentary Question on the Commons Order Paper asking when he proposed to answer my letter. As a result I got an immediate reply from Mark Hoban, the junior minister dealing with Atos matters, saying 'my current diary requirements mean I am unable to accept your invitation at this time'. That is simply civil service-speak for a flat No... I therefore waylaid Hoban in the lobbies after a vote and as soon as he saw me, he said immediately "I'm not seeing you". I was taken aback at his aggressiveness and said "But you can't possibly do this, this is a matter of the highest political importance and it's your responsibility to talk to and listen to key disability organisations about this matter, however contentious it might be". He simply replied blankly "I'm not seeing you", and repeated it 3 or 4 times. I kept on insisting "Why not?" and finally he said "I'm not seeing Spartacus". Again I was taken aback and asserted that in my view Spartacus had analysed hundreds of cases, prepared a very detailed and thoughtful analysis of the implications arising from these cases, and even if he disagreed strongly for whatever reasons it was his responsibility to meet them...

Meanwhile, the DWP continued denying that job centres had targets for sanctioning claimants on Job Seeker's Allowance, even though whistleblowers had indeed confirmed there were league tables in Job Centres and pressure on Job Centre staff.

Still in March, *The Guardian* reported that 'staff in a jobcentre in the West Midlands were this week told that the team who submitted the Stricter Benefit Regime "Refusal of Employment" referrals would be rewarded with Easter eggs...'.

A jobcentre source said: "This is an abhorrent trivialisation of the impact of such sanctions on the most vulnerable people in our community. We are not selling time share or insurance policies, these are people's livelihoods being rewarded by confection."

It was also reported that 'those claimants that do not understand the system ... are most likely to have their benefits sanctioned as they are easy targets.'

In April 2013, a whole raft of measures came into force as a result of the Welfare Reform Bill. These included the Bedroom Tax, Council Tax changes, and the scrapping of Legal Aid for people who most needed it e.g. disabled people who were getting their benefits slashed.

The much-loathed Esther McVey said, "many who get DLA and are officially classed 'disabled' are no such thing: only three per cent of people are born with a disability, the rest acquire it through accident or illness, but people come out of it. Thanks to medical advances, bodies heal." Again she perpetuated the myth that there were huge numbers abusing the system and also claimed that DLA "was the most abused benefit in Britain" though in reality it was one of the least abused. (In fact figures for benefit fraud had just appeared in *Liberal Conspiracy*, February 26th, showing that the rate for disability fraud was 0.5 %, one of the least abused benefits). But McVey was softening up the public ahead of her department's plans to remove half a million people from DLA. At the time I questioned why she was the Minister for Disabled. Would we have a man to be the Minister for Women? Or a straight person to be Minister for Gay People? Or a white person as Minister for Black People?

On April 3rd 2013, the terrible truth emerged about Mick Philpott and the manslaughter of six of his children in a plot that went horribly wrong. Never one to miss an opportunity to capitalize on a tragedy if it involved claimants, the *Daily Hate Mail* lived up to its name and sunk to new depths with its front page headlines: 'Vile Product Of Welfare UK'. The offence there should have been obvious to anyone with an ounce of common sense and decency. By inserting the phrase 'Welfare UK', at a time when huge cuts were being made to the Welfare State and impoverishing tens of thousands, this vile headline implicated everyone who claimed welfare - or Social Security as it used to be known - and therefore somehow guilty by association of committing such a heinous act. The fact that Mick Philpott and his wife received welfare was irrelevant. Tom Pride summed it up much more succinctly in his blog with the headline: 'Peter Sutcliffe - vile product of long-distance lorry-driving', demonstrating the ridiculous nature of such a headline.

Many of us submitted a complaint to the Press Complaints Commission.

Later that month, I was shaking when I opened the letter from the DWP, such is the fear they put us through, so it was a relief to find I found I'd been put in the Support Group. I was under no illusion and felt that Atos and the DWP needed to get appeals rates down and to show that the WCA had improved. Needless to say I had a massive 5 day migraine.

In May 2013 news came through Facebook about 53-year-old grandmother Stephanie Bottrill, who took her life because of the bedroom tax. She wrote it in one of her suicide notes to her son asking him not to blame himself but the government. She just couldn't afford the £20 a week that she needed and was worried about being homeless.

The DWP ploughed on nonetheless. In the same month they stated: 'Our schemes are helping people back to work but sadly some of those organisations offering jobseekers vital opportunities have been targeted by misguided campaigns...'. Responding to the ruling, Joanna Long, of Boycott Workfare, urged organisations to leave the schemes before the list was made public: "Workfare has meant less paid work for people across the UK, and exploitation for those forced to work for nothing. When the list of those using workfare is revealed, thousands of people will be reconsidering where they spend their money or make donations; hundreds will plan demonstrations. Companies and charities using workfare need to urgently reconsider whether they want to risk further involvement in these failing schemes."

Also in May 2013, two people with mental health problems won their case on the grounds that the Work Capability Assessment discriminated against people with mental health problems.

In June 2013 the Benefits&Work newsletter reported that 'We have links to a *Mirror* story about an ESA claimant who had a double heart and lung transplant but was found fit for work, wrote her letter of appeal crying in a hospital bed and learnt that the DWP would not change its decision just nine days before she died. Also to the story of the 62 year old woman offered a voucher to buy a tent in order to solve her housing crisis.'

In June 2013, I did a blog post in answer to a question posed by Broken Of Britain in relation to the DLA consultation some two years previously. I took one of the questions from the consultation and submitted my answer to the Broken Of Britain blog which they published. The question I focussed on was 'How do we prioritise support to those people least able to live full and active lives? Which activities are most essential for everyday life?'

I mentioned Maslow's Hierarchy of Needs as a good starting point. At the bottom of the hierarchy it's essential to meet the basic needs such as food, warmth (disabled people are often more inactive and are more likely to be spending long amounts of time at home and therefore are going to incur more heating costs), and shelter (housing needs must be met and adapted).

Moving up the hierarchy after the basic needs are met, come things like protection, security and stability. This is where legislation would be made to protect vulnerable people. Health protection would be another example e.g. being able to access doctors and dentists, and being able to have free prescriptions and support when having routine medical procedures.

It's only when the essential needs are met that a person, disabled or otherwise, can try and engage with the wider society eg being able to participate in social activities without it being assumed that a person is able to work. Both work and social activities can take it out of the disabled and vulnerable but social life can be tailored to an individual's needs without being pressured by government departments. An allowance could be the difference between a disabled person participating or not eg an allowance can help with transport or the accompaniment of another person.

Being able to participate in creative activities can lift the spirits and feelings of well-being of a disabled person, providing fulfillment and a sense of worth in the way some work can do. Again this can be tailored to an individual's needs without being pressured by government departments.

Feelings of achievement, self-worth and fulfilment can only be achieved when the essential needs are met.

In the same month, a Facebook friend, posted a picture of a bench with 'pneumonia bars' in the USA. Another friend said they had such bars on a bench in York. Underneath the picture was a statement which read:

The newly installed pneumonia bars, are indeed a form of violence, as their purpose is to prevent the homeless from sleeping on the benches, and, forcing them to sleep on the damp ground, thereby, risking contracting pneumonia.

How could they be so heartless that they would deprive the homeless even of a park bench?

In late June, there were some screeching headlines in the *Daily Hate*, I happened to have my flyers with me in my trolley regarding benefit fraud and I'd been waiting to post some in *Mails* given the right opportunity which this surely was. One can be fairly anonymous in *Morrisons*. My bit of direct action.

Later in the summer, IDS was criticized in the *Mirror* for 'claiming that the reason behind the explosion in demand for the lifeline service (food banks) was a growth in awareness rather than the effect of recent benefit cuts.' The Trussell Trust charity chief executive Chris Mould claimed a "clear and strong link between benefit changes and benefit delays, and people needing help from our food banks."

The row came as thousands of Britain's poorest children faced starving this summer while schools were shut for the six-week holiday. Charity bosses said they were "now seeing children in Lancashire with pot bellies, sunken cheeks and sallow complexions like youngsters found in famine-ravaged countries...".

On September 10th my sister got yet another ESA50 15 months after she won her appeal.

Meanwhile Atos were up to their usual tricks as posted in one group on on social media - such posts were regular and typical:

This is a possible ploy to help you fail the ATOS medical. At Manchester assessment centre Albert Square, just outside the car park at the front of the ATOS building there is a man who has been reported to be asking people

for directions, he seems to be asking those with crutches etc who clearly are
going into the building for a medical assessment. When he asks, he appears to
be watching you for eye contact etc. We suggest that this MAY be a ploy to
get you to chat to a stranger, and therefore fail the descriptors 6 & 7 on
communication and understanding others. We may be wrong but we do know that
in the Manchester ATOS waiting room there's a 50p stuck to floor to trick you
to see if you can bend down and pick it up ok therefore showing your manual
dexterity... the assessors are receiving incentives to find you fit for work
which are not removed if you appeal their decision, so it's in their best
interest to fail as many as possible...!

In October 2013 I posted another blog:

Welfare Dependent - who isn't?

If you're anything like me you'll be climbing the walls by now with that over-
used phrase so loved by the ConDems and the media: welfare dependency. We need
to challenge and expose some of these nonsense soundbites for what they are.

Think about that expression 'welfare dependency' for a moment. When
you analyse it you realize it's the most ridiculous expression on earth. I
mean what is normally meant by welfare? What do you understand by it? I
understand it to mean looking after the health and well-being of my fellow
human beings. Dictionary definitions will say 'the health, happiness, and
fortunes of a person or group' and 'statutory procedure or social effort
designed to promote the basic physical and material well-being of people in
need.'

So being dependent on that or at least that concept is a good thing,
isn't it? Of course, successive governments are using it to mean 'benefit
dependency' but again, put this phrase under scrutiny and its absurdity is
all too evident. Benefits are only, after all, the means to living, eating,
clothing, shelter, warmth. Show me a person who isn't dependent on these
things. Are MPs, CEOs, bankers or any other wealthy individuals you care to
mention somehow immune from this sort of dependency? Of course not.

Successive governments are using the phrase 'dependency' in the sense
of addiction, with all its negative connotations. If you think about it, it
is actually the wealthiest in society who are more 'addicted to a culture of
dependency' - a phrase, governments, and especially the Coalition, like to
bandy about a lot. Can it be called dependency at all when it is essential
for living?

Let's face it, if we substitute the word 'welfare' for the one of
'oxygen' - (we're all oxygen-dependent) - we expose the phase for its utter
stupidity.

Following on from that blog I did another one entitled 'The Party Of
Welfare - so what?' The Tories accused Labour of being the Party of
Welfare. Well, so what if they were? Instead of shying away from it,
I wondered why Labour weren't embracing it. Shouldn't they have
turned it back on the mean and nasty Tory rhetoric and simply have
said, 'Yes, we care about people and we're proud of that, we would

be deeply ashamed to be the party who took that basic security away from people. What sort of a government would be?' It was a missed opportunity. Such was the climate of harshness and brutality that while the two main parties were so busy locking horns to see who could be the meanest (and dragging in smaller bullies like UKIP) there was a gaping void meanwhile waiting to be filled with benevolence, compassion and humanity. (This was of course filled by Jeremy Corbyn in 2015).

In January 2014 I noted in my diary just how relentless and depressing it all was, which is why I'd not made a recent entry. Running up to Christmas and afterwards while offline, there was all the stuff about the rise in food banks and Labour called for an enquiry (to be mocked by a sneering IDS and Esther McVile as she got up and tried to blame Labour in a heartless response and telling the opposition that the best route out of poverty was work.) Food banks had risen in the previous years from around 40,000 to half a million. But then something even more incredulous happened. The EU were going to offer something in the region of 22 million pounds to provide more food banks and the government rejected it and decided to only offer 3 million instead. They rejected it because it came from Brussels and they didn't want Brussels 'telling them what to do'. So rather than having Europe 'interfere' they'd rather people starved, just to appease the anti-Europe brigade. It was obscene. Furthermore, IDS refused a meeting with the Trussell Trust, accusing them of being anti Welfare Reform.

The Guardian stated that IDS rejected any suggestion that the government was to blame. "I strongly refute this claim and would politely ask you to stop scaremongering in this way. I understand that a feature of your business model must require you to continuously achieve publicity, but I'm concerned that you are now seeking to do this by making your political opposition to welfare reform overtly clear."

January 2014 also saw the start of a relentless raft of poverty porn programmes which really took off after the 'success' of James Turner Street, dubbed Benefits Street. There was a huge backlash on Twitter. Tom Pride showed some of the comments on his blog *Pride's Purge* that were nothing but vile hate crime. Watching the programme, I found I empathized with many of the claimants. 'Fungi' had drug/ alcohol problems and had been abused as a child. Many of them were scrabbling round to make ends meet, their children were going hungry, some were threatened with eviction having been affected by the Bedroom Tax and there seemed to be a strong sense of community. For example, White Dee was helping out her neighbours by making phone calls on their behalf to the DWP and looking after Fungi's finances so he wouldn't blow it all on booze.

By February 2014, there was growing opposition from the

churches and the bishops and even the Pope about the devastating effects of the Welfare Reform Bill and the growing number of food banks. I noted how shameful it was that in this day and age and from the seventh wealthiest country in the world that people should be going hungry and should be punished for being unemployed especially when the government had thrown them in this situation.

In April 2014 G4S were awarded the contract for the new 'Help To Work Scheme' for people who had completed the work programme and not found a job. They were expected to sign on every day and be forced to do this scheme. Was it any surprise that G4S got the contract? G4S who dealt with criminals (and who had been guilty of huge criminal activities themselves) were now to be rewarded for criminalising the unemployed. It was ghastly.

On October 15th, 'Lord Fraud', the man who had referred to claimants as 'stock' said that disabled people weren't worth the minimum wage but could work for £2 an hour. He apologized but his Freudian slip was out of the bag and the disabled community was calling for his head. Labour's Angela Eagle said Lord Freud's comments were not "an unfortunate slip of the tongue" but "revealed the truth about this government's attitude to people with disabilities". Freud reportedly said there "was no system for going below the minimum wage". But he added: "...there is a group... where actually, as you say, they're not worth the full wage...".

Department for Work and Pensions sources said that 'Lord Freud... was not advocating working for less than the minimum wage, he was looking at whether the state should top up to those levels, if employers paid less - something that is not government policy.' Why then didn't he simply say that?

In December, someone called Lotte on Facebook stated:

I have terminal cancer, my prognosis is 0-3 years and I was diagnosed in March 2014 with my brain stem glioma. In April 2014 I was placed in the support group for 3 years and I have gone from being able-bodied to hopelessly disabled. I have many neurological deficits including diploplia, dyspraxia, dysarthria and dysphagia... this means that I have double vision and am going blind, I'm very clumsy and most days I drop everything I pick up, my speech is failing and one day I won't be able to communicate verbally at all and I have such difficulty swallowing that I now have a feeding tube. I cannot leave the house alone and I'm at risk of choking and need 24 hour care. They speak of me going into residential care, but they hope to keep me in my own home for as long as possible. The trouble is degenerative, nothing will get better, only worse, the cancer can't be cured. I'm 37. Now. I can deal with all that. I'm alive! And I can still do stuff!! What I cannot deal with is that I am on the Work Programme!!! I received this letter today... demanding I come to an appointment with the Work Programme on Tuesday or they'll stop my benefits. HOW SICK DOES A PERSON HAVE TO BE BEFORE THE HARRASSMENT STOPS??...

At first the WRAG left me alone, the manager was a good guy, he told me to go the MP etc. However, some weeks ago I got a call from WRAG, the girl said she was the new manager and she HAD to call me every 6 weeks to 'see how I am'. ...Now today I get this letter and I'M KICKING OFF.

The creepy bit is that in October 2013 as soon as I submitted my desperate, pleading, I'm so ill, ESA50 suddenly the WRAG harrassed me to come in. I spoke to the manager who said they could never sanction me if on ESA anyway?? Then he put me on phone contact only until I got SG, he even called me to ask if I'd had a decision on the ESA and he told me he couldn't do anything to get me off the WP until I was in SG, so he was a good guy. This new woman is just 'following orders'. How does she sleep at night??

In October 2014, Maximus were brought in as the replacement for Atos. In January 2015, Sue Marsh, disability campaigner and blogger, was hired by Maximus at a price of £75K. There was an awful lot of stick for Sue Marsh as well as support. Sue stated she was doing it to change things from the inside. Other well known campaigners such as Johnny Void thought it was she who was being played. On her Facebook page she stated that Maximus had asked her to be their Head of Customer Experience, and were giving her a 'fairly free reign to devise a strategy to bring about a wide range of improvements to the service from a customer perspective.' Her job would cover all aspects of customer experience and she vowed to give 'the same 300% passion and commitment to them that I have been giving to campaigning. I won't be writing about them, I'll be working with them.' She defended her decision by claiming that it was 'a campaigner's job to change things, not just to make a lot of noise... Everyone knows that I'm obsessive about changing this, giving me a job to keep me quiet would be to not know me at all.'

Clearly this was an enormous life-changing decision for Sue Marsh and her husband gave up work. Sue knew she would face criticism, but said she wanted to finish what she started and felt she was best placed with her 'knowledge and personal experience of what is wrong with the system at the moment and a rich research background to draw on from the Spartacus Network reports and all of the other amazing research done by DPOs, charities, individuals, groups and academics over the last few years...'.

As expected there were a mixture of responses on the blog. Here is one response (truncated):

I feel a bit uneasy about this. It is my view that no amount of improving the customer journey... will solve the real problem - i.e. it's not how the WCA is delivered that's the problem, it's the WCA itself. I do not know if your contract involves a gagging clause, but it seems to me that it will be near impossible to continue to agitate for change in DWP policy while working for one of its contractors. The head of medical services at Maximus is the same guy who was in the same job at Atos, and previously Unum; the staff delivering the same WCAs are the same; the centres are the same; it's all the same. The only real difference is that Maximus are getting about £100 million more than Atos did for the same work... Maximus does not, as other posters have pointed out, have a particularly good reputation elsewhere. However good at this job you will be, and however much you improve delivery of the WCA, you will not be in a position to deal with the fundamental iniquities inherent in the assessments, the lack of experience of the HCPs doing the assessments, the targets set for denying illness and disability, and the stupidity of DWP decision makers... You have been a very powerful voice for me and others like me on this and on the introduction of PIP, and I'm grateful for that... I am sorry to say that I can't help feeling that this new job means we have lost a voice which speaks for us in a media that cares so little about us and what we have to deal with on a daily basis... I wish you well, Sue. I hope this is a good move for you and your family. I hope your health doesn't suffer. As to whether you can really effect change, or are forced to become a mouthpiece for a rogue company which is implementing a disgusting policy, only time will tell...

Another response:

One of the biggest issues I have with many people who campaign is the same issue I have with Labour's shadow DWP ministers - the conflation of disability with illness. I am debilitated by chronic and serious illness, and you could argue that I am thus disabled, in that I am not as able as I used to be. But - ESA is not about disability, supposedly; it's about illness and the financial support ill people need while they recover or adjust to what may not be a very long life. Some of those people may be capable of work, some of them may desperately want to work but be unable to do so - but the WCA is not designed to determine any of that. It is designed to elicit any tiny bit of capability which is used as evidence that what the claimants and their doctors say regarding fitness to work is untrue. It's based on a disability denial insurance algorithm. It may well be the case that Sue can make 'the journey' a more comfortable one; it may be that she will be able to address complaints better - but she can't render a vicious policy better just by providing 'customer care'. She knows how harrowing a WCA can be - but it's not the delivery of the WCA that is the root of the problem - it's the WCA itself, the forms, the decision-making, the complete and utter uselessness of ESA as a benefit for sick people... I like and respect Sue. Her battles with her health have a lot of resonance with many of us - and I have appreciated her voice in our media and I am grateful for her work so far. But this? I don't know. I really don't...

In July 2015 we sent another email to our MP replying to one of her inadequate replies to our letter. Here are some excerpts:

Thank you for your letter of 26th June 2015... but we don't find your quotes from the DWP at all reassuring when there are leaked documents suggesting that disabled people are in the firing line to lose £30 of their disability benefits... They will be forced to live on £73 a week, losing over 30 per cent of their income. Can you imagine losing 30 per cent of your income, much higher though it is? This is pernicious and cruel and we are appealing to your

humanity and compassion... If George Osborne announces further cuts to
disability benefits, i.e. the slashing of the extra £30 for those in the ESA
WRAG group... then we will hold all Tory MPs accountable for not standing up
and protecting the most vulnerable...

We went on to say that in these more enlightened times, it is hard
to believe how widespread child abuse was in the 1970s. It is shocking
to think that's how it was back then. Yet there was a culture of
blame, excuse and denial, children weren't believed or they were
ignored. Authorities turned a blind eye and knew what was best for
children. Disability abuse is now the new child abuse. Believe it or
not, people will look back one day and say 'how on earth were people
allowed to treat disabled people like that?' Because to withdraw
their financial support when they have no other ways of earning is
abuse as it leads to poverty, neglect, deterioration of health,
homelessness, fear, hunger and in extreme cases, death. But it won't
be for want of trying. Millions of people have been calling for an
end to this absurd, brutal and obsessive austerity. But all that's
happening is the screws being tightened even further.

Still in July, the working poor were clobbered as expected in
the Tory budget, with tax credits being withdrawn at a lower threshold
than previously. Osborne thought he was being clever by raising the
minimum wage to a paltry £7.30 the following year and and to £9 an
hour by 2020 and calling it a Living Wage. Osborne's critics -
including the IFS - said that the poorest would be worse off because
the chancellor was withdrawing tax credits before replacing it with
a decent wage. IDS was cheering from the sidelines like a grinning
idiot saying 'fantastic' when it was anything but. Other measures
included freezing tax credits and public sector workers for four
years. As expected the ESA WRAG £30 component was to be abolished for
new claimants. This meant that disabled people who had passed the
Work Capability Assessment would be on the same rate as those on
Jobseekers Allowance. The Tories described the £30 as a perverse
incentive but the only thing perverse was their party. Furthermore
they announced cuts to housing benefits for all under 21s (except in
exceptional circumstances). So once again it wasn't the landlords
getting clobbered. They also cut corporation tax and inheritance tax.

In the September 2015 Benefits and Work newsletter the lead
article was: 'DWP'S NIGHTMARE SUMMER'. They stated that the DWP was
facing huge criticism over the ESA death statistics, which they
'tried to bury over the last bank holiday.' They reported that
thousands of claimants had died 'within weeks of being found fit for
work, leading to calls in the national media for the resignation of
IDS'. They further reported that it had been revealed that the DWP
had invented bogus ESA claimants praising the sanctions regime.
Leaflets featuring fake claimants had to be withdrawn. Finally, there

was 'the leaked news that the government's long-term violation of the human rights of claimants - and in particular the multiple cuts to benefits - are being investigated by the United Nations.'

On October 8th, day of local elections, I told the woman with a blue rosette outside the polling booth that I wouldn't ever vote Tory and went into a tirade about what they were doing, particularly IDS. She said he was very passionate and that a "lot of people in wheelchairs want to work... you know, there's nothing wrong with their brains". So, by that did she mean that 'they' don't have mental health issues? Or was she generalizing that all physically disabled people in wheelchairs can work as opposed to all the people with mental health issues who cannot work? In fact, what was she saying? What about all the people in wheelchairs who have both physical and mental health issues?

In January 2016, the Lords threw out the plans to reduce ESA for people in the WRAG group by £30 for new claimants in 2017. This would have effectively meant that those in the WRAG would get the same as people on Jobseekers Allowance - a paltry £73. It is astounding that this amount was considered a livable amount for young fit people on JSA let alone for seriously disabled people on ESA.

On February 3rd a former PIP assessor shared a post on the Atos Miracles page: 'I was PIP assessor as a nurse and left due to the disgusting way the targets were the priority... I detest the company and the way people at the end of the forms are critiqued and commented on in a derogatory nature in the offices and could not believe what I thought would be a compassionate approach to how people manage their lives and disabilities. This is certainly not the case, just target driven numbers and lots of health professionals leave, especially mental health nurses like me, as it is against a duty of care primarily to patients. I hope they lose all their contracts..'.

It is not uncommon to see former assessors blowing the whistle on what they have seen from the inside.

In March, the Lords ran out of options with the cuts to the ESA WRAG because the proposal went back to the 'house of conmen' who invoked parliamentary privilege just as they did for the bedroom tax.

Then cruelly, unbelievably, George Osborne announced the cuts to PIP to fund Corporation Tax and some other tax cut. The amount was exactly the amount needed to fund this - to the tune of £1.3 billion. The Tories were shameless by this stage. Thankfully there were Tory backbenchers rebelling, and one disabled Tory who was now an ex-Tory. He closed his website in disgust.

I had my own PIP assessment home visit in March, someone from the local Disability Service visited me and then the assessor from Atos who appeared pleasant and empathic. Luckily, I received a full award that time but three years later when I had a PIP 'review' I had a much tougher time even trying to get a home visit and then the 'niceness' of the assessor tricked me. I felt abused by her getting me into her trust, like one of those conmen who comes into your house with a charming smile but is there to get you to sign away your life savings. I lost the mobility element I'd had for twenty years and yet I had more conditions restricting me than ever before. Needless to say, I exposed the flaws in her assessments and her failure to take my GPs evidence into consideration and had my award restored. But not everybody can deal with the stress and anxiety. I don't know that I would have had the energy to take it all the way to appeal although it's what I advise others to do. Even two years on from the PIP review in 2019 I'm still waiting to hear from the NMC (Nurse & Midwifery Council).

The proposed cuts to PIP meanwhile rumbled on and IDS resigned. He was clearly trying to paint himself as the caring face for the disabled when he had, in fact, presided over brutal welfare cuts. IDS appeared on the Andrew Marr show, still portraying himself as a man with a conscience and that Cameron and Osborne were going in the wrong direction of travel by balancing the books on the backs of the poor.

But in *The Guardian*: Stephen McPartland, a leading Tory tax credit rebel, was also extremely critical of Duncan Smith, telling LBC that the sanctification of the former party leader was "disgusting" and he had "never seen evidence of this conscience people are talking about" during meetings about welfare in the past.

In February 2017, George Freeman, Tory MP, made some scandalous remarks about PIP's original purpose being for 'the really disabled' and 'not for people with anxiety taking pills at home.' I was incensed that he should make such comments when his own government had supposedly put mental health on a par with physical health with the Mental Health Discrimination Act.

This was his response to an Upper Tribunal ruling in favour of people with mental health problems who weren't getting any points for mobility and travel. The government had tried to ride roughshod over the Upper Tribunal's decision by tweaking the PIP regs as they wanted to deny people with mental health problems the benefit. It certainly looked as if there were grounds for discrimination under the Equality Act because what the government were in essence saying by denying people with mental health issues the same treatment as those with physical disabilities was that leading an active a life as possible with mental health wasn't as important as those who have physical disabilities.

In April 2017, *Panorama* did a programme on *The Benefits Cap*. Richard Bilton, reporter for BBC (who'd also done a programme, *Britain On The Fiddle*, something I wouldn't watch on principle with a title like that) actually suggested to a disabled woman who wanted to bring up her young family that it was a luxury! It was beyond outrageous. Mothers wanting to bring up their children? How very dare they? But what made my blood boil even more were the people adding their comments to *Panorama*'s Facebook page. That is why Bilton's report was so inflammatory because people believed that's how much people were getting in benefits but as I had to keep posting to the majority of them - 'the 20K mostly goes to the landlords. They're the ones who charge the high rent, for pity's sake.' Comments were also along the lines of being worse off than those on benefits and again I had to put them right thus: 'If working people can't afford rent they are ENTITLED to housing benefit top up. The Child Poverty Action woman said it in the programme.' But I supposed they didn't hear that because it didn't fit in with their scapegoating of benefits claimants which was the not-so-hidden agenda of the programme. Again the myth about their 'taxes funding these people'. People are extraordinarily blinkered thinking benefits payments are a one-way street. People on benefits and disability benefits pay VAT, utilities bills, rent, buy food, pay for fares, taxi fares, carers and so on. Much employment and services depend on the benefits of claimants to keep them afloat. Money is recycled. Other comments mentioned 'a sense of entitlement' as though families aren't entitled to a roof over their head, food in their bellies, warmth, basic human rights. In my day people used to 'moonlight' to sign on and nobody thought anything of it. That was fraud but the attitude now is to blame people who are just trying to do right by their families. And finally the comments about women who chose to stay at home with their children as if they were committing the worst of crimes. Do they value motherhood so little? It seemed to me so demoralising that these views were just as entrenched as they were at the beginning of my campaigning seven years previously, probably even more.

Prior to the election in 2017, I wrote a blog about why disability benefits are political. I was amazed how some people claiming disability benefits like ESA and PIP could still be in ignorance as to why things were so bad for them, why they they being put through repeated tests, why they had been sanctioned and so forth. For many they didn't see the Welfare Reform Act brought about by the last Coalition government as having any relevance to where they found themselves today.

I shouldn't have been amazed. It was all carefully choreographed by the Tories and the largely right wing media that supports them. It was in their interests to have the poor set against the poor, the working poor vs the out of work poor, the 'genuinely' disabled vs 'all those other people faking it', the poor vs the immigrants, the 'deserving' vs the 'undeserving', the young vs the old. So, the slow drip drip of poverty porn piped through our TV screens and newspaper, month on month, year on year, softened people up, made people turn on 'the other'. Divide and rule they have us. United we stand, divided we fall. It's as simple as that. And the Tories knew it and exploited it.

Many people were disengaged with politics and would trot out phrases such as 'They're all as bad as each other'. People would often say 'it was Labour that introduced the Atos and Capita assessment'. While this was true to some extent, previous Conservative governments had paved the way long before under the likes of Peter Lilley. On Wikipedia it states about Lilley: 'Shortly after his appointment, Lilley entertained the Conservative Party's annual conference by outlining his plan "to close down the something for nothing society". Lilley also replaced Invalidity Benefit with Incapacity Benefit in 1995 'in the hope of checking the rise in sickness benefit claims. Unlike its predecessor, Invalidity Benefit, this new welfare payment came with a medical test that gauged claimants' ability to work.'

Whatever scandalous horrors that occurred under New Labour's watch internationally, they introduced a raft of measures at home to reduce inequality. In terms of benefits, they introduced Tax Credits, Tax Credits for the over 50s, the Minimum Wage, an extra £28 for disabled people on JSA, free Legal Aid for people on benefits and other people on low incomes, voted against the Bedroom Tax, reduced homelessness and voted against the worst of the Welfare Reform Bill to name a few. Many of these measures helped the poorest in society and most of them were scrapped at lightning speed once the ConDems and subsequently the Tories came into power.

In 2017 Jeremy Corbyn pledged to scrap the WCA and put benefits in line with inflation. He wanted to bring back Legal Aid and get rid of punitive sanctions. He promised the WASPI Women £155 a week.

A lot of myths abound, for example, the one about there not being enough money in the pot for everyone to have what they need but again people are sold the politics of austerity for so long they believe it. But we are the sixth wealthiest nation in the world. We can afford to look after the sick and the vulnerable and let's not forget how many millions - if not billions - go unclaimed in benefits every year. It was never about austerity but ideology.

In May 2017 a woman with learning difficulties confronted Theresa May on her campaign trail about the cuts to benefits and how she wanted DLA returned as she couldn't live on £100 a month on PIP. Theresa May didn't know what to say, her campaign was carefully choreographed and she crumbled when confronted head on.

In August 2017, Labour's Debbie Abrahams stated: 'Shamefully for this government, Britain is the first and so far only country to be investigated by the UN for breaching the Convention on the Rights of Persons with Disabilities. Even worse, they chose to ignore the recommendations from the UN CRPD report, evading their responsibility towards disabled people in our country. The UN's report showed that the austerity policies brought in by the government in 2010 to reduce public spending, such as the destructive bedroom tax and the damaging cuts to social security and social care budgets were infringing on the rights of disabled people."

Ever since I heard about the Green Party's idea for Unconditional Income back in the 80s, I have supported the idea in principle. At the end of 2016 I did a submission for the case for Universal Basic Income from a disabled artist's perspective. In my submission I replaced the word 'universal' with 'unconditional' although they both needed need to be there.

Some argue against the idea of universal benefits because they don't think those who are well off should be in receipt of them e.g. the TV License, bus passes, winter fuel allowance etc. However, universal benefits are the most cost effective to administer, otherwise you get into the business of means-testing that is costly and divisive. That's not to say there isn't a place for some means-tested benefits as supplements or add-ons e.g. disability and housing elements. But the universal aspect of it should be just that, and unconditional. Universal Credit is a bastardisation of the universal principle. It's not universal and it's not unconditional which is why it's a wasted opportunity.

Obviously, the costs and the means-tested elements have to be thought through and worked out. Not everyone is going to agree at what constitutes a decent amount but something like the state pension figure is a good starting point for working age adults. Housing and extra costs for disability would need to be treated separately. A fair and affordable figure could be arrived at by learning from other European countries and those further afield where it's been pioneered previously e.g. Canada.

But as it stands at the moment, we have the poorest people in society, being coerced and sanctioned if they can't find work, even though everybody without exception, is entitled to shelter, food and warmth. It is outrageous in one of the world's richest economies that it should be otherwise. We quite rightly wouldn't let a dog be cold and hungry on the streets and yet successive ministers seem to think it is quite okay to have people hungry and homeless.

We have now reached a stage with the global economy and the rise of digital economies, where there isn't enough employment for all in the traditional sense of the word, and where's there's a lot of 'free'. The internet is full of free. This is to be welcomed for the consumer, though not so good for the creator or the adviser which is why the old model is no longer relevant in the 21st century. This was the case even prior to Covid. This is why it is time to separate 'work' from 'income', that is, work in the widest sense. Successive governments have used many a mantra to get the public onside regarding welfare reform, but for me one of the most pernicious is the 'something for nothing' one. The language is designed to rubbish and dismiss those unable to earn enough to live on. In reality, the reverse of 'something for nothing' can be found in every nook and cranny in society. People volunteer, they parent, they care for the elderly and the sick, they care for animals, offer advice, be it legal or access to justice, or study to improve themselves. E-books, photos, music downloads and instructive manuals are offered as free downloads daily on the internet. People are by nature altruistic and government ministers and rhetoric have been slow to acknowledge this, if they've acknowledged it at all. Sometimes they've corrupted it. As said previously, all I see is the nothing for something society wherever I look: people giving something in return for 'nothing'.

As an artist myself (in the wide sense), I also have a special interest in UBI from that perspective. Art is not only therapeutic but makes people feel valued and worth something. It can be done from home. Most artists with disabilities or long term health problems are never going to make enough to live on because of precarious health and because the arts are precarious.

Unconditional and Universal Basic Income would mean people could take risks, instead of living in fear, knowing that they didn't stand to lose all should they fail. Fear incapacitates. Bullying, coercion and sanctions also incapacitate. The separation of living needs (warmth, shelter, food, clothing) from the higher pursuits in life i.e. how one spends one's time is long overdue. I don't buy the argument either that 'nobody would work' if we had UBI. If work is such a good thing, then people will want and choose to do it, as they already do, that is, work in the widest possible sense. It is absurd that in the 21st century we still have an old-fashioned 20th century model of work, where people leave their houses to work for an employer for 35 hours a week. Yes, that is one form, but work has diversified greatly in the last few decades and the working from home has only been hastened by the pandemic.

Surely it is time to value and celebrate that which is 'given away' for the benefit of all? Isn't it time we had a real and intelligent debate about work in the wider sense of using one's time valuably and/or for the benefit of the whole community instead of seeing how many more hoops the DWP are going to make the long term unemployed and disabled jump through just to get money to live on?

Ref: BENV / 21

Update March 2021

My writing of the diary gradually fizzled out in 2017. That may be because I got out of the habit, I grew tired or that the changes that'd come in thick and fast during the passage of the Welfare Reform Bill had already been implemented. But make no mistake, we're still feeling the impact today.

There's been untold hardship and many more deaths. One of these was Errol Graham who died in June 2018 aged 57. He was an amateur footballer when he was young. By his mid 50s he had mental health issues, had become reclusive and was unable to leave his Nottingham flat. He had no income for food and wrote a desperate letter to his DWP assessor asking of them: 'Please judge me fairly… it's not nice living this way.' He couldn't attend his WCA and his benefits were cut off. He weighed four and a half stone when bailiffs found his body inside his flat. He had starved to death in one of the richest countries in the world.

In August 2019, also in Nottingham, Philippa Day, aged 27, was found collapsed at her home beside a letter rejecting her request for an at-home benefits assessment. She died after two months in a coma. She had been diagnosed with unstable personality disorder and type 1 diabetes, for which she'd been receiving DLA. But in January 2019, after she'd applied for PIP, her income was reduced from £228 to £60 a week. In June 2019, she called the DWP to say she was "starving" and "couldn't survive like this for much longer". She was asked to attend a face-to-face assessment despite it being "distressing" for her and her mental health problems were "exacerbated" by the process. The coroner concluded that call handlers repeatedly failed to flag that Philippa needed "additional support" due to her mental health problems. The coroner also found that the failure to administer her benefit claim in a way that avoided exacerbating her mental health problems was the "predominant factor" that caused Philippa Day to overdose.

Covid19 then came along in 2020, exposing the terrible inequalities and what ten years of austerity has done to the poorest communities. In 2020, the UK's Office for National Statistics showed people living in more deprived areas experienced double the rate of Covid mortality than the more affluent areas. Covid19 also exposed the unfairness of the system. People who needed to self-isolate after being exposed to the virus complained they couldn't live on £95 per week Statutory Sick Pay (one of the lowest rates in Europe). Other people who would be left with no income if they didn't go to work and who weren't eligible for furlough were directed to Universal Credit. This was boosted by £20 per week to cover the hardship caused to those affected by Covid-19 but once more it exposed how woefully inadequate the rate of UC was prior to this. The extra £20 per week has made a massive difference to poor families and is, for instance, the difference between eating adequately or not. But even at the time of writing this is only being extended as a temporary measure.

Meanwhile, for claimants going through an endless revolving door of assessments, the Covid restrictions provided a welcome break as face to face assessments were paused, and claimants could breathe a sigh of relief for a while. Even so, telephone assessments have gone ahead, and some claimants have reported hearing confidentiality breaches and other voices in the background from Health Care Professionals doing these assessments from their homes. Others have come across the same tricks over the phone by the private companies. For instance, claimants have read their reports where assessors 'saw' how the claimant moved around over the phone!

While Covid19 has given us a breather from the punishing regime - reminding us what life can be like without the constant threat of an assessment hanging over us - too many of us fear that austerity will be back in some form. The chancellor will tell us all how generous he's been but at some stage will remind us that he has to balance the books. And sadly it doesn't bode well for claimants, not until and unless we have a genuinely progressive, anti-austerity government.

Poverty and the Pandemic: The Legacy of Shirkerphobia

James Morrison

Britain 2021: soaring in-work poverty; falling life expectancy in deprived areas; the resurgence of rickets, scurvy and other 'Victorian' diseases; and children going to bed hungry as their parents face invidious daily dilemmas of whether to put food before fuel. Teachers, nurses and care workers queuing at foodbanks; record levels of homelessness; and disproportionately high COVID-19 death rates among BAME and other precarious groups forced to troop into work throughout the pandemic and hemmed into multi-generational accommodation in areas of high-density, poor-quality housing. None of the brute realities that have been exposed and exacerbated by the events of the past year were inevitable — and all might have been wholly avoided, if only successive governments had adopted different visions of the kind of country they wanted the UK to be.

As we are forced to endure endless Johnsonian platitudes promising a fabular 'new normal', backed by a 'levelling up' programme that will tackle the impending post-COVID economic turmoil by 'building back better', let us not forget: the unconscionable levels of poverty and disadvantage visible to all of us today are (in the short term at least) largely the responsibility of the party he leads. During the now widely discredited 'austerity years' presided over by David Cameron's Conservative-led governments - a period from which Johnson himself seems (disingenuously) keen to distance himself - ministers embarked on a systematic, deliberate and vindictive discursive mission to portray Britain's working-age social security system (disparagingly re-framed as 'welfare') as an unaffordable luxury, and anyone unfortunate enough to have to rely on it as, by turns, 'shirkers', 'skivers' and 'scroungers'. To cheers from their acolytes in the popular press, the Coalition government embarked on a swingeing programme of cuts to the benefits system (framed as 'welfare reform') which, over Cameron's six years in office, shrank the working-age social security bill by a third - in the process, plunging tens of thousands of families into levels of hardship that even the government's own statisticians recognised as poverty and (in some cases) destitution[1]. Chief architects of this hegemonic political project were the then Chancellor of the Exchequer, George Osborne, and Work and Pensions Secretary Iain Duncan Smith - a man who had constructed much of his political 'brand' (following an unsuccessful spell as Tory leader) on his claim to have experienced a personal

---

[1]   Mackley, A., Foster, D., Gheera, M., Keen, R., Kennedy, S., and Wilson, W. (2018) 'Effect of Welfare Reform and Work Act 2016'. Available at: https://commonslibrary.parliament.uk/research-briefings/cdp-2018-0072/ (accessed: 3 February 2021).

epiphany during a confrontation with the realities of poverty on Glasgow's chronically deprived Easterhouse estate. In one year alone (2013), at the peak of its assault on the welfare state, the Coalition unleashed the following onslaught of cuts and reforms, in a sustained, unrelenting effort to reconfigure the extent and limits of social protection that working-age households could expect from future safety nets: an ongoing year-on-year real-terms freeze on benefits uprating for unemployed, sick and disabled people; a (subsequently reduced) household benefit cap of £26,000 a year; a 'bedroom tax' (or, in government-speak, 'spare room subsidy') reducing Housing Benefit entitlements for households with an additional bedroom, including those used to store equipment or cater for caring needs for disabled people; the rolling out of 'mandatory work activities', backed by three-strikes-and-you're-out sanctions designed to end the 'something for nothing culture' alleged to exist among the unemployed[2]; the abolition of council tax benefit for low earners and those without work; and the introduction of a (now widely reviled) all-in-one payment for low-income households, Universal Credit. In all, 42 changes to the working-age benefits system were initiated by the Coalition between 2010 and 2013 alone, according to a contemporaneous audit by the Child Poverty Action Group[3] – 'reforms' which imposed real-terms cuts totalling £22 billion a year and, in the process, slashed the incomes of 450,000 people with disabilities (Disability UK) and 400,000 of the poorest families (Chartered Institute of Housing)[4]. All the while, efforts to drive down the benefit bill still further saw long-term sick and disabled people continue to be processed by profit-driven firms, such as Atos and Maximus, along an unceasing production line of fitness-for-work tests – euphemistically dubbed 'Work Capability Assessments' - as the death toll of people dying from their conditions or committing suicide after losing their payments continued to soar, by some (government) estimates to more than 81,000[5]. So dire were levels of poverty left in the wake of these, and later, cuts and reforms that, following a lengthy fieldwork visit to Britain, the United Nations Special Rapporteur for Extreme Poverty, Professor Philip Alston, condemned ministers for pursuing a policy programme that 'led to the systematic immiseration of millions

---

[2]   Gov.uk (2013) 'Benefit sanctions – ending the 'something for nothing' culture'. Available at: https://www.gov.uk/government/news/benefit-sanctions-ending-the-something-for-nothing-culture (accessed: 3 February 2021)

[3]   Butler, P. (2013) 'Every welfare cut listed: how much a typical family will lose per week', www.theguardian.com. Available at: https://www.theguardian.com/news/datablog/2013/apr/01/every-welfare-cut-listed (accessed: 3 February 2021)

[4]   Ibid.

[5]   Gov.uk (2015) 'Mortality statistics: ESA, IB and SDA claimants'. Available at: http://archive.is/j0nAF (accessed: 4 February 2021)

across Great Britain'[6].

But it was the instrument of discourse – made manifest through a meeting of minds between elite political rhetoric and the narratives of the tabloid media (both press and TV) – that enabled all of this to happen. By first constructing, then mobilising, a popular consensus based around the supposedly indisputable logic that all that mattered, in the aftermath of the 2007-8 financial crash, was the size of Britain's (historically unremarkable) budget deficit – and that the only way to address this was through the single-minded pursuit of spending cuts, rather than tax rises – ministers had paved the way for the ideologically driven attack the political Right had long dreamt of mounting on the post-war welfare settlement. What followed was a deluge of – sometimes subtle, but frequently blatant – anti-welfare propaganda, articulated through what often seemed like a calculated pincer-movement of political opprobrium and tabloid invective. In the weeks and months leading up to the full-frontal assault of 2013, there were signs of a concerted ramping up of the 'language of shirkers and scroungers'[7], often in keynote speeches. Most notorious, perhaps, was the maliciously divisive juxtaposition drawn by Osborne in his 2012 speech to the Conservative Party Conference between low-paid shift workers, 'leaving home in the dark hours of the early morning', beneath 'the closed blinds of their next-door neighbour, sleeping off a life on benefits'[8]. A foretaste of this had come three months earlier, when the mask of 'compassionate Conservatism' Cameron had carefully crafted during his years in Opposition slipped during a testy exchange with then Labour leader Ed Miliband at the parliamentary dispatch-box. In it he had sought to align Britain's two main parties with either side of the imagined dividing-line between the unemployed and low-earnings households generally – two groups that (lest we forget) are both reliant, to varying degrees, on social security due to the risibly low incomes on which they are forced to subsist. Jabbing his finger at the Opposition leader, Cameron constructed a soon-to-be oft-repeated rhyming couplet that revived a decades-old trope straight out of Margaret Thatcher's playbook[9] – asserting that while 'we back the

[6]   Ohchr.org (2019) 'UN expert laments UK's "doubling down on failed anti-poor policies"'. Available at: https://www.ohchr.org/en/NewsEvents/Pages/DisplayNews.aspx?NewsID=24636&LangID=E (accessed: 4 February 2021)
[7]   Garthwaite, K. (2011) '"The language of shirkers and scroungers?" Talking about illness, disability and coalition welfare reform', *Disability & Society*, 26(3): 369-72.
[8]   Osborne, G. (2012) Osborne, G. (2012) Speech to Conservative Party Conference, 8 October, https://www.newstatesman.com/blogs/politics/2012/10/george-osbornes-speech-conservative-conference-full-text (accessed: 3 February 2021).
[9]   Thatcher, M. (1975) Speech to Young Conservative Conference, 8 February, http://www.margaretthatcher.org/document/102484 (accessed: 3 February 2021)

workers', Labour 'back the shirkers'[10]. With one jab, the discourse of shirkerphobia was born[11].

As the long-heralded tidal-wave of 'welfare reform' kicked in over ensuing months, such oppositions - sometimes reworked as 'strivers and skivers', but often reduced to more timeworn antonyms such as 'hard-working families' and 'scroungers' - were repeatedly recycled, not only in government pronouncements but in tabloid headlines and, increasingly, through a new sub-genre of 'factual' television docusoap, which came to be dubbed 'poverty porn'[12]. In analysis carried out for my 2019 book *Scroungers: Moral Panics and Media Myths*, I found that the word 'scrounger' appeared in national and regional newspaper articles 2,103 times in 2013 alone - a fivefold increase on the year that heralded the start of the crash (2007), when it occurred 406 times, and a near-doubling of its 1,214 occurrences in the year the Coalition was formed (2010). Significantly, the term 'shirker' - the Coalition's favoured iteration of the 'scrounger' - also peaked in 2013, hitting 593 mentions in the press, compared to 229 the previous year; 173 in 2010; and just 112 in 2007. Similarly, 'skiver' soared to 570 appearances in 2013 - more than tripling from 163 in 2012. It had been used 136 times in 2010 and 120 in 2007. While each of these terms subsided somewhat in their media prominence during ensuing years, they remained historically high at least until the election of Cameron's short-lived majority government, in 2015 - during which year they were still used in 1,187, 267 and 210 articles respectively[13]. The ongoing prominence of these pejorative terms throughout this period is just one measure of the extent to which an increasingly normative and accepted 'scrounger discourse'[14] came to permeate the national conversation, as the interrelated subjects of austerity, the deficit and welfare reform continued to influence - and, on occasion, dominate - the direction and tenor of public debate. Around the same time, Channel 4 launched its first major foray into popularising poverty as primetime entertainment, in the guise of the reality show *Benefits Street*, whose many subsequent imitators - spread across not only commercial channels but the BBC - would do more than any other form of popular culture during this period (including the press itself) to establish what sociologist

[10]   Douieb, T. (2012) 'Workers and shirkers', *Huffington Post*, 11 July, http://www.huffingtonpost.co.uk/tiernan-douieb/workers-and-shirkers_b_1664564.html (accessed: 3 February 2021)
[11]   Quoted in Morrison, J. (2019) *Scroungers: Moral Panics and Media Myths*. London: Zed Books.
[12]   Jensen, T. (2013) 'A summer of television poverty porn', *Sociological Imagination*, 9 September, http://sociologicalimagination.org/ archives/14013 (accessed: 3 February 2021)
[13]   Morrison, J. (2019) *Scroungers: Moral Panics and Media Myths*. London: Zed Books.
[14]   Ibid.

Tracey Jensen has characterised (after Pierre Bourdieu) as a 'doxa' of anti-welfare 'common-sense'[15]: doubling down on Coalition rhetoric to frame working-age benefit recipients, especially the unemployed, as workshy (and often fraudulent) wastrels. A measure of the growing public appetite for such caricatures (beyond *Benefits Street*'s ratings, which peaked at 4.3 million or a 17.2 per cent audience share) is the extent to which such terms featured in Google searches, with a prolonged spike between January 2012 and June 2014 – the timeframe during which the successive anti-welfare policy assaults launched by the Coalition played out[16]. It was not just newspaper editors and ministers who obsessed over shirkers and scroungers, then, but the public too - as an interest in stories stigmatising the unemployed and disabled as non-contributing drains on finite taxpayer-funded resources at a time of constructed national emergency was continually primed by elite agenda-setters determined to distract attention from (and displace blame for) the root causes of the country's economic woes.

 As is so often the case, however, the discursive power of this narrative ended up owing as much to accident and happenstance as deliberate discursive engineering by the powers that be. After several years of obsessively seeking out 'scroungers' and 'shirkers', cashing in on the commercial newsworthiness of these topical political narratives, while emboldening ministers to go further and faster in demonising and punishing benefit recipients, the tabloids were rewarded in 2013 with the ultimate scrounging poster-boy – in the baleful figure of Mick Philpott, an unemployed father of 17 who had killed six of his children by staging a fire at his Derby home in an effort to frame his former partner. The hysterical tabloid coverage which followed news of Philpott's actions, and attended coverage of his subsequent trial, was dominated by a distorting focus not so much on his manifestly criminal actions as the suggestion that they were intrinsically related to, and perhaps even symptomatic of, the fact that he was a benefit claimant. In this way, Philpott's deviancy was widely portrayed not as the (thankfully) exceptional case that it was but rather as emblematic of wider-scale pathologies held to be native to and/or typical of the unemployed as a whole. Hence the perpetually benefit-baiting *Daily Express* cast him not as 'Britain's most evil father' but as 'Britain's most evil scrounger', while the *Daily Mail* framed him as a 'vile product of welfare UK' and *The Sun* elided the supposed lesson from his case that over-generous benefits can 'debase humanity'[17]. Inevitably, it did not take long for the Philpott case to be

[15] Jensen, T. (2014) 'Welfare commonsense, poverty porn and doxosophy', *Sociological Research Online*, 19(3): 3.
[16] Morrison, J. (2019) *Scroungers: Moral Panics and Media Myths*. London: Zed Books.
[17] Quoted in Morrison, J. (2019) *Scroungers: Moral Panics and Media Myths*. London: Zed Books.

appropriated as a totemic case for more nakedly political purposes, too: in a wildly coincidental, or cynically choreographed, visit to Derby around the time of Philpott's conviction (depending on which account one believes), Chancellor Osborne used the opportunity to raise 'a question for government and for society about the welfare state, and the taxpayers who pay for the welfare state' about the wisdom and fairness of 'subsidising lifestyles like that'[18].

In Philpott's case, then, Britain was presented with the ultimate 'scrounger' folk devil: greedy, selfish, unabashed and criminally callous to boot. He represented the perfect personification or montage of supposedly interlocking forms of vice – and the legacy of his case has continued to act as a locus for the more stubborn strands of anti-welfare sentiment ever since. It is to monstrous caricatures such as this that ongoing suspicions of the nature and motives of working-age benefit recipients – especially the unemployed and those unable to work due to sickness and disability - owe their potency to this day. By extension, it is on the dishonest, inaccurate framing of such extreme and atypical cases as supposed exemplars of endemic or widespread problems of abuse in the system that much of the policy legacy of the Coalition, and that of preceding and succeeding governments, can be blamed. We can glimpse this legacy, in all its gory Technicolor, as we gaze out on the socially and economically ravaged Britain many people inhabit today – through eyes newly opened (for some at least) by the uneven casualties of COVID and the lock-downs and other restrictions that have disproportionately affected those already experiencing the worst inequalities (of income, housing, education and health). As I type, fiscal hawks in Boris Johnson's government are still doing everything in their power to resist growing calls for them to extend the one-year boost to Universal Credit they introduced to cushion the blow for the many people swept by the pandemic onto out-of-work benefits (often for the first time in their lives). Meanwhile, Work and Pensions Secretary Therese Coffey has suggested that her principal reason for preferring this to the one-off payment of £500 or £1,000 reportedly favoured by the Treasury is to avoid disincentivising people left without work due to the pandemic from seeking it – arguing that it might deter them from 'rushing out to take a job or increase their hours'[19]. Encroaching mass redundancies, widescale furloughing and interrupted earnings are at once, then, reframed not as the sorry outcomes of a dramatic public health emergency and resultant economic crisis, let alone of structural forces per se, but (once again) as at least

[18]   Quoted in Morrison, J. (2019) *Scroungers: Moral Panics and Media Myths*. London: Zed Books.
[19]   Quoted in Butler, P. (2021) 'One-off Covid benefit may stop people working, says minister', www.theguardian.com, 3 February. Available at: https://www.theguardian.com/society/2021/feb/03/one-off-uk-covid-benefit-may-stop-people-working-says-minister (accessed: 3 February 2021).

partly a symptom of individual behavioural defects; of the pathological cultures of 'welfare dependency' so persistently blamed for unemployment by right-wing politicians through history. From Keith Joseph's 'cycle of deprivation'[20] to IDS's 'something for nothing culture' to Coffey's imaginary of the COVID-era chancer, happily extending their prolonged period of involuntary furlough for a few more weeks for the sake of a £500 handout, in place of the regular uptick in Universal Credit they actually need: some things never change. Even at a time as desperate as this, the spectre of 'the scrounger' still lingers; not only refusing to die, but being revived and reanimated in new, ever more preposterous, guises. The real-world impacts of policies predicated on - and enabled by - a discourse of deserving versus undeserving poverty may be all around us, in plain sight, and on such a scale that they are slowly waking more of us up to the range and depth of inequalities that have for so long been downplayed or denied. But for as long as we continue to tolerate, even encourage, these stereotypes - as a culture and a society - there is a real danger that poverty and inequality, in all its forms, will only get worse.

JAMES MORRISON

is a writer and academic, currently working as a Reader in Journalism at Robert Gordon University, Aberdeen. A former national newspaper journalist, his research focuses on media and political discourses around marginalized and disadvantaged groups and the relationship between popular narratives about them, their own lived experiences and public attitudes towards them. His books include *Scroungers: Moral Panics and Media Myths*, *Familiar Strangers, Juvenile Panic and the British Press: The Decline of Social Trust*, and the forthcoming *The Left Behind: Reimagining the Socially Excluded*.

---

20   Quoted in Welshman, J. (2007) *From Transmitted Deprivation to Social Exclusion: Policy, Poverty and Parenting*, Bristol: Policy Press.

from Unspoken Companions: Poetry and Unemployment

Alan Morrison

After seven years of what might be termed the 'welfare hate', with over 80,000 deaths (and suicides) among sick and disabled claimants between 2011-14, approximately 2,380 within six weeks of the DWP and Atos declaring them "fit for work", it is only in recent months that the British pathology of what I term 'Scroungerology' has shown vague signs of a pausing for thought.

Undoubtedly some factors contributing to this latter cultural hiatus are the United Nations report condemning the Coalition and Tory Governments' abuses of disability rights through disability-targeted benefit cuts, and veteran social-realist director Ken Loach's Palm d'Or and BAFTA-winning film intervention, *I, Daniel Blake* (in some ways a polemical update on Jim Allen and Roland Joffé's superlative *The Spongers*, broadcast 1978, which juxtaposes the story of a single mother and her children targeted by punitive disability benefit cuts against the backdrop of the taxpayer-funded Queen's Silver Jubilee, and which is more than ripe for repeat).

These have come as timely reinforcements to several veteran campaigns – Disabled People Against the Cuts, the Spartacus Report, the Black Triangle Campaign, Calum's List et al – that have fought valiantly over the past seven years to put the catastrophic impact of the disability cuts in the public domain, in spite of the DWP and a complicit mainstream media's best efforts to 'bury' such issues.

Nevertheless, we have a long way to go politically and attitudinally as a society until we can wrestle back some semblance of a compassionate and tolerant welfare state which looks after the poor, unemployed, disabled and mentally afflicted, and without recourse to stigmatisation and persecution. The front line of 'scroungermongering' is the thick red line of the right-wing red tops, most heinously the *Daily Express*, and, of course, every English person's favourite hate rag, the *Daily Mail* – the ubiquitous negative drivers of most public opinion.

To be on benefits today, no matter what one's personal circumstances or disadvantages, is almost a taboo, and one exploited ruthlessly by the makers of such televisual effluence as *Benefits Street, Benefits Britain: Life on the Dole*, and the reprehensibly titled *Saints and Scroungers* (one campaigner, Sue Marsh, has tried to re-appropriate that dreadful term on her admirably defiant *Diary of a Benefit Scrounger* blog).

In spite of a faint sense of relief felt across the unemployed and incapacitated communities at new Work and Pensions Secretary Damien Green's announcement that there will be no more welfare cuts beyond those already legislated, there is still cause for trepidation when said legislated cuts, of £30 per week to new Employment and Support Allowance (the old Incapacity Benefit) claims, kick in this April - certainly, then, 'the cruellest month' this year.

By something of a coincidence, my [new] poetry collection is precisely on the theme of the welfare and disability cuts... *Tan Raptures* gathers together poems composed during the past six years of remorseless benefits cuts and welfare stigmatisation. Some of it is from an empirical perspective, my having been for much of this period in the no-man's-land that is the 'Work-Related Activity Group' (abbreviated disparagingly to 'WRAG') of Employment and Support Allowance, where those who are deemed unfit for work for the time being but not necessarily permanently are placed (I am a lifelong sufferer of pure obsessional disorder, an unpredictable and debilitating form of OCD).

Poetry and unemployment often go hand-in-hand, if that's not a contradiction in terms, since writing poetry is a form of occupation (alongside editing it, publishing it, teaching it, mentoring it, workshopping it etc.), even if an often impecunious one as paid opportunities are few and far between. Indeed, the fact that poetry has very little 'market value', and employment or occupation in capitalist society is almost entirely defined in terms of earning money, almost all full-time poets are, paradoxically, 'unemployed'; at least, in purely superficial material terms. Through the sadly seldom-consulted prism of humanistic occupational theory, poetry is certainly an 'occupation' in the authentic sense of the term.

Many poets have been unemployed at points in their careers albeit 'poetically employed' at the same time. Indeed, unemployment is often an 'occupational hazard' of being a poet, and many either still are, or certainly have been in the past, intermittent benefit claimants. Capitalism has no time for poets since it deems them unprofitable and economically unproductive (in any case, it has their occupational replacements: advertising copywriters). ...The sometimes inescapable relationship between poetry and unemployment - bards on the dole - is almost never spoken let alone written about by poets. Poetry and unemployment are unspoken companions. But many poets will stifle a bitter laugh at the notion of a Department for Waifs and Poets (DWP).

In *Tan Raptures* I refer to the DWP as the 'Department for War on the Poor', since that is undoubtedly its primary purpose today. The collection includes polemical paeans to many victims of the Tory benefits cuts and sanctions, such as Glaswegian playwright Paul Reekie (suicide), ex-soldier David Clapson (death from diabetic complications/malnutrition), and the Coventry soup-kitchen-dependent couple, the Mullins (suicide).

The eponymous polemical poem is an Audenic dialectic in 14 cantos on the social catastrophe of the benefits caps, pernicious red-top "scrounger" propaganda, and Iain Duncan Smith's despotic six year grip at the DWP. It is also a verse-intervention of Social Catholicism, as epitomised by Pope Francis, in oppositional response to the "appalling policies" (Jeremy Corbyn) of self-proclaimed 'Roman Catholic' Duncan Smith.

The title *Tan Raptures* plays on the biblical notion of 'The Rapture' - the 'raising up' of living and dead believers to meet their maker in the sky - satirising the ubiquitous 'tan envelopes' that strike fear into claimants on a daily basis as passports to a twisted Tory notion of 'moral salvation' through benefit sanction...

Abridged version of original article published on *International Times*, 2017: http://internationaltimes.it/unspoken-companions-poetry-and-unemployment/

RUTH AYLETT

Place and date of birth: London in 1951. Aylett teaches and researches computing at Heriot-Watt University. She is widely published including a piece in the 2019 Bread and Roses Anthology and in the *Morning Star* on the day of the 2019 General Election. Also in all sorts of magazines: *Butcher's Dog*, *The Poets' Republic*, *The North*, *Agenda*, and various anthologies.

Social Security

Stuck to chair
Waiting and waiting

Names are called, not yours
The shouting man strong-armed out

Your earlier heart attack is quite irrelevant
Just answer questions. We award the marks.

Rule Britannia

Britannia went down to the social
took her kids and asked for some bread
told there'd be money in five weeks time
went home and strangled them dead.

Britannia got zero from zero hours,
her landlord demanded the rent,
evicted her when she couldn't pay,
so Britannia went out on the street.

Britannia begged outside Tescos,
asking for coins from the shoppers;
too cold to sleep on the pavement
blasted the lot on some uppers.

Britannia went down to the social
and threw a brick through its glass,
swore at the people who worked there,
shrieked at the ones who walked past.

Britannia convicted of vandalism,
banged up for not paying the fine;
she hanged in her cell, but so what?
People do that here all the time.

Rule Britannia, Britannia rules the waves
Britons never never never shall be slaves.

MICHELLE BAHARIER

is a dyslexic contemporary artist and poet, and has also expressed herself creatively in performance, sound, sculpture installation, drawing and painting. As a socially engaged artist Michelle creates projects with communities. This includes performance art, sometimes in form of walks and other public art forms. She is able to voice the extraordinary, the ordinary, the unheard and bring neglected stories and histories to life. Michelle has been part of the D.I.Y arts and squatting communities. She observes human conditions and our journey through life, interwoven with our identities and in her case, as a disabled, working-class Jewish woman. Michelle studied Fine Art at Exeter College of Art and Design, and her Post Grad was at the Slade School of Fine Art. She has exhibited in the USA, Europe and the Middle East. Her sound piece called Sedition, part of Sound moves, is in the archives of Tate Modern UK. Michelle has authored many books, arts, poetry and cooking. She won the Julian Sullivan Award at the Slade School of Fine Art where she published her first poetry book, and the NatWest Bank Award for Visual Arts. She was censored from an art exhibition run by the *Big Issue*, as her work about homelessness was seen to be too controversial. She founded the mental health charity CoolTan Arts, run by people with disabilities. CoolTan Arts published a women's poetry book, *Hysteria*, which won 27 awards, notably the 2015 GSK Impact Award. She famously started the Largctyal Shuffle walks, CoolWalks and Southwark hidden stories. She features in all the Brixton Poets pamphlets.

It is happening here and no one's acting

I am just an administrator,
Not a murderer
I am just acting within the rules
I am an instrument of government
I carry out the rules
Because I am an instrument of government
I am just a work coach, doing a job
I am just one pay cheque away from a claimant
I am just an instrument of government
I carry out orders
That's what I do
Lest I lose my job
I don't make decisions,
I just follow orders
It's the Case manager above me
Protected in call centres
A great place to hide
It's the decision maker above them

Overseen by the case manager,
Overseen by the team leader
by a senior Civil servant
Overseen by a Minister
Who's overseen by the Prime Minster
Who was voted for by the people
who is the murderer
through complicity
who is the bystander who falls into line
who gives out food tickets
who stands in line
A decision maker, a work coach, an administrator, a case manager
Are all just following the rules
which they must oblige
Developed by Senior civil servants as directed by ministers
They troll though journals of lives they know not
Of struggles and hunger to which they turn a blind eye
As recommended by the work coach, the case manager to the
decision maker,
Give them the sanctions as it says in the rules
D stands for death, W for Work and P for Prison... we are
sending you to Department of Death through work Prison in your
own home.
I note a senior civil servant claims he is bullied,
Yet all civil servants have blood on their hands
As subtle ways to dispose of the disabled the dysfunctional and
the Prisoners
All executed by stealth.................
and the murderers are the
administrator,
the work coaches, the case managers, the decision makers,
the civil service,
the ministers and the prime minister
who was voted in by the people
        Who is the murderer.

XANTHI BARKER

was born in London where she still lives. She writes short fiction that has appeared in various magazines and anthologies. Her story *One Thing* formed part of Open Pen's first novelette series. In June 2021 her memoir *Will this house last forever?* will be published by Tinder Press.

The Archway Tower

It's the first day of the summer holidays and this is the tallest building we've ever been in. Tall enough that the tip is swallowed by the grey-black tower that sways over our snapped back necks. My brother says, Look! it's falling on us, but before I can see it our mum reappears, yanks our flimsy wrists inside.

Inside, where the ceiling is low enough to see every mark and crack, every cobweb, the shoulders of the building collapsing under its own weight.

The shoulders of the people here are collapsing too. You can see it in their bodies or the way their words come out too fast, too heavy, too harsh from their anxious mouths. Our mum leaves us to wait while she joins the queue, but even from across the room we can feel her heart whacking EMERGENCY so it echoes in each of our chests. We crouch behind the fat square cushions of the benches, their stained fabric sticky and scratchy at our cheeks, playing at spies until she comes back glazed with relief, thrusting paper at us, a biro the size of my finger.

She's passed the first round. Now all we have to do is wait.

We take turns with the biro, layering scribble over scribble, inventing animals with limbs and trunks and eyes and hoofs in combinations that turn our giggles into shrieks. Our mum forgets herself for a minute, adds a pair of antlers to our beast's back legs, reveals hidden eyes, and the curl of her lip, dazzle of her eye — sudden but definite, a current buzzing through us — is like being at home for a moment, out in the park, anywhere else but here.

Here where a man has just slammed his fist into the screen at the counter, turned and lurched back down the queue shouting and shouting, pounding his fist into his palm, his face getting bigger and smaller with rage until someone bigger and angrier but cleaner, quieter, uniformed and solid with intention, intercepts him, marches him out.

I don't know what scares us more: the lurching man with his lurching anger, or the uniformed man with his uniform anger

— the unpredictable bile, or the cold machination of control. We sit still in our seats. Stop drawing. Stop laughing. Watch and wait.

The queue shrinks and swells. This fever of emotion, heavy wanting in the dully lit space, the thin grey carpet. I let my eyes trace the squares of it, count widths and breadths, how many chairs in the space, how many windows, doors, buggies, old people, babies, bins. How many cameras, as my brother points out, his spy mouth tucked underhand, out of sight.

Our mother in her smart jacket and blonde hair brushed out. Our mother with her handbag and lipstick. Our mother with her soft smell that says mother, home, sleep, warmth, waiting. Waiting. We must not speak to her. No reason but we know: we must not speak to her. Then our number is called. Stand up! We've got to go, she says.

The lift goes up. Another floor. The ceiling lower. An empty office. Or only an office, and I can't believe there could be people there, in the silence, in the beep beep beep. More chairs with their thick padded sticky cushions, more waiting, waiting, waiting. A man comes to take our mother. We look at each other. Stay there, wait.

Wait and wait.

Water from a paper cone cup. My brother slips off for "an investigation" and comes back with it, turning me hot with jealousy. Where did he get that cup? He points towards a tall, swing door. I'm afraid, but not enough to outweigh my desperation to hold that cold watery weight myself. I push the door. Fill the cup. Sip.

Walk back without spilling a drop.

When our cones are empty, we flip them upside down and put them on each other's heads, feel the final dregs dripping through to our scalps, shiver and giggle and let them drop. Take each other's and break them — or, my brother breaks mine and so I break his, biting off the tip and looking through it like a binocular.

What if she doesn't come back?

The lights flicker off.

On again.

Off.

On.

The building breathes, we can hear it. My brother says it first and I shut up to listen. It's breathing. Whirring. No, breathing, breathing.

The lurching angry man from earlier walks past us, lead

by another man in a suit. It's him, my brother says, though at first I don't believe it. But my brother says, look, see the three burnt holes in his left shoe.

Just when we can't wait any longer, our mother comes back. She barely stops, passes us in a gust, a flutter of her hand, and we follow, back to the lift, another six flights up. We blink at her, asking, What, more? What? What?

She has a look that means don't ask. That means what we are afraid might go wrong could be going wrong at this exact moment. We curse ourselves for stealing all those extra cone cups.

I'm sorry, I say, and she softens for a moment. Strokes the silky skin she likes between my ear and my neck.

It's not you, she says. It's this.

She flips her wrist and the papers flurry in her hand, typed words and boxes as faint as our chances. Everything could still go wrong, that's what her elastic-band snapped voice amounts to. Everything meaning the entire cracked box of our life and wrong meaning some spiky, complicated, seeping form of lack.

My brother and I know only that it's something to do with words like debt, bills, benefit, outstanding, eviction, notice, penalty, broke, broken, bank, can't and don't, and how it does not seem possible though we know it's true: how words like that, how words at all, can put a person, our mum, in an ambulance.

This time we follow her to the man's desk. The skin of his neck sagging over the collar of his too tight shirt. His kindness, but something too warm in it, like a glass of orange juice left by the radiator. He makes ticks and crosses on the paper, in accordance with his questions and our mum's answers, his frown the ridge we've got to hang all our hopes on.

He claps, once, out of nowhere, something like reassurance, and our mum thanks him, but we are not reassured. Did he take her hand across the table? Or did she only withdraw, close in on herself, as though he had done?

We scan his eyes for signs, find them only finding her.

I climb up onto her lap, take the pen and insist on filling the form myself. I know everything, I say: name, address, phone number, marital status: divorced. Do you receive child maintenance from your ex-partner? We have been taught to scorn that question, so I turn my practiced nonchalance on the man. "Are you joking?"

Our mum lets her laughter join his but pushes me from her lap, clears her throat and he returns to the form, ticking, crossing, humming, tick, tick, tick.

My brother starts a thumb war behind her chair, and in the time it takes for everything to be worked out, I lose twice, win once and my brother twists my thumb until the skin evaporates in the burn. He is about to sink his nails into the wound when our mum gestures for us to get up, telling us it's time to go. "Loser," he hisses, but I don't squeal or kick him like I usually would. Anyway — it's going to be okay. That's what the steadiness of our mum's gait says. I hold my blistering red thumb out, triumphant, as we wind our way back down the building.

Outside, impossibly, the sun is still high. We cross the road and go to Greggs, where our mum buys a giant sunshine cookie and breaks it in two. She gets a chocolate eclair and my brother and I eat half the sun each, dribbling crumbs, cone cup saliva, relief, all the way back down Holloway Road.

BRUCE BARNES
was born in Leytonstone, London in 1948, his work has recently appeared in *London Grip, Pennine Platform,* and *Strix.* He is retired having previously worked in advice centres in London, and is now a trustee of an advice centre in Bradford, West Yorkshire.

Raft

raft (colloq) large collection, crowd, (from raff-rubbish, perhaps of Scandinavian origin)

As if the word was a floating accumulation
of the last dream, 'raft' sailed out of bed with me.
Guttural and Nordic, I could gargle with it.
At breakfast, the business news and 'raft'
sounding unflappable, as rolled up umbrellas,
and with a meaning that tasted like gilt-edged cereal,
the bowlfuls, day in day out,warding off oblivion.

Mid-morning, Ms G and I, her son and the crowd
push down fron Highgate against the 'Social'
and its locked swing doors. There is someone's
scribbled note about opening late and I know
that they hurry fron unavoidable circumstance
to make us manageable,letting us in as two and threes.

We wait again on the tenth floor, Ms G quietly patient,
her son intrigued by the textured ceiling tiles,
and I take in the view. A seascape of London
ebbs against the grey watery glass. The houses pile in,
regularly,but my eyes work at the mist and distance
searching for something afloat out there.

"Do you see the Nat West Tower
and Lloyds Building" My arm strains in that direction
but falls back as I realise that those on board
have got no reason to care. Ms G and the crew
have seen enough of 'ships of rescue'
and save their breathe for waving goodbye.

Review

(for John)

A fortnight ago, the letter he couldn't read,
tried in two pages to say: Zilch for furniture.
I said, "Why not try a review?". He surveys the city
from his flat: "Do I need this?" His expansive 'this'
was an unseen shared, the bloody obvious,
translated to a language he didn't know.

John, and I, are glued to a waiting room bench,
that's screwed to the floor. Elsewhere's activity:
a tachograph idles in Mannningham Lane,
papers lie on a Parliamentary table,
no one objects, so their foolscap bumbles
into rules. And John is crying.

Big tears sheet over his lived-in face,
like a river flooding its old water courses,
plopping into the cups of his hands,
"I can't handle this." (But he won't tell me
what 'this' is!). I watch as the crying
he struggles with, runs through his fingers.

Having regard to all the circumstances of each case,
we still wait in a world that's rule made:
we can't inquire after its haecceity.
I could ask what's been graffitied on our coccyx hard seats.
Sinking further back into illegible scrawl,
wiry indices massage the small of my back.

For a while, the waiting room settles to thisness,
being like the Benefits Agency, anywhere else.
A child spins a swing bin's stainless steel top;
Mam says "Stop!"; he says "it's nowt" and because
it's no less than silver light shimmering,
he picks from the universe what he wants 'this' to mean.

The visitants

It's almost a surprise

to see them, crowded in a Lincolnshire field,
ogling the train that I'm travelling on.
Their place is beyond that smudged line
of poplars, in inner city interview booths:

Earls Court or the Bakers' Arms, Leyton, flash by,
and with their shoes soaked in the first sward,
they wait to explain some unfinished business,
it's complicated, but if I want the low down

I have to play my part: make them comfortable
with weather talk, (they've come streaked with drizzle),
then start with: 'what's brought you in, today'?.
No useful answer but what the mind has thrown up.

Prompt: so, why not start at the beginning?
In the early fumbling to understand myself,
there was curiosity about others, a discomfort
with closeness that a sense of order relieved,
until bureaucracy sent me home snivelling,
'it ain't fair' about me, them, and the system;
but advice work walked in to put flesh
on expressive faces, on that generalisation.

Query: was the manipulation of rules
a labour of love, or a nice little earner?
Both, but not all the time, if truth be told.
The pleasure of getting a result,
was marred by stress, if I went too near
their precipice. Yet at the edge of adversity,
I found life stories I had never known,
that my hidebound imagination had craved.

Ask: why now, after years of not listening,
when the soft give of carriage seat, a coffee
from the trolley barely interrogates
their hardship? Is it a job unfinished?
They have not come to get forms filled in,
nor something nebulously sorted,
and in the instant of faces, there is a wanting-
I've got their stories and they want them back.

BOB BEAGRIE

was born in Middlesbrough on 23 June 1967. He has published numerous collections of poetry, most recently *And Then We Saw The Daughter of the Minotaur* (The Black Light Engine Press 2020), *Civil Insolencies* (Smokestack 2019). His next collection *When We Wake We Think We're Whalers from Eden* is due out from Stairwell Books in 2021.

The Queen of Hearts

'The sad truth is that most evil is done by people who never make up their minds to be good or evil.' Hannah Arendt

'Sentence first, verdict afterwards' Queen of Hearts
Alice in Wonderland, Lewis Carroll

She asks not from personal malice nor individual
        vindictiveness
but out of a genuine concern for the common good, the state
of the nation and in such a casual off-hand tone, the way a
        barista
behind the counter in Starbucks might enquire if you desire
sugar with your caffe latte, and her brow creases a tad
as she speaks, as if out of tender regard like a firm but kind
primary school teacher from a well-to-do picturesque village
doing a stint in your challenging inner-city academy, who
        knows,
is absolutely convinced, you can do better if only you'd
        knuckle
down, try that little bit harder because everyone has it in
        them,
everyone has the capacity to succeed, especially in these days
of equality, but it's her thankless job to separate the wheat
from the chaff, her responsibility to implement the correct
procedures because without the likes of her the system
would crack under the weight of all those trying to take a
        lend
making claims for what they assume they're entitled to and so
she asks the question in a cotton-wool voice that seems to
suggest a real practical solution, 'So why is it that you
        haven't
managed to commit suicide yet?', later she'll sit with her
        family
after dinner watching the soaps on the box, indulge in half

            an hour
of Candy Crush to help her switch off, lie in bed drifting
            into sweet
dreams of being a Disney Princess or a real-life one just
            like Lady Di.

BRIAN BEAMISH

was born in 1974 in Plymouth and currently lives in London. He hopes
to flee to Wales as soon as possible to be closer to his family. Brian
has been published previously in *Emergency Verse: Poetry in Defence of
the Welfare State* (Caparison 2011), *The Robin Hood Book: Verse Versus
Austerity* (Caparison, 2012) and on *The Recusant* website. He studied
philosophy at university before tuition fees destroyed egalitarianism
and worked for 23 years in the private sector before life events placed
his life on its proper course. He is now a full-time counsellor in
private practice. He hopes daily that power will yield to compassion,
and wishes that Jacinda Ardern could be World President one day.

Winter, stale

Stone-smooth step to a corridor of echoes
Duck egg blues in a dry urinal
I wait, gloaming, behind the too-varnished doors
Brewing bitter ail and wells of arid tears
Why, happy man be's dole!

Shabby tweeds and leather scents
Emerge from secret smoking rooms
Happy for a fourteennight's reprieve
Street-ejected through the wire glass
Why, happy man be's dole!

Back to strain and shadows
Villages of whispered lies
Waiting for easeful retirement
Signing on and signing off
Why, happy man be's dole!

OLLY BEAMISH

was born in Lowestoft, Suffolk. He spent thirteen years in the RAF as a radar technician, then with the MOD Navy. Always a reader and writer and dabbler in poetry, retired to write novels.

Unkindness

Unkindness is the cut
When the clerk says, But
Have you perused the board?
Yes, I say.
But, really there's no way
That I can afford
To go to Timbuctoo
To be a CEO
For an oil company drilling
Holes. But really I'm willing.
How about a chef in a posh hotel?
Sounds great, but — well.
I can't boil an egg
And I've only one leg.
Can I go now? Please?
Not yet. A ski instructor?
Steel erector? Orchestra conductor?
I did your job once. A Clerical Officer.
But now… Life was buggered up. Life!
Went drainwards. You see, I've a sick wife.
As if you cared. Not relevant. Life's shite.
I'm unemployed. Not a bleeding parasite.
A television producer? Astronaut?
Are you qualified in torture?
Gestapo agent? Is that for me a future?
No. (*shuffles forms*) That's my job.
(*Stabs pen in blotter. Examine, it works*)
Now sign here and hop it, do
Outside there's a half mile queue
(*Smirks*)

KITTIE BELLTREE

was born in London in the 1960s. Her poetry and prose has been published in a range of journals including *Poetry Wales, Under The Radar, The Morning Star, The North* and in the anthology, *Cut on The Bias: stories about women and the clothes they wear* (Honno, 2010). Her debut poetry collection, *Sliced Tongue and Pearl Cufflinks* (2019) is published by Parthian. She works as a Specialist Tutor for neurodivergent students at Aberystwyth University.

Stephen Carré, 2010

That silence
it's a
racket
it's the
sound of
swinging
lead
a dead
tone
the line's
gone **he worked**
as a tele-
communications
consultant
before that
silence
it must
be
bro-ken
his   head
oscillating
over a
black
hole **he**
couldn't
ans-wer
the
door or
the
telephone that
silence
it's
terminal

it promises to
reduce dependency
he lived
off
his
savings
for 2
years
before
claiming that
silence
it's the
ass-ess-or
noting no
evidence to
suggest
the client's
health
condition
due to
their
depression is
[...]
life
threatening **he**
spent
days
on
end
in the
same
room &
couldn't

leave
the house that
silence
it's a
brown
envelope
found
fit
for
work
with-out
a phone
call
with-out
contacting
his
doctor
psychiatrist
or comm-unity
mental
health nurse **he**
couldn't
talk
to
friends or
relatives that
silence
it's the
hermetic
space
between
medical
opinion
& the
work
capability
assessment **he**
committed suicide
after
they
re/jected
his appeal
that silence
it's the

DWP
flouting
the coroner's
urgent
warning they
must
obtain
medical
evidence to
prevent
future
deaths **he**
couldn't
ask for
help that
silence
it's a
criminal in-
difference
to
the lives
of 1.5 million
people when
the
government
pushed
on with-out **his**
dad says Stephen
would
still
be
alive if they'd
bothered
to
contact
his GP that
silence
it's the
poker-faced
wall
the
dead-
pan
re-verb-er-ation

```
the                    to   t r y
long                   & co mm u n i c
hard                   ate w i t h  t h
strug/gle              e D    W    P
```

David Barr, 2013

They knew about it and did nothing about it […] If we let a defective bus in the road [and it killed someone] we would be up for manslaughter; that's why these people should be taken to court

— David Barr's father, a bus driver, commenting on failures to address serious safety concerns raised over the Work Capability Assessment

      A points system
      A physiotherapist, a DWP decision-maker and two
Government ministers
      Ignoring the red lights
Burning rubber
      35 minutes to make the assessment
      18 minutes to write the report
      15 points to pass the test
      No substantial risk
Rubber stamping
Driving his son to the edge
      Anti-psychotic sedatives, sleeping tablets
antidepressants and a history of mental distress
      Found
      Fit
      For
      Work
Ignoring the red lights
He got a bus to the bridge, walked to the middle and jumped

Phillipa Day, 2019

She was told to claim P.I.P. because her D.L.A. was due to stop

And they lost her forms

She told them she had diabetes, unstable personality disorder, depression, anxiety and agoraphobia

And they stopped her benefits

She was told she must make a new claim

And they would not reinstate her payments

She told them she was *literally starving and cold*

And they said they'd heard it all before

She told them she was *£5000 in debt*

And they said she'd been sobbing during the call

She told them she *literally cannot leave the house*

And they rejected her plea for an at-home assessment

She told them she *genuinely can't survive like this for much longer*

And they did nothing

She was found unconscious next to a letter from the DWP

And they told her she must attend a benefits assessment

She was in a coma for ten weeks

And then she died

PENNY BLACKBURN

was born in West Yorkshire in 1970, although she has lived in the North East for over 25 years. She works in a further education college, teaching young adults with learning difficulties and behavioural problems, many of whom experience huge barriers in accessing benefits and support. She has been published widely, including online with *Riggwelter, Atrium* and *Ink, Sweat and Tears* and also in print with *Poetry Society News, Broken Spine* and *Fly on the Wall*. She has pamphlets coming out in spring 2021 with Yaffle and Wild Pressed Books.

Jumping Through Hoops

Each significant piece of information
must be accurately placed
within the correct, identified box
of the specified form
— available Wednesdays, bi-weekly,
when the moon reaches the nadir.

Forms must be brought in person
to our top floor office (no lift)
3 miles from the nearest road or rail link,
open every 5th Friday (mornings only).
Come no earlier or later,
for such untimely supplications will be refused,
returned unread.

Should your form be accepted
your application will be considered
by uninterested, sorry - disinterested staff,
thoroughly trained to ignore
the individual circumstances of your case.

Any dispute on decisions must be made
via official recorded complaint.
Most certainly not via Facebook, or tweeted.

You will receive a reply within our scheduled number of target days.

At which point your request
will be most carefully
deleted.

SARA BOYCE

Sara Boyce is from Donegal but lives in Belfast. Her poems have appeared in publications including *Between Light and the Half Light* (2015) two CAP anthologies, *North West Words* (2019) and *Other Language* (2020). She had a poem long-listed for the Seamus Heaney Award for New Writing (2018).

Brown Envelope Culture

Nestled in that bowl
between Divis and the Craiganlet Hills,
Belfast's citizens are more divided than ever.

Words still evoke visceral reactions,
Now though, mantras have been replaced
by the more mundane.

Ditchwater dull words
like 'brown envelope'
trigger a gut response:

Belfast Citizen One:
tummy flips,
heart flutters,
head pounds,
blood crashes
through your arteries,
glands go into overdrive;
saliva and sweat.

The sound of your gate creaking,
of the soft swish of the letterbox brush,
of something settling on your doormat,
all fill you with dread.

You finger the thin envelope
flip the kettle on and light a fag,
try not to think the worst;
Sundays are the best days
when there is no post.

The alphabet's a jumble before your eyes –
ESA, DLA and PIP,
death by a thousand letters,
a thousand paper cuts.

You set the letter against the mantle clock,
And try to recall,
before you push away the chair,
When your precious life
stopped counting.

Belfast Citizen Two:
tummy flips,
heart flutters,
head pounds,
blood crashes
through your arteries,
glands go into overdrive;
saliva and sweat.

The sound of an email zinging,
of a soft briefcase unzipping,
of palms being rubbed together,
all fill you with anticipation.

You finger the thick envelope,
wave that finger and
call for drinks all round,
try to quell your excitement;
Sundays are the busiest days
for your show houses.

The alphabet's a jumble before your eyes
NAMA, NCA and PAC,
You blink, fix your cuffs
and they're gone.

The weekend rolls in again,
and with it, that damp Lagan fog.
Some will lug home shopping bags from Iceland,
while others will blow their fixer fees in Ibiza.

Dangerous People

like Brigette, wearing a hand-knit
Bollix to Brexit beanie,
doctorate in her back pocket,
told she is over-qualified
by a clerk in a pair of winkle pickers.
Brigitte thinks *he* is over-dressed.
And Gareth, in his *Just Do It* runners,
whose Senior Project Manager
views him as over-empathetic,
tells him he needs to be more detached
from the six-year-old who tries to hide
from poverty, under a pool table,
his eyes emptier than dinner plates.
And Finn, who doesn't need to act,
so over-wrought by grim thoughts
of another precious life lost
to Capita's conscious cruelty.
And Mary, who is over-critical
of the small fact that 8000 people
are waiting for an appeal;
she thinks its indefensible.
And Flair, highly over-reactive,
insists on bringing up our dead
at the Christmas dinner table
gets on like a Brazilian bishop
asking awkward questions, like
Why are they poor?
And Bertie, who over-simplifies
complex policy decisions,
talks of Beveridge's vision,
says the clue's in the name —
'Social Security.'
Towser thumps his tail twice.
And Maria — seriously over-invested
in celebrating the innate good in
working class neighbourhoods;
knows that context counts for a lot.
And Nuala, over-idealistic,
likes to keep her powder dry
smile her wry smile at power
till she makes them wobble
on one leg.

Over-involved
every single one of them,
in the lives of others
they have never met.

C.D. BOYLAND

was born in Coventry and now lives in Cumbernauld, near Glasgow. He has
been published in magazines like *Gutter* and *The North*, and anthologies
such as *New Writing Scotland*. His debut pamphlet *User Stories* came out in
April 2020. Described by one reviewer as 'smart insights delivered with
uncluttered fluency', *User Stories* is available now from the independent,
Edinburgh-based small press Stewed Rhubarb (www.StewedRhubarb.org).

Three Sonnets for Universal Credit

#1/.

Your payment is what you are allowed
not what you need, a 'standard' applies
a fixed amount is what you are allowed
'fixed' as in set, as in stone. An extra
amount is available if you have extra
needs, such as children — but a standard
number of children is all that is allowed

Your circumstances are assessed every
month, changes in circumstances can
effect what you are allowed and must
be reported, failure to report a change
may mean that you have to repay what
was previously paid to you, unreported
changes in circumstances are not allowed.

#2/.

Told I was going onto Universal Credit, told there
would be a wait, no way of getting help meantime,

no money at all, five weeks absolutely nothing
coming in, no choice, go to the Foodbank, no gas

no electric on, after a while couldn't even get out
to the Foodbank, down to around six stone, in the

deepest, darkest place, on the verge of ending it all.
A neighbour knocked on the door and I just burst

into tears, such a terrible state, but the thing is,
I had always worked, I'd had some good jobs, what

the government wanted me to do. But I can't work
now, constantly anxious about money, trying to

keep my head above water and hoping to find a
new place to live when I have the debts paid off[1].

#3/.

£52/week, enough to buy
cold, a little crack in the
deposit on some loneliness
keep their brittle fingers
like chalk outlines, stop
their toes. £52/week
mental health, a pair
to tie around your neck,
your hardship on, new
newspaper. £52/week
without a door, a blank
every day that buzzes
head, enough to carve
cut the shape of you into
a little death, a little
pavement, put down a
a little treat for the kids
warm, preserve them
the wolf from nibbling
enough to buy some
of iron shoes, a weight
new bones to hang
fears to be folded like
enough to buy a room
space at the start of
like a migraine in your
out a bloody silhouette
the official statistics.

[1]Sonnet #2 is a found poem, made using text published at: https://www.
bigissue.com/latest/hellish-system-reality-life-universal-credit/

PETER BRANSON

is now a full time poet, songwriter & traditional-style singer. His poetry has been published in Britain, USA, Canada, Ireland, Australia, New Zealand and South Africa, including in *Acumen, Agenda, Ambit, Envoi, The London Magazine, Reach, Sarasvati, The Warwick Review, Iota, Frogmore Papers, The Interpreter's House, Magma, Poetry Nottingham, South, Elbow Room, The Curlew, The Fenland Reed, The New Writer, Crannog, Measure, The Raintown Review, The Houston Poetry Review, Barnwood, Main street Rag, The Able Muse* and *Other Poetry.* His *Red Hill, Selected Poems* was published in 2013 by Lapwing, Belfast. His latest collection, *Hawk Rising,* also from Lapwing, was pub. in 2016. He has won prizes and been placed in a number of competitions over recent years, including a 'highly commended' in the Petra Kenny International, first prizes in the Grace Dieu and the Envoi International and a special commendation in the 2012 Wigtown. He was shortlisted for the 2018/19 Poetry Business Pamphlet and Collection competition. Two further collections are forthcoming: *The Clear Daylight* (Littoral Press, 2021), winner of the 2020 Littoral Press Full Collection Nature & the Spirit Poetry Competition, and *Marrowbones* (Sentinel Poetry, 2021), first prize winner in the Sentinel Poetry Book Comp 2020.

Scapegoats

Floral tributes have been left where the body of a rough sleeper was found near the Central Museum and Art Gallery in .... One homeless charity claimed the man was attacked by three thugs and struck in the face with a hammer days before he died. Lindow Man, also known affectionately as Pete Marsh, is a preserved bog body discovered near Wilmslow, Cheshire, on 1st August 1984 by commercial peat-cutters.

To my good friend John Beech

Pete Marsh was overkilled like you, his head
stoved in, garrotted, throat slashed, bled, then drowned,
the mangled, marrow-less remains, like creased,
discarded leathers in a barn, outweighed
by sods, intact, adulterer or thief,
prisoner of war or murderer perhaps,
or witting sacrifice to sooth false gods,
conserved and chronicled behind plate glass.
Your death was brewed by local youths who struck
you with a hammer on both cheeks. You froze
here three days later like a worn jute sack,
your middle-aged rough sleep exposed, where folk
who cared at last laid flowers, your epitaph
'Since Last Year, Nothing's Changed!' yesterday's news.

No Use Aged Forty-two
A carol
Tune: 'The Recruited Collier' - traditional, adapted.

For Linda, the Sally Army lady who shakes her tin at us

The brass band's playing in the square,
Sing Merrily on High,
King Wenceslas, The First Noel,
Watch Ships Come Sailing By.

Chorus:
> *Well it's winter now with Christmas here,*
> *No angel's wings for you,*
> *O Come, O Come, Emmanuel,*
> *No use, aged forty-two.*

Your bed tonight a cold stone floor,
Shop doorway off the high street,
With cardboard for an eiderdown,
Brown paper for a sheet.
Chorus:

You crave long summer days, warm nights,
Some shelter from the rain,
Bleak winter is your terror time,
Chills bones and dulls the brain.
Chorus:

What brought you here, so far from friends
And family, tell me why
You've slept outdoors alone for years,
Blank stares from passers-by?
Chorus:

"Lost everything, job, wife and kids,
The demon in my head;
No other way, I had to leave,
That's what their voices said."
Chorus:

"I read their faces, people round,
Grow louder by the day:
To them I'm an embarrassment
They wish would melt away."
Chorus:

Folk wash their hands, police move you on,
Leave charities to cope;
Your world inside one carrier bag,
Can't live on faith and hope.
Chorus

First verse repeated

Chorus: (modified):
    Well it's winter now with Christmas here,
    No angel's wings to cope,
    O Come, O Come, Emmanuel,
    Can't live on faith and hope.

Fixed Odds

For George Pickering

He wheezes like a straining chuffer train,
exposure, cold and rain, cement, brick dust,
asbestos spores, that constant hack and spit
into the grate, his lungs clogged to the pores.
Old banger, too much choke, he trawls for breath,
his eyes coal fires, his nervous hands as coarse
as scaffold boards, "A martyr to his chest,"
safety on building sites back then a joke.
Life sentence, cramped Oddfellows' terraced house,
tin bath and outside lav, two-up two-down
with rising damp, "Don't let the bastards grind
you down" his toast, he's now, brickie by trade,
dry soil broadcast above a waiting grave,
part sagging chair beside the fire, part ghost.

NICK BURBRIDGE

was born in Malta in 1954, is an Anglo-Irish poet, playwright, novelist, journalist, short story and song writer, who lives in Brighton. He is the author of three books of poetry: *On Call* (Envoi Poets, 1994), *All Kinds Of Disorder* (Waterloo, 2006) and *The Unicycle Set* (Waterloo, 2011). His plays include *Dirty Tricks* (Soho Theatre), *Vermin* (Finborough), and *Cock Robin* (Verity Bargate Award Runner-up). He writes for his own fringe company, and his work has been broadcast often on BBC Radio. His novel, *Operation Emerald* (Pluto), was published under the pseudonym Dominic McCartan, while he collaborated with Captain Fred Holroyd on *War Without Honour* (Harrap/Medium), launched at the House of Commons. His work has featured in literary journals, including *Acumen, Ambit, Agenda and Stand*, and Arts Council anthologies *New Stories 5* and *6* (Hutchinson) and *20 Stories* (Secker & Warburg). As a singer/songwriter he has made eight albums with his band McDermott's Two Hours, several in collaboration with The Levellers, who covered 'Dirty Davey' on their eponymous number one-selling record. His songs are widely recognised as a significant contribution to the folk revival. (www.burbridgearts.org)

Song For Judgement Day

My friend Flynn's on the last train in
with his tattered coat and stick
He might be a visionary
He might be a lunatic
But in the canyons of his mind
he's seen it's judgement day
Redemption now he's out to find
before this land is swept away

And the longer he stands by the track
the more he feels alone
He knows there's no journey back
Now the last train's gone

So he trails to the city square
where herds of bigots stand
tattooed arms ramped in the air
screaming for the promised land
And penned in side-streets by the law
black-clad figures heave
They can't say what they're fighting for
But what it is, they still believe

Stationed in the suburbs
the silent army stand
banging pots and hollering
beating hand on hand
Flynn sniffs the scent of hypocrite
It's one that he knows well
Take mercy when you're offered it
then let the angels go to hell

And he sings:
Purgatory - catastrophe - *auto da fe - salva me*

So Flynn's under the red lights
where the gutter's full of dirt
prince and minister, pimp and skite
stained slip and sweatstained shirt
He makes out with a redhaired whore
She says, You're awful small
Says Fynn, I'm getting old now, sure,
You're lucky there's anything there at all

So he limps to the library stack
where the keyboard warriors fight
Beggars fleece him, thugs attack
He takes to his heels in flight
And he crosses the cathedral green
and thinks of Notre Dame
He's sure this is the final scene
and prays, Dear Lord, thy Kingdom come

So on goes Flynn with coat and stick
and his overflowing cup
He's knows he's terminally sick
so he stops and he throws up
And as he struggles with his fears
he takes a final piss
so cheek and cheek are streaked with tears
How did it ever come to this?

And he sings:
Purgatory - catastrophe - *auto da fe - salva me*

Song Of Icons

So this is their land of freedom
Marked by the chosen ones
the salt-stained iron master
and all his tainted sons
The martyr set in plaster
and the minister in bronze
And lost between dark earth and stone
the unknown millions

If we pull together
we can tear these figures down
cast them in the water
and watch the bastards drown

They make sure their children learn
they come from noble stock
They sail away to starve and burn
to save and not attack
If they return with galleys
and the whip to lash the back
they swear it is to civilise
the heathen and the black

They tell you being just and pure
gives them their cause and right
not wrought by laws of nature
but by reason, creed and might
For what makes them superior
They vow they have to fight
So onward Christian soldiers
from the darkness into light

But while they plough through plague and fire
and walk over the meek
to build their barren empire
with the labour of the weak
where plot and pitch lie underground
we wait, we work, we seek
the moment when the lost are found
and all these walls must break

So, my friends, this is the hour
the circus is in town
paper tiger, man on wire,
plate-spinner, mop-haired clown
Now the animals desert
and the big top tumbles down
we rip these crumbling bars apart
break mace and flag and crown

And as this fabric turns to dust
our rivers swell and rise
so the iron masters crack and rust
the soldier falls and the trader dies
And we set sail on an inward tide
across an open sea
where we haul back our strength and pride
we stand as one and take the knee

Austerity Song

It's darker hour by hour now the red sun's down
and the grey men from the towers send their runners into town
They've orders to uncover us so all the people learn
there's a cheat round every corner, and a skiver at each turn
And all across the city we can hear them rail and shout:
We're here to nail you beggars now, we're here to drive you out
No quarter and no pity, you're like a bleeding sore
We're going to hit you hard, so you don't come back for more

This woman waiting at her gate goes out to them in tears:
I raised all my children here, it's been my home for years
They say, So you've no reason now, you're just a waste of space
You've had your day, we'll make you pay, or we'll take back
        this place
And right across the city now they tally room by room
and each one of us that fails they drive out into the gloom
No quarter and no pity as they move from door to door
clubbing down the frail and stealing from the poor

You're bone-lazy, you're not lame
Ditch the stick and lose the chair
and hang your heads in shame

You're not crazy, and you don't need care
You waste our time and money
Now try living on thin air

This old man's at his window when the henchmen come to call
He tries to reach the stairway but he stumbles in the hall
They kick away his crutches and hoist him in the street
put his back against the wall: Stand on your own two feet
And right across the city they seek out the halt and weak
It's time to pay the piper now, there's nothing for the meek
No quarter and no pity, if you breathe you're fit to give
We need all you've been taking, it's no way for you to live

This mad lad in the precinct's chasing voices in his head
He's been looking for asylum but he couldn't find a bed
And when he sees them coming he cries: Save me from this hell
so they pin him and they seize him and they throw him in a cell
And right across the city, if you bend or lose your mind
it's just a masquerade, or you're past saving, and you'll find
no quarter and no pity, there's no place for your distress
They'll drive you to the margins where you walk your wilderness

But when a new sun rises we break cover lost and bruised
It's then that we discover we have nothing left to lose
And so we rise together with a weapon called the word
we call, we march and gather, till we know that we've been heard
right across the city now, so all the people learn
there's a brother round each corner and a sister at each turn
No quarter and no pity - all we ask is our birthright
and till we bring the grey men down we'll struggle, flail, and fight

Bone-lazy, no, we're lame
We need the stick, we use the chair
we won't hang our heads in shame
And if we're crazy, we need care
It's our claim to time and money
We're not living on thin air

RACHEL BURNS

Place and date of birth: Newcastle Upon Tyne, 1971. Burns' debut pamphlet, *A Girl in a Blue Dress*, is published by Vane Women Press. She is widely published, recently in *Butcher's Dog, Fragmented Voices, The Poetry Village* and *The Blue Nib*. Her poem, 'Pegs' was selected for The Poetry Archive, Wordview.

The flat stinks of old men and cigarettes

I sit on the windowsill
lengthways, legs and feet stretched
back against the wall,
outside the streetlights fizz into life.
Leaves rustle against the window
and kids on BMX bikes wheelie up and down.

I walk from room to room, cold concrete floors
and try to imagine what it feels like living here.
I trace my hand over the taps in the windowless
bathroom, running a hand over cold Formica.
The kitchen looks out over a shared garden
a scruffy patch of grass and a privet hedge.

I open the double doors into the one and only bedroom,
try to picture a bed, a cot and a mobile playing Brahms
the walls painted lilac.

I phone my social worker from the payphone
to say the giro had come but it's short.
He says there is no mistake and I hang up.

Inside the cupboard in the hallway
I find the gas and electric slot metres
and a dead man's walking stick.

We do not know when normal service will resume

Today I saw an archangel
preening himself on the lake
the unfolding of the wing
as white as the white of a human eye
stretching out
slowly dipping into the water
then once clean   folding back into his body
and later the letter arrived from the hospital
with an apology from royal mail
a sharp V cut into the envelope
and the letter unfolded itself like a broken wing
like the wrong kind of origami

Demolished

I see cranes and bulldozers hard at work
the old benefit offices demolished
into a pile of rubble and scattered bricks.

A fire truck douses the wreck,
thick clouds of smoke
rise up like ghosts of welfare past.

I remember going cap in hand to the DSS
for a crisis loan in the days
you were given a number
& sat in rows chatting and smoking
with other desperate comrades.

There was no money, the rent was due
you've not eaten for days,
the bairn is out of nappies,
you were scraping the bottom of the SMA
baby milk tin, literally.

You hold the baby up to the security glass,
like an offering so the benefit officer
can see. She looks at you both like dirt
and tuts, tut, tut, tut.

Gives you a number, and you're back in line
smoking like a chimney to calm your nerves.
Every now & then someone kicks off
& is thrown out by Security.

They keep you waiting until the final hour.
When your number is called
your heart almost stops,
you snatch the Girocheque & race
to the Post Office before closing time.

Buy bread, nappies, baby milk & ten cigarettes.

I don't smoke anymore.
I stare at the smashed-up wreck
of the old benefit offices, at the pile of rubble,
the scattered bricks.

I weep (though can hardly believe it)
for the loss of the safety net,
for the clippy mat ripped right out
from under our feet.

PHILIP BURTON

Born in Dunfermline, Fife, in 1945, raised in Thanet. Burton has been a hippie, a labourer, a professional student, and a Catholic head teacher in Lancashire. He came to writing through the OU, and via the WEA courses of Copland Smith. He recently received a commendation from Heidi Williamson in The Poetry Society Stanza poetry competition, 2020, for his poem on the theme of dyslexia. In the last twenty years he has been widely published in literary magazines – 360 of his poems in total, including editions of *PN Review* and *Stand*, as well as in anthologies for adults and children. He has twice had poems included in Hammond House poetry anthologies, and has won many awards, including First prizes in the Teignmouth Poetry Competition, the Lancaster Litfest, the Sentinel, and the Star Magazine humorous poetry competition. In 2019, he concurrently held four First prizes in national or international poetry competitions: the National Arts Centre Jack Clemo poetry competition 2019, the Horwich Writers Hate Crime Awareness poetry competition 2018, the Sandwich (Kent) 2018 Poet of the Year award, and the Barn Owl Trust poetry competition, 2017. He won Third prize in the 2019 Hastings Poetry Competition, and Third prize in the Ware Poets 2020 Open Poetry competition. His poetry publications include *The Raven's Diary* (joe publish 1998), *Couples* (Clitheroe Books Press 2008), *His Usual Theft* (Indigo Dreams Press 2017) and *Gaia Warnings* (Palewell Press 2021).

Turn Of Events

The roundabout man, they say, drinks rum
and litres of black stout. Never touched him
nor met his inner circle, only rode once on
his cock-eyed steed. A purple moon shone.
I watch him oil-check the dobby roundabout,
kick-start its massive petrol heart.
A luminous menu of rises and falls collapses the night
into nine revolutions each minute.
Between blinks the queue is added to. The man will judge
his perfect passenger load. Too much
and the gearbox fights itself. Beyond complaint
some who can't swallow being asked to wait
between arrival and thrill
try to wallop the guy on the carousel.
Fair excitement and bare violence
are two filaments of the same circling bulb.
On sanguine days the blood gets swabbed up
and vomit confined in pine-scented dust.

Years flick by, then I find him
in the paranormal din below the viaduct
where his rotating world had set him down.
Grown old, he clings to his easy grace,
beyond safety nets, content to hear cars
glide in shivering, stippling, glare
above his operator's cabin –
an Argos cardboard box with scribbled horses.
Sit on, he says. *Give it a spin.*

MARIA BYRNE

or DeafWiganPoet is a performance poet in the northwest. Is part of the Wigan
community of poets. And a Student of Music at TMP, which is a Wigan based
college of art. Appeared on Radio Warrington and BBC Radio Lancashire,
and other projects relating to the local art galleries.

Education

Education,
It's important
For employment,
And is the
Embodiment,
Of hard work
And a good work
Ethic,
But it seems
Working hard
Is not enough,
And help to get in work
Doesn't cover full time
Education.
Now, if you work hard
To educate yourself
You're a mouth not
Worth feeding,
A useless eater.

LOUISA CAMPBELL

has two published mental-health-related poetry pamphlets: *The Happy Bus* (Picaroon Poetry, 2017) and *The Ward* (Paper Swans Press, 2018). Her first full collection of poems, *Beautiful Nowhere* (Boatwhistle Books, 2021), is about a traumatic childhood, leading to becoming both mental health nurse and patient. She lives in Kent, England.

Work Capability Assessment

They may as well strap you to a wooden chair,
slap you about a bit,
dim lightbulb over your head.

Tell us exactly how far you can walk
before you must stop
for the pain...

Did you know
there's a wheelchair
imagined for you?

If they imagine you
having the strength to propel it,
you fail.

ANNA CARLOTTA
is an artist and got a Fine Art Degree as a mature student over a period
of five years at the University of Plymouth. She has suffered from anxiety,
panic disorder and some agoraphobia since the age of 18. She was greatly
affected by the Welfare Reforms to ESA and PIP, and had to appeal the ESA
WRAG to get into the ESA Support group. She dreaded moving from DLA to
PIP, and had a daily fear of a brown or white envelope dropping through
the letter box for assessments etc.

Poem to the Tune of Liverpool Lullaby

It's quite a struggle every day,
Living on the JSA,
The sanctions start to eat away,
And leave us with no money.

For those who have no silver spoon,
Grimmer days are coming soon,
The food banks full and there's no room,
And Patel smiles so snidely.

TINA COLE
was born in the Black Country and now lives in rural Herefordshire. She
likes to write about people and relationships good or bad. Her collection
I Almost Knew You (2015) focussed on those themes. Published poems have
appeared in U.K. magazines such as, *Brittle Star, Creative Countryside,
Poetry Café, Mslexia, Aesthetica, The Guardian* newspaper and in several
poetry collections. She is a member of the group www.borderpoets.org.
In 2019 she won the Oriel Davies Writing Competition and the Welshpool
Poetry Competition judged by Liz Berry. She has recently won the Yaffle
Press Poetry Competition and was highly commended in the Candlestick
Press call for poems on getting older. She is the organiser of the annual
Young Peoples Poetry Competition - yppc2019.org. Her second collection
will be published by Yaffle Press later this year.

Communication

I have come to talk benefits

I am not fluent in benefits, but I know
a bit about foreign, I can say estrangerio in Portuguese.

I have escaped lands sick with war and tyrants
yet my life here is still one-part sugar to ten parts vinegar.

Cooking is not my strength either – you should try another
department, as an illegal you have no recourse to public benefits.

My people were like small rivers rushing into a hundred
seas, so many washed up black-sheeted on foreign shores,
their tide is sloshing and rising.

You are talking in riddles, the vocabulary you carried here is
            as gaudy
and deceptive as those Matryoshka you people sell at markets.

Why am I always on the way to somewhere else? The same streets
grow old with me, the same neighbours turn away, close their
            curtains
against falling stars, step over gutters that run a filthy red brown
sluice, no words of comfort pass the borders of your teeth.

You are not in the right place, you should have phoned ahead
            to book
a longer appointment, next time we will need a translator.

My body is mapped in old ways of being where Summer's
song is an aria of fire and blood, of ancient survivors
with a frayed past, you cannot unpick us, we are seamed together
in your high voltage cities where cardboard ziggurats grow
in the freezing yawn of doorways.

Yes, well, thank you, your time is up for today, maybe make
another appointment for next week?

HOLLY CONANT

BORN Leeds 22/12/91. She has just had her first poem accepted by poetryandcovid.com, which is due to be published later this month. She is a student at the University of Leeds and a single parent. She is currently being treated for autoimmune related issues and MH needs. This poem is about coming to terms with her neurodiversity, which has begun to happen through the process of shielding.

A Door

opens on both sides but I
have no hands, no fingers to
grasp the notion of a handle. I
experience *a priori*. Your side
has a window. Mine
has a slate board which I
bang my head
against.

A letterbox posts through both sides.
If I post a letter this is the wrong
way, or at least, no-one else
understands. But I
am expected to act on orders with
a standard header, sanctioned by
someone who has spelt my
name wrong.

A peep-hole works on one side. I
search. I try to observe the
difference to make sense
of everyone else, but logic has no place
through this looking glass. The
world is obtuse and I
cannot see beyond the
postman's uniform.

The door is locked on both sides. It has no
keyhole.

JONATHAN CROOSE

was born in Flintshire, North Wales, and now lives back and forth between the edge of Dartmoor and the flat fields of Norfolk, UK, where he grew up. His poetry has been published by *The Bangor Literary Journal, Spelt, Poetry and Covid, Poetry 24, Word Bin, Places of Poetry* and *Loud Coffee Press*. He works as a university lecturer, theatre-maker and musician.

I know it's not you

That bastard back
has floored you, strapped you to the rack.
I hear you,
I know how that spinal crack has laid you up,
handcuffed, clamped and locked you in a box
with just the single window
and a view of neighbour chimneys and tv aerials
and a small, barking, fucking dog
that marks every moment
like the incessant tick-tock
of a torturer's clock.

I know it's not you,
I know
that the body you have lived in these long, lonely months
now belongs to someone else,
hostage to the jangling nerves of an unknown visitor
who has long outstayed their welcome.
I wish we could call the cops.

I know its not you, my sweetheart, my love,
whose body, strong and supple,
whose muscles, grip and bend,
always moving and graceful like willow,
are the true temples of your soul,
I know the true language of your place in the world,
Is annexed now by the chemistry required
to repel invaders.

But let me tell you:
you are still here, I can see you,
I can hear you knocking at the window.
I see your elegance under fire,
the blade of your well-timed wit,

your patient pulse of kiss and lockdown grey,
the flourish of your pen.

You are still here, my love
and there is light ahead.

Tier 4 Is Class War: A Public Service Broadcast

It has come to our attention, in the corridors of power
that there has been some… contradiction… about who sets the
rules,
so first of all, before we start, and I open up the floor,
can I just remind you all *exactly* who is who?

God has given *us* the right, through privilege of birth
to be in charge and supervise his vision, here on Earth,
and you, unfortunately, happen to have fallen
into a lesser category,
somewhat… down the ladder,
and are therefore
of less worth.

So now is the time to realise: who is the bloody *boss*?
Who makes the final reckoning in terms of profit and of loss?
This is no time to fuck about, complaining endlessly
about your needs and aspirations.
So stay there,
on your knees,
and get some bloody education.

They taught us, back at Eton, to understand one thing:
that we are made of better stuff: Prime Ministers and Kings,
and you are *little* people: lack
eys and underlings;
this is the natural order, the proper way of things.

There is very little point, you see, in trying to undermine
a thousand years of history, the deep ancestral line.
What sort of snotty upstart would dare to contemplate
a challenge to the natural hierarchies of state?

So when I say 'jump!' you say: 'how high?'

And when I say 'desist!' you say: 'should I also
carry in your bags, or press your shirts, or kiss
that very special place
that really hankers
to be kissed?'

Now, every now and then there comes along a chap,
with ideas above his station,
and we really can't have that.
Someone who really stirs the pot, someone who fucks it up,
some nasty little bloody oik who gets the Proles worked up,
someone like Marcus Rashford,
with his ridiculous ideas
that children have a right to eat.

Oh dear, oh dear, oh dear!
Does he really think that anything from up there in the North
can make us raid our pockets for the brats he's bleating for?
Does he think we're soft? An easy touch?
Or not right in the head?
To imagine that we'll give these kids
a slice of daily bread?

We are made of history, gun metal, flesh and sugar,
of steel, and oak and ocean craft,
of statue, chain and trigger.
We are made of old estate, of fox hunt, shares and shackles,
we are made of stronger stuff
than passes,
goals
and tackles.

Marcus Rashford's big mistake is to imagine that we care,
that we're moral, that we're ethical, empathic and aware.
Marcus Rashford's big mistake is to imagine that we're good,
that a bit of public pressure will make us do the thing we should.
Marcus Rashford's big mistake is to make a bloody fuss,
we don't give a bloody shit
if you're not one of us.

So let's just get this one thing straight:
you and I are not the same;
to be frank I'm quite surprised I have to point this out again!
On behalf of the Prime Minister its an absolute disgrace,

that Marcus bloody Rashford,
doesn't know his bloody place!
So there'll be no three-course dinner
for the rug rats in the North,
no fruit or bloody vegetables, or nonsense of that sort,
no winter fuel allowance, no balance of nutrition,
let them starve,
it will bring down the excess population.

And before you gasp, before you howl,
before your jawbone hits the floor,
when you voted for the Tories
this is what you voted for!

EOWYN DAVIS

is a poet and campaigner for the rights of the disabled and disadvantaged.

Solidarity

Solidarity! is our call
Let's do battle for us all
We'll tell them all one by one
How we want things to be done
We'll shout loud in their deaf ears
All the things they want to hear
That we are suffering the fate they chose
Watching us drown under brown envelope woes
Laughing as they recount numerical facts
Of homelessness rising because of bedroom tax
Smirking with shouts of glee
As more of us sink into poverty
We strive to make them play fair
So we can have our fair share
The one thing we forget
Is rich men have no regrets
So while we continue our fruitless struggle
They are deciding which of us to haggle
Making us dance hey diddle diddle
To their money spinning tuneless fiddle.

Struggle Street

My mate lives on Struggle Street
Does not get enough to eat
Scrabbles deep among supermarket bins
For the odd dented baked beans tins
Clops around in holey scuffed shoes
Patched up with yesterday's news
He really needs a nice warm coat
To protect his scrawny body from being smote
Against northerly winds of poverty that blow so cold
Making his young face grow prematurely old
Powers that be cast their judgmental eye and sent
Him for a tick box assessment after a works accident
Kicked him off his ESA
And forced him instead to claim JSA
Made him pay the bedroom tax
Refuting all plausible facts
My mate lives on Struggle Street
Eking out his meagre ends to meet
While his government makes him magically disappear
As they enjoy their high life of champagne and cheer.

We Are Here

We are here
We are there
In solidarity, yet alone
Cocooned in our insomniac discomfort zone
Unable to escape pain
Limited by disability, time remains
Fathomless, unheard, voices scream
Swallowed by the night, as others dream
Darkness consumes our hurt
And we try to blurt
Out fears and woes
To unfeeling throes
Of dispassionate faces
Reminding us we are worthless "spaces"

I want the chance to address

I want the chance to address
The right Honorable IDS
To get right in his face
Ask him to set out his case

Why?
I want to chance to request
The Right Honorable IDS
Explain to me
With his false "piety"

Why?
I want him under duress
That right honorable IDS
To see the suffering he has caused
The poor and the sick with his new laws

Why?
How does it feel IDS
To wade through your troubled mess
Up to your neck in the flood
Of dead, broken Britain's blood

Why??

Back to the workhouse

Back to the workhouse
Broken battered bodies go
Labours of despair

Cuts

Welfare reforms
Money cut
No spare bedroom
Hopeless, somewhat
Not fit for work
Disability
No more DLA
Or Motability
Sanctions, non compliance
Endless waits
Assessment
No Investment
Counting costs
Uncaring government
People, hungry
Homeless, spent, lost

SARAH L DIXON

was born in Stockport and is based in Huddersfield. She had recent acceptances for *Bloody Amazing* and *Mancunian Ways*. Her books are *The sky is cracked* (Half Moon Press, 2017) and *Adding wax patterns to Wednesday* (Three Drops Press, 2018). Sarah's inspiration comes from ale, being by/in water and adventures with her son, Frank (10). www.thequietcompere.co.uk

Word association

You tie
my favourite pet
to a sign
marked
'government interference'.

Make my first gig
when I was discovering
who I was
about proving
my identity.

Take the model and colour
of the Mini
that gave me freedom
and drain the happy flight
from these memories.

What is your memorable word?

And have we sullied it
enough for you yet?

Is it still happy?
If so, we have more work
to do here.

Not for you

Not my favourite scarf
or my best corduroy coat.
No eye-liner eyes
or powdered blush.

I take notes
in a stocking-filler notebook.
No rounded pages,
flowery covers or unicorns.
A simple ring-bound A6 volume
with a plastic cover.
For you no flourishes, no hearts,
no sketches of aardvark noses.

In the front I write
'commitments'.

Commitment
not to love
as partner
or mother
but
a commitment
to invest less time

with both lover
and son.

These letters refuse to join.
Record in stark print
my vows to Theresa May.

Priceless

The skip of happy heels.
Your version of the Hokey Cokey.
A second hug
at the classroom door.

Our walk to school
Your questions about marrying trees,
how we know the Big Bang happened,
Why Donald Trump is so bad.

The battle to see who can find a gap
in clothes to put frozen hands
on hot bellies first.
Illicit delighted screams from the other.

Swimming lessons.
You are confident diving for weights,
launching from the side.
Check I am watching all the time.

The way you adjust
to so much change.
New house, school, friends.
New routine and you call it home now.
Being just us two.

ELAINE EDWARDS

Elaine always knew that she was an artist, writing took over when health declined. At first a reluctant poet, the therapeutic effects of sharing have kept her writing. Her 40s and now most of her 50s lost to illness and yet found. The grim reaper flirted with her many times, then changed his mind. She is delighted and determined to enjoy life in ways that she still can.

When You Are Very Ill

When you are very ill
the burden is on you
to collect evidence
to be ignored
much of the time
on any claim you make
in case you are
claiming for laziness' sake
No duty solicitor
for the crime of being ill
When you are a criminal
innocent or guilty as alleged
you have access
to someone to fight
your right
to live a life as free
well still in many cases
When fighting for
innocents justice
the law often
blocks that way
that many who have sway
to get away
are the crime
lords of this and
the last century
When will decency
have a say?

I had that A5 white envelope today

you know the one
I said you know the one
it's the bullshit form
to see if they can declare me
fit for work again and
make me go to tribunal
court for the disputed claim
to get things sorted out again
to be allowed to live
while unable
to fend for myself
or it could be okay...
I have good representation
from a point of understanding
for the first time in this process...
Insert string of swear words here
I am not as scared as before
but still it is a time
of severe abuse trauma
to be dredged up in another layer...

At the end of my armies

At the end of my armies
my terror-wrists
the pain in my neck
shoulders some of the blame
my fingers are held to ransom
costing loads to pick up a mug
invisible disability is smug
when systems pull another rug
from wobbly valiant recuperations....
I wasn't planning on bringing swinging hips
into screaming twisting cramps
as my ankles cry defeat
Achilles heel painful feet...

Dear DWP

I know you want to kill me you see
I've been through your system three times before
Each time a breakdown suffering more
Doctor or judge last tribunal
apologised for distress caused.
I am ill
Disabled
Not a criminal
on trial for fraud
obliged by the rules
provide truth
If it changes from unwell enough to die
in the blink of an eye
to fit for work and self care
I wouldn't be wetting my pants
as I scream in distress
four days after your attack advance
if I were able to live without help
Carers
kindness from strangers
who won't leave me to die in a heap
just because I'm unwell enough
to not only not earn my keep
but be trampled by sheep
who think it's fine to trample fragile minds
lead them to their slaughter
or reach another brink of death
as they face their last breath
As you steal dreams of support
to hold their seams
as life tears them apart
along you come wicked upstart
to stab them in the heart
Give the beggars crumbs
from the mouths that live in slums
You eat your hearty meals
from treasures that you steal
to give the rich a hand
to bring the gallows to this land
as you the executioner bring the axe down
on the heads of the sick and dying
Lack of compassion this must end.

PAT EDWARDS

was born in Aberdeen on 1st March 1958. She is a writer, reviewer and workshop leader from mid Wales. Her work has appeared in *Magma, Prole, IS&T, Atrium* and others. She has two pamphlets: *Only Blood* (Yaffle 2019); *Kissing in the Dark* (Indigo Dreams 2020). Pat hosts Verbatim open mic nights and curates Welshpool Poetry Festival.

If Dad and I had to go through it all again

We've got to go to the Dole Office he told me,
so I held his hand while we queued outside.
I watched the men vanish like food absorbed
by amoebas. The Dole Office enzymes broke
them down in return for a few quid each week.

I can't remember how Dad actually got the cash;
maybe it was diffused through membranes or did
it arrive as a postal order. It meant I was entitled
to free school meals, the ignominy of collecting
tickets from the teacher's desk echoing my Dad's

shame, the process by which we were labelled
Single Parent Family. The 60s were another time,
but if Dad and I had to go through it all again,
the endocytosis would be digital, online biology;
the science of poverty no more advanced by time.

Biographical context to the poem:
I was born in Aberdeen on 1st March 1958, out of wedlock. This was the reason my parents travelled so far from Glasgow where they lived. They moved to Bournemouth to work in the catering industry but Mum died when I was five. As a single parent family we relied on benefits all my childhood and whilst I was a student training to be a teacher. I now live a comfortable middle-class life because my Dad stuck by me even after Mum died, and I got an education. My poem questions how little has changed for poor families claiming benefits, despite modern technology, and likens the shame of the process to the way microscopic organisms feed.

MICHAEL FARRIE

originally set up the ESA & DLA Survival Guide Facebook Group roughly at the time he was facing an ATOS assessment which is the yes or no as to whether you can continue your life or not. Even with a positive brown envelope thousands if not millions face this situation and they have to negotiate the complex benefit bureaucracy and often the arbitrary pushbacks. In facing this situation together and offering advice and support, the ESA DLA UC & PIP Survival Guide became a strong community and now offers benefits advice to thousands.

The Ladybird Book of MP's Expenses - Iain Duncan Smith

Once upon a time there was a man called Iain who worked in London, that is the capital of our country, he is a very busy man indeed, in charge of benefits and employment, he works in a very busy office but is very often out and about, doing important business he tells us.

Busy men like him don't have time to eat mere tea and toast of a morning, so Iain visited a lovely little cafe, so lovely it was, that most of the prices for the meals and drinks were printed in double figures. But that didn't deter Iain as he couldn't resist tucking into a particularly sumptuous breakfast and he soon felt very full, Mr Duncan Smith was very happy indeed when he realised that the breakfast he had just eaten and most delicious it was too, would not even cost him a single penny.

"£39" said Duncan triumphantly, now where did I put my claim form and, bother, I forgot that I could claim for the paper too! Iain looked thoughtful as he further schemed, "Don't you need a pen to write with?" he said thoughtfully, "Why didn't I claim expenses for that too, what a buffoon I am, I laugh at myself sometimes, I really do".

Iain felt quite satisfied about his cleverness but he started to look slightly cross for a moment as he realised he may have been just a little bit naughty "I'd better not tell anyone about this" he said wisely, but alas for him he had not seen the man from our other book you may have read, Mr Newspaper Reporter, who was sat just one table away from him pretending to enjoy his tea.

A day later the news was all over town about how Iain had spent 39 pounds of money belonging to the public just eating his breakfast! But Iain smiled wryly, for he worked in Westminster, and there you were allowed to claim expenses for almost anything, even a brand new motor car or a newly dug moat surrounding a castle if you had your wits about you. If anybody complained he thought and I could find that they were receiving benefits that I am in charge of, I could sanction them, he thought cunningly...

He shot Mr Newspaper Reporter a mischievious glare: "Write what you like about me" he said, as he decided that if he was to be criticised, he would simply carry on as he was anyway, for he had one thing on his side that most other people didn't, he is right, he thought, and everyone else is wrong, believing that is what being a politician is all about, and that means that I cannot be criticised by anyone because they are wrong anyway.

With these thoughts rolling around in his mind, Iain found himself at rest again and decided to order a triple espresso with Albanian goat's cream even though he would then have to claim another £15 on top of the £39 he had already claimed for the food part of his breakfast which had contained a delicious blend of lightly fried caviar surprise on almond oil soaked wholemeal breaded pheasant tart.

To read the rest of the book, visit Iain Duncan Smith's GoFundMe page and pledge just £39 towards the great man's next breakfast in London. And the rest of his amazing book will be sent to your Amazon Kindle.

BARRY FENTIMAN HALL

was born in York in 1969. He has had twangy legs for the most part since and latterly a whole bunch of fibro type stuff. When not too fogged on drugs he works in a library and as one half of the literary consultancy Wordsmithery. He is also the editor of Confluence and currently poet in residence at Rochester Riverside. Works: The Unbearable Sheerness Of Being (Wordsmithery, 2016), England, My Dandelion Heart (Wordsmithery, 2018), Sketches (Wordsmithery, 2020). His writing has appeared in the following magazines and anthologies: Confluence, Crack The Spine, Whirlagust II, Dissonance, Dreich, Please Hear What I'm Not Saying, Ink, Sweat, & Tears, Marble, The Cormorant, Coronaverses, Foxtrot Uniform, The Blue Nib, Until The Stars Burn Out, City Without A Head, Writers Café Magazine, Thanet Writers, Green Fields, Squiffy Gnu, Black Light Engine Room, Anti-Heroin Chic, Vita Brevis.

The Twitch Is Back (I live my life like this)

I live my life like this
My damaged nerves are easily hurt
The palpitations in the theatre
were not caused by the art
of the performance
or the sugar of the sweets
My heart races needlessly
when distracted by thoughts
about rights and wrongs and politics
All the small sharp things
The missed ink
of business plans and forms
Official lego bricks designed to trip
the barefoot and the sick
My fingers tremble when
I place a hand on heart for comfort
To no effect
I have lived my life like this
My face betrays no sign
that my body is wrecked
The punch comes from offstage
maybe not meant but sent
in any case
Knocks my head to the side
Bends my neck till it cracks
I have kept a lid on it so well
that it shocks when
people see that I can't keep still
I live my life like this
And at least for now
the twitch is back

Low Mood

Weeping tired and cheekshot is no way to go about the day
        Weaving through the shopping school,
                uncertain where your feet might drop
A river runs though your bones, or maybe an electric current.
          It could be the 8.50 to Doncaster
             We all vibrate in a unique way
Heartfelt in hands and feet and belly
       The beat reaches where it shouldn't crunching
                in the ears like boots in snow
It always brings us up short when we have gone on,
        to see something that brings back the grieving days
          The last ribbon always clings to the railings
            You are never alone with a skull full of ghosts
You want to get it all down on paper, give it a name
          It is the inescapable rain that brings a shiver
               at the touch of the first drop
It is every shade of dog that looks back at you from the darkness.
          Every memory of a time when you didn't
             Every kind of blue
The grayscale form has no need of this
    It gives no space for the things you need to say
        It asks only that you will not be too much trouble,
       and shamed already you comply and write,

                "Low mood"

RONA FITZGERALD

was born in Dublin in 1954 and now lives in Glasgow. Her poetry is published in UK, Scottish, Irish and US, in print and online. Highlights include *Aiblins: New Scottish Political Poetry* 2016, *Oxford Poetry XVI. iii Winter* 2016-17. *Resurrection of a Sunflower, Pski's Porch* 2017. *The Passage Between*, Issue 1 Spring 2018. *Poems for Grenfell Tower*, Onslaught Press 2018, *#Me Too*, Fair Acre Press, 2018. *Blue Nib* magazine, Issue 39 September 2019 and Digital Edition June 2020. *Poetry and Covid*, September 2020. In July 2020 she was one of the winners of the Federation of Writers short story competition.

What if

I didn't emerge ahead of time
and my lungs were better developed?

I could drink cow's milk without wheezing
or eat legumes without dying?

Midges didn't bite me, no outraged red blotches
merging with my coral walking shirt?

The wily wind wafted pollen over my head
no runny nose or sneezing?

My alveoli relaxed, my lungs could breathe
without the aid of inhalers?

What if I transferred to another body -
pristine, flaw less?

Would I still be me?

The Ailments

there's eczema, asthma, hernia
and tricky veins

there's Reynaud's phenomena
arthritis and muscle pains

there's food that make me ill
and others that would kill

but I'm more likely to say
that I'm rarely, ever, ill

I do my indoor bike
with application and zeal

I walk every day, cook from scratch
our evening meal

you could say it's unfair
a tough life, a hard road

but I really don't do badly
I take my time, rest then reload

okay, I can't wear wool
feel the cold, my white cells are low

but I manage to keep busy
wrap up, keep the flow

words abound, movement prevails
love and friends fill my day

yes, it's a bummer,
life's a challenge everyday

but I'm still alive, active
and vigorous in my way!

JAMES FOUNTAIN

Born in Hartlepool in 1979. Researched the first PhD on British modernist poet Joseph Macleod (2010) and is currently editing and re-releasing Macleod's works with Waterloo Press. Fountain's poems have been published in *The Recusant, The Journal, Dream Catcher, London Grip* and *The Blue Nib*. His first chapbook, *Glaciation*, was published by Poetry Monthly Press. His second, *The Last Stop* (Original Plus), was chosen as runner-up by Imtiaz Dharker at the Ilkley Literature Festival Chapbook Competition in 2018.

The Catch of Commerce

The leafy cabinets of English scenes
slot together like forgotten dreams.

Slender conifers sway on distant hillsides,
curlews soar, calls rising ever higher.

In the city, people teem from glass blocks
oblivious to the frivolity of financial gain.

Swayed by the rhythm beaten on a drum,
attempting to win to show they know the score.

The land by the shoreline has been bought
already, developers prepare to begin building.

As embattled fishermen land empty-handed,
the roar of cars from the commuter's road

reminds them of a new catch.

Taken Out of the Fight

A trio sit on a bench by Hartlepool War Memorial,
trying to look busy and failing. The sheer
embarrassment at their unemployment and
inactivity is pasted crudely across acne-ridden
faces and longing stares, as I walk past.

I'm a few paces away, in the red borough council
building, where earlier I had heard plans from
the mouth of the chief executive, hopeful
of change, but realistic that rejuvenation
would take time. As I exited, these three were,

of course, still there, an hour later, one for all,
and, if they remembered, all for one, beside
a monument to struggle, another form of work,
to those who fought and died for their country.

But the fight had been taken out of these three.

Watching Mothers of Knife Crime Victims on TV

A broken bone in my back jogs downwards occasionally,
as I watch mothers of knife crime victims on TV,
wishing I could say our pain is the same,
as birds sing outside on the slate.

Is pain equally dealt? My only pain can be
held in place with a careful hand, and will
go away, while theirs can never be healed,
lives ended with children's deaths

after a game of chess, then Russian roulette,
a fight-to-the-death, with weapons of choice,
and later, a mother standing over,
her song forever silenced.

NAOMI FOYLE

was born in London in 1967 and grew up in Hong Kong, Liverpool and Saskatchewan. Her many publications include *The Gaia Chronicles*, an eco-SF quartet set in a post-fossil fuel parallel Mesopotamia, and three poetry collections: *The Night Pavilion*, a 2008 PBS Recommendation, *The World Cup*, and *Adamantine*, which was launched in 2019 in the UK, USA and Canada. A long-time Brighton resident, she teaches Creative Writing at the University of Chichester and is currently co-project manager of LIT UP, a mentoring and publishing scheme for poets of colour at Waterloo Press.

Brokenshite

"I don't see [homelessness] in those terms [of political policy]. I see it as a combination of concerning elements in terms of addiction, family breakdown issues."
        - The Rt Hon James Brokenshire [Con], Housing Secretary 2018-19

Lily tugging your tartan shopping trolley   down Church St
in search of a sucker   for an Irish accent   a soft touch
      who'll queue for a Big Mac and fries   while you cough
      in the cold   outside Liverpool Central   mutter
      other, private orders   down your mobile phone –
      your hair a faded flame
            your face a stranded currach,
                  your good self unwashed 'for months'
      the Council's winter street campaign   *Always Room Inside*
                  'all a pack of lies' . . .

Sebastian   yogi on a cardboard mat   outside my local Co-Op
sanctioned by the Portslade office   for being ten minutes late
cheerfully unrolling   a grey sock   with raw beef sausage fingers
      to display the scarred proof   of your forthcoming operation
      to remove busted pins and plates   ever re-scheduled
      until your chest infection clears –
            which in this weather might take a while
so cheerfully accepting   tangerines, sandwiches and Eccles cakes
      before gifting your box seat   to a young woman
            in a bobble hat and puffer jacket and zooming off
      who knows where   on a white mountain bike . . .

Simon   the spectral son of Shane McGowan   or an apparition
      out of *Great Expectations* who materialised beside me
in the Café Nero queue at Victoria Station   and with a shining smile
      sparked by the clunk   of a coin   in a paper cup
         became my personal avatar   of gummy, grimy joy . . .

And you whose names I'll never know
         the pale man kneeling   outside Pret á Manger at Kings Cross
         head bowed, hands cupped   a silent island
              in a frothing river of commuters . . .
      the man biting back tears   on the pavement slabs
         outside my bank   carefully unfolding and refolding
            his creased receipt   for six weeks of hostel nights
               tucking its tatters   back in a pocket
                     next to his heart . . .
      the invisible campers   under the arches at Black Rock
         building a wall   of empty wine bottles
               around their tents . . .
      the grizzled legless Rastaman   zig-zagging his wheelchair
         up St James's St   stopping traffic   with the smashed grin
               of a gold medal Paralympian

      the numb young woman   asleep or not on a bench
      outside the law courts   who, the winter's night
      I joined a small crowd   determined   to help her
         refused to open her eyes   or speak
            whom I know now   as a blue nylon cocoon
      and a pair of black pumps   neatly parked on the pavement
               I strain to cycle past up-hill . . .

      How long will you always be with us?
                          Where are you now?

DAVID GARBUTT

Place of birth: his grandmother's living room, London, 28 Aug 1951.
Occupation: Retired. He worked as a software developer and consultant
for 25 years in Switzerland. Publications: *Readers & Writers Magazine,
Horizon, One to One, Word For Word* anthology (Berkshire open lit
competition, winner plus four highly commended). *P* (Journal). Recent
work on *Medium* (@DavGar51). He recently had a poem shortlisted for *The
Rialto* Nature & Place competition 2021.

The Last List

This is the last list
like a sword,
but unlike a life,
it ends with a point.
It begins with a statement:
This is the last list
and it whines down the page
like the decided groove
on a record, closing in.
Contrathetically: it faces out
tries to impose
it allocates the things.
It fibrillates the heart
that writes. Vibratically
it asks - why only now
turn to the world
to say - *From now*
do this and this,
and all this very lastest list
of things my way.

Ah! That is lost.
Lost in the movement
of the coil around the
elliptical pin. Lost in the
rotational momentum
of that whole,
black,
spiraling thing

Bus 36 at Solitude Park

"I've two weeks left".
Her hands are holding
each other
her eyes are holding
me, letting tears go.
"In another three years
I could have retired".

> *What we are holding*
> *is small, not just each other.*
> *We are holding a butterfly*
> *the scales falling off its wings, its eyes*
> *trying to escape, trying*
> *to find getting wings*
> *is not the final stage…*

"Will you look for another job?"
I ask, flailing.

"Yes, I am, lots of interviews!
It's a full-time job…
We can telephone".
"We can talk—anytime."

Its my stop, she gets off,
I stay on. I'll walk back.

Later, in the park, we talk.

"I'm looking too, no interviews
yet. All the times before
It was positive—at the end I mean,
I hated change, but now…
We are always caterpillars".

I break a rule,
confess I'm not strong,
a False Monarch,
not even from here. She starts, looks at me
tilted.

"Look, it helps, being angry; it's a stage:

after tears, after guilt,
after crushing the butterfly,
but what's left is an egg".

"Let's go and eat leaves"

MOIRA GARLAND

Moira Garland is a retired lecturer, once trade unionist, ex-melodeon
player, now poet and short fiction writer. Her work appears in such
magazines as *The North* and *Strix*, and anthologies including *Black
Lives Matter, Release a Rage of Red, And the Stones Fell Open, Bloody
Amazing,* and *The Forgotten & the Fantastical #3.* Her beginnings lie just
within the birth of the NHS, and the sound of River Mersey foghorns.
@moiragauthor.

Fray

He writes about a safe place.

The words unravel.
He writes about failure
in liminal spaces
fledglings hunted
by cats in hedges,
failing
        falling
into hidden places until

he has to apply himself
for jobs
wear a stitched-up suit
so he will not go ragged
refusing haulage trucks
performers who lie with words
skills
application
training
sanctions

sobs in his chest
he ducks for cover
steps up
boards the frenzied express
plunging him into the fray.

RAINE GEOGHEGAN

is a poet, prose writer and playwright of Romany, Welsh and Irish descent. She was born in Tradegar, South Wales on 27.02.56. Nominated for the Forward Prize, Best of the Net & the Pushcart Prize, her work has been published online and in print with *Poetry Ireland Review, Travellers' Times, Under the Radar, SkyLight47, Poethead* and many more. Her work has also been featured in the film *Stories from the Hop Yards* with Catcher Media and based on the work of photographer Derek Evans. My poem 'A Memory of the Hop fields' was made into a film by the Wellington Primary school in 2019. She performs her work here in the UK and Ireland. She is registered disabled after a fall down the stairs and has had ME/CFS for 24 years. Prior to this she worked in theatre and the performing arts, acting, dancing, directing and teaching. Her pamphlet, *Apple Water: Povel Panni* (2018) was a Poetry Book Society Spring 2019 Selection. *They Lit Fires: Lenti Hatch O Yog* was published in December 2019, with Hedgehog Poetry Press. Her first full collection, *The Talking stick: O Pookering Kosh*, will be published by Salmon Poetry in March 2022, as well as an anthology of Romany Women's Writing which she will be co-editing. Website: rainegeoghegan.co.uk - twitter.com/RaineGeoghegan5

The Glass Delusion

Don't touch me   I may shatter,
speak to me   walk around me,
but don't touch me   I may shatter.
I may break.

You can look at me   even look through me,
                 just don't get too close.
Shss, speak softly, quietly
don't raise your voice   I may shatter.

Sit close   but not too close.
I need plenty of space.
Don't judge me …   if you do
I may shatter.

If the light shines   at just the right angle
you might see yourself reflected in my face.
Please don't scream   I may shatter,
if I do   you'll have to pick up the pieces.

[Inspired by Radio 4's programme 'The Glass Delusion' — The "glass delusion" is an extraordinary phenomenon in which people believe themselves to be made of glass and thus liable to shatter.]

fatigue

ME/CFS - Chronic Fatigue Syndrome - a debilitating multi-system, long term chronic disease. Overwhelming fatigue that is not improved by rest.

    was something i relished,
nestling in my bed
after a long day,
sleeping a healthy sleep,
knowing that i would return
to the world.

    now it is something monstrous
attacking my body,
furring my tongue,
clinging to my lungs,
embedding itself in my brain,
gnawing at my bones.

    the enemy within waits
in my marrow, corroding the cells.
it has claws like knives
and breathes fire.
i am trapped.
there are bars around my bed
and the door, like my mind, is shut tight.

    I lie here day after day,
sleeping an unhealthy sleep,
tasting the bitterness of rust.

Ludgate Shopping Centre

She parks the car,
places blue badge on the dash.

The boys jump out,
slamming doors.

> *She feels the first prick of tension.*

Into the lift,
grey and smelling of disinfectant.
Status Quo singing 'Down, Down'.
Did she really like this band once?

> *Relief as they come to the first floor.*

Her son is happy, has a friend,
he's about to spend his birthday money.

The smile on her face is for him.

The boys rush into shops,
scan shelves;
he wants computer games,
and new trainers,
a gentle reminder of how much cash he has.

A girl screams;
she jumps, nowhere feels safe.

> *She starts to fade, legs feeling like damp sand.*

> *'Stay upright'.*

They want to go into another store.
She promises them a pizza if they're quick.

She waits.
A cold wind stings her face.

*Imagine a quiet room... somewhere in Ludgate
shopping centre.
A place to lie down,
where limbs, bones rest inside skin.*

She considers going into the store.
Images of glass doors swinging,
bright lights, babies crying and musak,
forcing itself into ears, eyes, head.

*A deep thirst and a
yearning
for soft earth, grass,
the healing tones of green. She
sighs as if breathing out will help
her remain solid.
Her legs give way.*

*Crumpling to her knees,
she slides down the shop window
and in front of her, his feet.*

DECLAN GERAGHTY

is a writer, poet and spoken word performer from Dublin. He's had poetry
and flash fiction published in *Dublin in the coming times*, *The flying
superhero clothes horse* and the poetry anthology *2020 Visions*. His
latest work is included in the short story collection *From the Plough
to the Stars* which was published by Culture Matters. He's currently
working on a flash fiction collection entitled The Bowsie which will be
published in 2021.

Davey

Are you on the dole
Or maybe you don't even have enough stamps to get it
Combing for scraps like the seagulls in the field
Circling the crazy woman throwing bread in the air
And they make that sound
That beak sound.
Are you happy?
Are you surviving?
Are you looking after yourself?
Do you still see any of the old faces?
I'm sorry about your brother
How's your ma?
And your sister in Oz?
My life beats like yours
It pulses good and bad like the weather
And we're Irish so you can just imagine the weather
The clouds that hang over me
Just like the clouds that hang over you
And if there is a Jesus
Like that born again Christian stuff you follow
I hope he takes you into heaven
And your brother will be there
And you can do all the things you used to
Hopefully without the arguments.
And what you were years ago was a warrior
But now were getting old and weak
But they still can't take that way from ye
The fact that you were a warrior.

Blood on the dole

Do all blokes on the dole go to heaven
Do they clean up after the saints
On some celestial jobs bridge
The gates of Saint Peter won't polish themselves
And if they go to hell, are they there because of the sins
        of the poor
The sin of being poor
The sin of not being born into a family from a leafier more
        well to do place
Is there purgatory for all blokes on the dole
Or did they already just live it
And it says god will forgive them
He'll take them into heaven and forgive all of them
And does he forgive the blokes on the dole
And the girls on the dole
For some imaginary middle class crime
A crime that doesn't exist.

Just because they said it doesn't make it right

I know what it's like
When they take that power away from you
The power of being a proud man
And they put you in your box
In your compartment
Labelled
Branded for themselves
To make them feel good
About their own weak egos
Their own weak minds
And sometimes it looks like there's only enough to kill yourself
        with cheap booze and bad food
And the restaurants and shops you pass may look intimidating
As your weekly payment seems to go in one hand and out the other
Sometimes you feel like you're trying to make something from
        nothing
Sometimes you feel like nothing
But you are something
Something very special
And if you can think your way out of this trap

You'll look back and probably laugh one day
Or probably even cry
Depending on the humour you're in.

MARIA GORNELL

is a poet from Liverpool, she has been published widely in the small
press and has poems included in such anthologies as *Clinical, Brutal An
Anthology of Writing With Guts* (2011), *Soul Feathers*, an anthology for
Macmillan Cancer published by Indigo Dreams (2011), *Emergency Verse:
Poetry in Defence of the Welfare State* from *The Recusant/* Caparison
(2011), and *Binders Full of Women* (2012). In 2012 her pamphlet *In the
Absence of Wing* was published by Erbacce Press. Maria is a trained sound
therapist and uses some of her poetry in therapeutic settings.

In Sickness and In Wealth

Ever felt like a flower not allowed to bloom?
as you call out my worth in numbers
faceless decisions
the Mcdonaldisation of the world
punch keys into my heart
bureaucracy through my soul life
gorge my eyes out with relentless
hammering to my bones
send me brown paper letters
signed with a death wish
wish me sickness in health
take away my power
silence my voice
scapegoat me into a box
dehumanise me
strip me of my identity
tell me I'm a drain
a worthless egg
crack my spine
and send me on journeys
that lead nowhere
give me a bus ticket
to purgatory
while you make a profit
on my disempowerment

wrap me in chains
insult my intelligence
because you can't be sick
and clever at the same time
send me more brown letters
to reinforce my absolute
uselessness on earth
which you are employed
at the will of an unemployed world
take away my options
limit my chances
send me to a food bank
of unhealthy processed gluten
that will make me more
fat and sick
tell me I didn't fulfil my duties
take away my human rights
this is England 2018
In sickness and in wealth.

MARK GRIFFITHS

Born 30.6.70 Essex. An eco-socialist and hardcore Republican residing in Swansea. His poetry has appeared in *Red Poets* and the *Morning Star*.

Old timer

With the onward zap of digitisation,
We cannot hear the constant tick,
Racing passed our defined lines,
Shocked by the everywhere voids,
Not on track online somewhere?
Connected ......frozen,
Riding uncontrollably,
Chase the next rage,
Comfort in the thrill of precipice,
As the movement advances unabated,
Ignored as we are busy amused,
In the brand of relentless innovation,
Skills are being killed to 'future',
We are blissfully diverted,
 unable to nourish sustenance,
Physically withering under onslaught,
Fearing to share,
But sharing our fears,
Heading headlong forwards,
Knowledge a debris,
Discarded as passe,
Shame relic trying to survive...

NR 2012

No compassion for the jobless or the vulnerable sick,
Who have recourse to bare subsistence of carrot and stick,
But we glorify and idolise the pampered percent,
Who wilfully avoid dues not willing to share or relent,
They demand we must create Growth,
If we want a crumb from the loaf,
The elite establishment are beyond reproach or punishment,
As the debt despair legacy voids us from survival entitlement.

Arbitrary power imprisons the male and impoverishes the female,
That may dare riot against welfare state fail,
But encourage the reckless finance gamble
That rapes the public purse scramble,
The establishment enshrines we repay,
Any supposed debt every sweating day,
But leaves the rentiers and corporations untouched,
With power capture they cripple, state-crutched.

SUMAN GUPTA

was born in London on 2 January 1966. He teaches at the Open University
and has mainly published in an academic vein, recently *Digital India
and Poor* (Routledge 2020). A few decades back he wrote poetry which was
occasionally published. Then the muse largely left him alone. Now he
writes in something like verse only when academic investigation seems
unequal to the issue and rarely feels confident enough to try and get it
published.

The Contemporary History of Austerity in Britain

In 2009: on the way from Cheltenham to Westminster / a man
poked us in the eye / with elegiac and earnest fingers.

[Earnest] not just about the 'me', but the 'we' / not just
about the market, but about society … too

[Elegiac] there are deep, dark clouds / steering our country,
reaching the sunshine / on the far side

[Earnest] here's a whole new, never-done-before approach
/ because the world has changed completely / the age of
irresponsibility is giving way to the age of austerity

[Elegiac] we risk becoming once again the sick man of Europe /
our children will be weighed down by a millstone / of debt /
the way out / is through massive change

[Earnest] I'm frustrated it's not happening / I'm impatient to
get on with it / today I want to explain what the change needs
to be / the age of austerity demands responsible politics

[Elegiac] despite the gravity of this debt crisis / despite the consequences of not dealing with it / they can't stop the politics of spin … smoke and mirrors … treating people as fools

[Earnest] this country expects more from us / than a hair shirt and a stern lecture / Personal responsibility. Social responsibility.

[Elegiac] Is vision dead? Does the age of austerity force us to abandon our ambitions?

[Earnest] No. We are not here just to balance the books. / The question is: how does government achieve in the age of austerity? / And the answer is: by delivering more for less.

In 2010: allegory took over.

Suicide squats in a malodorous apartment overlooking sweet Thames. She hums to herself. Her face is blind. Her lips red, looks free, skin white as leprosy. Through broken panes she spies. She haunts and hunts serially. Evicted and Hungry are in the subprime light. Evicted levitates a bit. She floats in hot air outlets. She is there but not quite there. Hungry sighs a fading sigh. She becomes pristine by degrees. She tries her food bank debit card. Evicted patronizes winter shelters. She spits true grit in summer. They are young. They are old. They have many clones and some hybrids. Some are NEET, some messed up. Their universal credit shatters their universe. Suicide watches their aimless regress. She hums. She slashes interest rates. She bails out those that aren't too big to fail. She licks the diaphanous miasma called Austerity. Smoky austerity rises and falls like a breathing torso. Like Thames tide, forevermore. Suicide looks for her next victim. Evicted and Hungry evade her gaze. Suicide passes with indifferent eyes. Her serial killer tell is untold. Evicted and Hungry can only kill themselves. By mistake. Suicide kills Mental Health Issues instead. Mental Health Issues writes a crisis report. And a death note. Her mind is labyrinthine. She meets Suicide and smiles. She is murdered over and over, serially. She is subjective. Evicted and Hungry are objective.

In 2019: news style.

Universal credit wait fuels poverty and food bank use. Welfare changes drive food bank use. Demand for food banks reached a record high. Britain forces disabled to food banks. Appoint a Minister of Hunger. There are more food banks than McDonalds. I hung around outside, embarrassed to go in. Food bank use by children over holidays surges. People who come here have been abandoned. Parliament has no substantive, freestanding obligation of fairness. Austerity to me is a working person having to access a charity to have enough food to eat. Poverty increases among children and pensioners across UK. Worsening child poverty harms learning. Growth of in-work poverty is UK's statistic of the year. You can't blame the government for poverty. More than 4 million in UK are trapped in deep poverty. Millions of UK adults are functionally illiterate but problem ignored. Level of NEET young people hits three year high. National minimum wage laws allow lawful discrimination against young people. Zero-hour contracts take a huge mental and physical toll. UK income inequality rises as benefits cut hit poorest. A third of premature deaths in England are linked to social inequality. Inequality driving deaths of despair.

UN Rapporteur: Given the significant resources available in the country, the sustained and widespread cuts to social support, which have caused so much pain and misery, amount to retrogressive measures in clear violation of the United Kingdom's human rights obligations.

In 2020: the language of science.

Austerity is the Virus.

MARTYN HALSALL

has concentrated on writing poetry, and about poetry, since retiring from
a lifetime in journalism that included 17 years as a staff correspondent
on *The Guardian*. His latest award was winning the Norman Nicholson
Society 'Lockdown' competition in October 2020, when he also published
his latest collection, *Visible Music* (Caldew Press) about experiencing
cancer. He lives in rural West Cumbria, and enjoys travelling in
Scotland.

Cross Reference

This chancer tried it on: no fixed abode,
no job since leaving the family joinery business-
light yokes, some rough-hewn crosses on commission.

We made some background checks; a gang of them
fancied themselves as anti-capitalists –
washed-up fishermen, footnote poet, a fraudster

who pulled the purse strings to his own advantage;
and a gaggle of groupies, one just off the streets –
his Mum among them, trying to fathom it out.

Seemed to walk everywhere; no driving licence;
fantasy skills base – turning lame to sprinters,
making some lepers radiant, raising the dead.

No-one in their simplest minds trusted the Iscariots
who filed his application. He never showed
up for an interview, ignored our e-mails.

We heard his scheme went pear-shaped. Never a whisper
of a VAT return. The benefits squad
was poised to mount its own investigation

when they got the heads-up (someone under cover) –
justice done by betrayal. Some bribery did him,
and a trumped-up treason charge, cross-referenced, nailed him.

OZ HARDWICK

was born in Plymouth in 1960 and came of age in the Thatcher era, during which he became over familiar with the DHSS and dead-end jobs. He became a mature student just as student loans were being introduced, and has lectured in English and Creative Writing at Leeds Trinity University since 2000. He has published five poetry collections and four chapbooks, including *Learning to Have Lost* (Canberra: IPSI/Recent Work, 2018) which won the 2019 Rubery International Book Award for poetry, and his latest, *Wolf Planet* (Clevedon: Hedgehog, 2020).

Curriculum Vitae

Work is a series of shapes pressed out of laminated card, the resistance of stiff keys on a cheap clarinet. It's the makeshift shelves in a pop-up shop and the knock on a door that will never be answered. When I'm asked about previous employment, I show the tiny scars and the Tupperware lunchbox, the loose polo shirts that have been washed too many times; and when I'm asked for references, I state latitude and longitude, and quote an essay on Camus that my old French teacher read with a Scouse accent. Work is a Perspex hopper in a weigh-your-own store and the swept vegetable leaves after the weekend market. It's the gaps between slats of a jerry-built chalet in a rain-swept holiday camp. At the Jobcentre, a man in a tracksuit breaks computers and a young girl cradles a snake in a fish tank. The Devil makes work for idle hands, but my hands are shaking as my name is called.

BRUCE HARRIS

started writing creatively in 2004 after a career in teaching and educational research, including extensive research-based publications. Since then, he has been consistently successful in short fiction and poetry competitions, and extensively published in print and e-zines. He is author of several short story collections, *First Flame* (2013), *Odds Against* (2017), *The Guy Thing* (2018), a collection of 'rites of passage' short stories published in aid of the Huntington's Disease Youth Association, *Fallen Eagles* (Book Guild, 2021), a novel, *Howell Grange* (Book Guild, 2019), and poetry collections, *Raised Voices* (2014), *Kaleidoscope* (2017), and *The Huntington Hydra* (Caparison, 2019). For personal reasons, he donates the takings from his published books to the Huntington's Disease Association.

M.E. Revisited

How well I knew it, that special silence,
the void where the unsaid words used to howl;
the passing glances, the downcast eyes,
the really fit people rejoicing in modesty.
How tired I became with being tired,
pining away in a squander of time
with all that I was or had hoped to be
made down to muscles like naked bones rasping.
An insult of judgements easily made;
such parcels of pettiness, the bad tabloid jokes,
and too many nights half-alive in the small hours
trying to find a shelter of answers.

You return to the routines, rescued by kindnesses
and removed from the million germs of the innocents;
You work out what damage is irretrievable
and mend the reparable fences you find;
the telescope turns; so tiny and distant
that shrivelled existence, immobile perplexity.
No more the indifference to present or future;
no more the examining of pasts and portents.
The questions continue; occasional, then rare
and you repeat the answers you gave at the time
and so they look puzzled, as if they'd been there,
as if they'd an answer to make your life rhyme.

Kafka's Garden

In Her Majesty's Government's labyrinthine corridors
where the muddled mazes reflect the thinking
a person diagnosed with an incurable illness
by an experienced specialist hospital consultant
after an established and verified genetic test
is not necessarily entitled to benefits
even though there is no treatment available
and the illness is known to cause many issues
with cognitive and physical repercussions.

All evidence and testimony is rendered irrelevant
against the 'qualified health care operatives',
the 'qualifications' carefully unspecified,
whose brief is all too obviously a wrecking one
for whoever and whatever the case put to them.
Even though the benefit on offer is a pittance
inadequate for less than one day's health care
HMG wants its invalid citizens to jump
through hoops of fire for its scattered pennies.

I wonder if Kafka had his own refuge garden
with cultivated lawns and bright tended flowers
where he could repose and rest his aching mind
away from the bureaucratic jobsworth hordes
wrapping victims in knots and silently sniggering
as they watch the vulnerable caught in their webs.
Would Franz be selecting an ideal burial plot
for every Minister of Obfuscation
to feed his daisies and nourish his brassicas?

If someone were to appear on the Ministry steps
with a limb neatly tucked underneath each arm
precariously supported on an old zimmer frame
would a 'health care operative' consider it appropriate
to help them up the steps, or would that negate
the victim's chances of governmental scrapings?
If a time server tin brain suddenly went berserk
spraying benefits around like Scrooge after treatment
would he be re-assigned to cemeteries and parks?

German Jewishness, insurance and the law
would be enough to deal with for any mortal mind
and if Prague had no places for attainable peace
the craziness around him would have driven him crazy.
A water feature, perhaps, a bower or a nook,
a comfortable deckchair for taking his ease,
watching birds doing uncontroversial things
or the insects doing their daily dozens
with studied and careful objects and intentions?

'A duty of care', I've heard the politicians call it,
'a moral obligation' to support all citizens,
though an illness with no cure doesn't qualify, it seems
for public support of investigative research
even though it keeps killing citizens every year
and has been with us now since cholera and small pox.
I'll visit Kafka's garden, fold my arms and turn my back,
dreaming in the greenery, and ignoring all the noises
of bucks for ever being passed in the buildings behind me.

Invaders

Clouds of doubt replace our certainties,
their mists envelopping our shore's definition
and compromising all our taken for granted
expectations of a quiet retirement.
His island mind is threatened by strangers
occupying places he thought were his
and we wait like silent villagers hearing
the trudge of smugglers in the dead of night.

Would you trust your movement co-ordination
to control a boiling pan of water?
Would you assume your span of concentration
enough to read through a slim, small volume?
Pouring liquid, walking a while,
standing still without support,
cutting, slicing, knotting, tieing,
all false friends and newly fled.

All the imprisoned are not in prisons,
all the deprived not about nutrition
and while self-infliction never really excuses
the moral duty of hoping and helping,
in the Huntington case, it doesn't even begin
to be the most remote consideration.
Huntington is random, unjust and vicious,
a conviction imposed on unblemished innocence.

The clock ticks on to the rhythm of life
as we continue to seek to enjoy its beat
and deny its beating; we hope to stand
on the patch we have made, its boundaries
respected, its integrity intact.
The invaders lay claim to her, him, them,
regardless of guilt, gender, age or reason
and then turn on those who presume immunity.

DEBORAH HARVEY

Poems widely published in journals and anthologies, broadcast on BBC Radio 4's *Poetry Please,* and awarded several major prizes, most recently the 2018 Plough Prize Short Poem Competition. Her four poetry collections, *The Shadow Factory* (2019), *Breadcrumbs* (2016), *Map Reading for Beginners* (2014), and *Communion* (2011) are all published by Indigo Dreams, while her historical novel, *Dart* (2013), appeared under their Tamar Books imprint. Her fifth collection, *Learning Finity,* will be published in 2021. She is co-director of The Leaping Word poetry consultancy, which provides support and advice to page and performance poets, groups, organisations, schools, universities, promoters and anyone interested in any aspect of poetry. https://theleapingword.com/ https://deborahharvey.blogspot.com/ www.facebook.com/Deborah.Harvey.Writer

A Foretelling of the Second Coming of Christ in which He will Cleanse the Department of Work and Pensions

After Matthew 21, v12-13

The only light is from the stairwells
between each floor of the blocks of flats
and the leftover moon, and the flame of your anger
which is crackling with devotion that is holy.
Take these table tombs in the churchyard.
Right now you could tip them over
with a flick of your finger
one after the other, if you tried.

Must it take a furious god
to cut loose justice, send it clattering
on its dusty broken wings,
overturn the desks of the assessors
and drive them from their dens
like cheats and thieves?

MARTIN HAYES

was born in London and has lived around the Edgware Road area of it all
of his life. He has worked in the courier industry for over 30 years and
is the author of four books of poetry: *Letting Loose The Hounds* (Redbeck
Press, 2001), *When We Were Almost Like Men* (Smokestack, 2015), *The Things Our
Hands Once Stood For* (Culture Matters, 2018) and *ROAR!* (Smokestack, 2018).

the telephonist who works more than 16-hours a week

there is a hole in her hull and she is tilting in the harbour
unable to go out to sea anymore
she is letting in water
and every month the hole gets bigger

she has a leaking hull
and doesn't know what to do
the captain of the ship
having left leaving two crew-members on board
the system doesn't seem to want to allow her
to fix it
because after she has paid for the mooring costs
and the interest on the loan she took out
to buy a new set of sails
there is never enough left over
to buy any wood and nails, tar and brushes
that could help her patch it up, stem the flow
of the water

all she wants
is to become seaworthy again
but it seems the system is designed
to make the hole even bigger
so that more water can get in
ruining her furnishings
and spoiling all of the food on board
until there is nothing left to sleep on
or eat anymore

now that she is in this mess
the system doesn't want to allow her
to mend her hull
preferring instead
to let her tilt even more

until she finally takes on so much water
that she will go under
and sink to the bottom of the harbour
along with the rest of the wrecks

units of damage

in memory of Errol Graham

they found a small wooden box by his bed
that you or me would've kept something nice from our past in
his 4-stone body was laid out on the floor beside it like a mat
the coroner said
it contained two back teeth and the pair of pliers
he'd used to pull them out with
cut off he turned even more in on himself
tipped his world even further up on its head
long ago he'd stopped cycling the 2-hours it took
to see his grandkids
tins of fish found in his cupboard were 4-years out of date
what a state
what a State we pay our taxes to
to look after men who can't look after themselves
while turning blind eyes to avoiders
leaving holes in the fence for them to push their cash through
then pinching pennies back off the poor

DWP pulled the cash, said his situation didn't demand an
immediate payment
the claim he'd put in wasn't relevant to his situation
of course it was fucking relevant - he was our people - a
citizen
not just a unit of dough
but you deal in units of dough don't you
units of cost, units of damage
your pockets have holes we feed cash into that end up in the
stomach's of Lords
not inside Errol's stomach
but fed to your saggy-titted tousled-haired confederates
your bitches in bearskins waving about a contract

you think we don't know this
all of us seen as units of cost
units of damage
you outsource to companies who employ people that stink of
nothing but training
who've had all of their humanity trained out of them
then you put them on the phone
to script-speak to people like Errol

look at yourself…
you did this to one of us!
because of an unyielding script
because of a points system that's had its eyes taken out
because it's always just another day
of power and numbers to you

the first casualty of first lockdown – April 2020

Janey calls me up on Teams
she's in a state
she received an email in from HR last night
telling her that she's gonna be laid off
because the company needs to keep an eye on the wage bill
to ensure it remains a going concern
once lockdown passes
they might be able to reemploy her in the future
but need to see how things develop
or don't develop

I tell her I didn't know about it
but thought that something like this was coming
not just for her
but for the many

Janey starts pouring out words that feel like questions
how she's worried about what she'll do
for the food money, the rent
how her little two will cope
she's already started feeling the urge to self-harm again
and when the job money goes
she doesn't know if she'll be able
to navigate around all of those forms again

waiting in DWP limbo
waiting at the food bank
while the fridge remains empty
and she descends back into that fog

I don't know what to say to her

though the Thames has welcomed back its first dolphins
and the smog has lifted from over San Francisco Bay
and though the flora and fauna seem to be erupting again
the sky is dark
and from over the horizon
there is coming soon the biggest storm
we have ever seen
one no correctly filled out form
will be able to contain

I decide, at this stage, it's probably best
to sympathise instead
because those wolves at the DWP
are gonna eat this one up as a snack

TATTY HOGGARTH

is a ranting Punk Poet based in Bradford. Started performance poetry in 2010 and has supported acts such as Attila The Stockbroker, Captain Hotknives and David Rovics.

Vaccinate your children

You should Vaccinate your children
It seems straight forward to me
Vaccines save lives
They've eradicated polio from our society

Vaccines have created a world where we are protected from disease
So when anti vaxxers spout lies, it causes me great unease
It's scientifically proven, vaccines work
When they say it causes Autism, it drives me berserk

Their argument is so simplistic
What's wrong with being autistic
This is who I am, I am of equal worth
Not through vaccinations but through the accident of birth

They want to try and cure us, change who we are
But me and Autism can never stray too far
And I'm glad because it makes me, me
Right from birth, we were meant to be

Sometimes I don't react well in social situations
But that's no need to say we don't need vaccinations
Sure we do, vaccines save lives
They've got a problem with aspies, I can see it in their eyes

So no matter what they say, I know this for sure
Autism isn't a disease, we don't want a cure

ANGI HOLDEN

writes adult and children's poetry and fiction and won the MMB Poetry Pamphlet Prize for *Spools of Thread* and the Victoria Baths Splash Fiction Prize.

Letterbomb

Each day she watches the postie cheerfully
striding up the path in his fluorescent jacket,
his knee-length shorts the colour of Bath Stone,
his walking boots worn pavement-soft.

Each morning she waves in response
to his raised hand, listens for the letters
to land on the 'Welcome' doormat.
She waits for his whistle to recede,
for the clunk of the garden gate,
the rattle of striker as its latch catches.

Each day she picks up the bundle of post.
She sorts leaflets and flyers from magazines,
dumps offers of cheap broadband,
of double glazing and funeral plans,
into the paper recycling bag.

She considers the envelopes,
plain and windowed, some white, some brown,
her name and address hand-written or printed.
One has the familiar type on the reverse:
If undelivered, please return.
This is the one she has expected.
She crumples, scattering post across the floor.
It is an hour before she gathers
enough strength to tear it open.

Dear Client

We need to see you.
It is important you attend.
There is doubt about your entitlement;
your benefits may be affected.

Although it is not compulsory
I would like to invite you
to discuss your options.
Please arrive promptly.
If you cannot,
please contact me immediately.

Bring your passport and utility bill.
We may be able to help with the cost
of childcare or travel.

You can bring a friend or relative.
It might be helpful to know
Jobcentre Plus offices can get very busy.

ZEKRIA IBRAHIMI

is a 62 year old anarchist who has been diagnosed as a schizophrenic by an often uncaring psychiatric establishment, and he revels in being a rejected outsider. Ibrahimi is Afghan, and disabled, and he writes much about what it is to be a refugee - one of the international homeless.

A schizophrenic considers Covid-19 (part one)

I'm sectioned in the loony bin,
I'm rubbish to be locked away,
But outside, madness must begin,
Getting more rabid every day,
Outside, streets are as wild as sin,
And panic like garbage has sway,
But in PICU, calm seems to win,
And burnished hope salutes the day

A schizophrenic considers Covid-19 (part two)

Schizophrenic - that is how I'm defined,
A 'loony', sectioned far from the world's gaze...
Now, shops, streets, must have gone out of their mind.
Hospitals are burnt out, and in a daze.
Politics is in flames, and, as if blind,
Stumbles, without sense, along twisted ways,
Through manic hecatombs, where cold ghosts wind.
Masks and vaccines are dead-ends in a maze...
All of society should be consigned
To a 'nuthouse', while Covid's fires blaze...
In the TV room, I watch Covid grind -
Like a disaster everyone obeys -
Towns into cinders, and, then, will have whined,
Once nurse brings meds, on heaped trolleys and trays.

[Note: These poems are on the theme of a mental health unit actually seeming 'saner' than the condition of society in general, under this universal lockdown. In a nasty way, people have been given a quite oppressive taste of what it is like to be sectioned, in that they have been involuntarily confined for so-called 'health reasons'. Indeed, just as campaigners protest against the sectioning process in psychiatry, anti-lockdown groups criticize excessive restrictions on households. This sectioning/lockdown parallel is a disturbing one.]

SALLY JAMES

was born in Wigan on 01 08 1942. She has an M.A. in Creative writing from Bolton University. Her chapbook of poems, *Coal Dust and Confetti* (Thynks Publications, 2014), speak of the harsh realities of mining in the Lancashire area. *The Wasamaroo and other poems* was published by Scott Martin Productions in 2018, they are poems for children from 8 years onwards. She has a CD of humorous Lancashire dialect poems which she did with her husband under their name Tin Pot Poets. She has had poems published in numerous small press magazines and webzines including *Orbis, Pennine Ink, Worktown Poetry* (Bolton), and the Open University poets' anthologies. In 2020 she won a poetry competition and will be having a poem published on a plaque at Bolton Station.

Government Information

Popping through my letter box
quietly without exploding
the brown envelope
lay silently on the mat
not moving just lying.
I trembled at the sight
questions tortured my mind.
I picked it up, it wasn't hot
or cold or pained my fingers.
I placed it on the kitchen table
it looked harmless enough
propped against a stained mug.
I dared myself to open it.
Words danced through
my half-closed eyes
informed me as I am shielding
there is help available if needed.
I relaxed, celebrated with cold tea
waited for my food box to arrive.

First pay packet

The little brown envelope
lay by the glass fruit bowl
mam saw it and smiled.
Her dolly tub fingers
opened it with care.
"Two pounds seventeen
and sixpence" she said.
Gave me a ten-shilling note
went back to the mangle
turned the iron wheel.
Soap bubbled in cold air
steamed her glasses.
"Buy a washing machine
with my wage" I urged
"you could get one
on the never never".
Her woodbine breath croaked
"I may do just that".
My little brown envelope
became her release from drudgery
her mangle a symbol of the past.

KATE JAY-R

is an author and has written extensively. Her novel *The Other Side Of Carrie Cornish* was inspired by her personal struggles with the benefits system, and her own experience with long term mental and physical health problems and those of others. She has been campaigning online against changes to welfare changes since 2010. She prefers to call it Social Security even though she regards that as a misnomer, as it's more like social insecurity these days. She wrote another novella related to the benefits system over twenty years ago entitled *Lost The Plot* which appeared in an avant-garde magazine *Texts Bones* published by Skrev Press. As well as writing many novels she has written short stories, some of which have been shortlisted for awards. She also writes poetry. She set up the Facebook group Nothing4Something nearly a decade ago for disabled artists and those with long term health problems. The group is now called Don't Go Breaking Our Arts where members share their poetry, writing, satire, art and photography. Kate also loves music, singing, cats, LFC and photography, not necessarily in that order.

excerpt from **Lost The Plot**

Governments Lose The Plot: It began with Thatcher. In the days before her, people moonlighted. We're not talking ill people as in folk on Invalidity Benefit, as it was known back then, who got on with the business of being ill quietly – we're talking healthy young and not-so-young men. Nobody batted an eyelid. Unemployment rose to over 3 million under Thatcher and the people thought it was bad. People discussed the changing pattern of work in the eighties, they talked about moving to more part-time work, increased leisure time, early retirement. Many people were forward-thinking. More recessions followed and in the early 90s, Peter Lilley and Michael Portillo publicly attacked their latest scapegoats: the so-called New Age Travellers who, God forbid, were enjoying themselves. Enjoying themselves? While not working? Surely this wasn't allowed. Surely they were taking the piss. But meanwhile, unemployment was creeping up and the government were happy for the borderline sick to be pushed off the books onto the new Incapacity Benefit. No Prime Minister wants high unemployment. It doesn't look good. Then along came New Labour. They were more right-wing than any Labour government in my living memory, in fact far more right-wing than Ted Heath's government. New Labour wanted to disassociate themselves from the bad years in the wilderness, the loony left, the Militant Tendency and the rest. They kow-towed to big business, the bankers, the market economy, market forces; they wooed *The Sun* or was it vice versa? They didn't undo the foundations of eighteen years of Toryism. The spotlight gradually crept up on those claiming Incapacity Benefit, who'd been hidden from the malicious glare of the Tory Red Tops. Articles began appearing about people getting Incapacity Benefit 'just for anxiety, stress and depression' as if somehow these were non-illnesses. Cue David Freud. He latched onto, or should I say imported, ideas from the States where Welfare to Work was big; one idea in particular was that the focus of people's fitness to work should be on what they can do, not what they can't. Sounded all very noble and reasonable, and supported by disabled people saying how much they wanted to work. Cue the Employment & Support Allowance for new claimants. Phew. That let existing claimants off the hook, didn't it? They were protected by law, weren't they? Besides, these people had paid into the National Insurance Scheme and so were entitled. Weren't they? Cue the Private Health Assessors whose name everyone knows - but let's call them Axima for these purposes (axing being what they're particularly good at). Axima were and still are employed to use their tick-box assessments to lop the disabled off their benefits. Average time to complete assessment said to be twenty minutes. Eye contact from assessors said to be nil or minimal. Seemingly innocent questions from said assessors, such as 'Do you watch *Coronation Street*?' used as proof that a person must be fit for work if he or she answered in the affirmative on the grounds that he or she could sit for half an hour.

"Stop, stop, hang on a minute, Mr Axima Man," says protester, waving hand in the air to get his attention.

This is duly noted by Mr Axima Man. Claimant can raise hand in air ergo must be capable of work.

"But but - Mr Axima Man - my mother is over eighty and she can wave her hand above her head and she watches Coronation Street and sometimes she digs in the garden."

Mr Axima man considers this. Makes a note. Claimant has given me an idea. We could round up all the over 70s and 80s, even 90s at a push. They could all do their bit. After all, we're all in this together.

"But but Mr Axima Man - what have washing and dressing and sticking your hand in the air or bending down to pick a coin off the floor got to with the cumulative, day-in-day-out wear and tear of work?"

Mr Axima man makes more notes. Pain. Fatigue. All subjective. All in the mind. We will call it functional disability and place ourselves above GPs who have had training for years, as opposed to gods like us who have only had a few weeks training.

"But but Mr Axima man," says protestor, stamping foot. Mr Axima man duly notes the flexibility of the claimant's leg and foot as evidence that claimant could work, maybe treading grapes, or, if push comes to squash, trampling a few claimants heads underfoot. "But Mr Axima Man. All this - it's like measuring the outside temperature with a ruler, ergo invalid."

Axima Man notes: claimant is able to communicate.

Nil Points.

"Mr Axima Man? If you give me zero points, or points under 15, I will appeal. So many cases are overturned at appeal-"

Axima Man makes note: if they go to appeal and win we will send them out another letter within weeks. Days if necessary. In the end they will buckle, if we hound them long enough.

"-which Mr Axima Man, rises even more when claimants have representation."

Axima Man is scribbling away now. Notes: Government is doing away with Legal Aid for cases like this. That'll stop them rolling their wheelchairs or banging their white sticks with glee. Maybe suggest government do away with appeals altogether.

"And while we're at it, Mr Axima Man, will you tell your ministers how we vehemently disapprove of the way they whip up enmity against addicts, alcoholics and the overweight. We can see right through it. It's the 'undeserving poor' again. It's a return to Victorian times."

Axima Man ignores this. He has had enough here.

Claimant: "Take P.I.P."

Axima Man (thinks) - We intend to.

Axima Man - "The community has been consulted. We want to target those who need the most help."

Claimant - "You mean the rest of us can fuck off."

Mr Axima Man (thinks) - In a word, yes.

Mr Axima Man - "We want to make the test more objective. We want it to be fairer."

Claimant - "Nobody believes that bollocks. The mark of a civilized society is measured by how it treats its weakest members. Edmund Burke, I believe."

Axima Man - "SHUT UP! SHUT UP! ARBEIT MACHT FREI".

But -

But this is a horror story.
You didn't come for a horror story. Did you?
Or a rant.

excerpt from The Other Side of Carrie Cornish

...On the Saturday, Carrie is shuffling around the landing in her dressing-gown and there is this tempest brewing in her gut. She already heard the clonk of the letterbox and now she sees a clump of post hanging through its mouth, brown envelopes foremost, like a tongue poking out at her, mocking her. And always on a Saturday.

She feels the soaring dread at the thought of turning over the brown envelopes and seeing The Department of Work & Pensions address on the underside of one of them. She wishes it were Sunday —a safe-from-bills-and-official-letters day. No letters are good letters any more, since the advent of emails. At best they are junk mail or pleas from charities. But she knows—even before pulling out the thick tongue of letters from their maw. Knows that one of them is bad news. That the time has come. The tide is against them—her and Sandy. Her especially, with her invisible illnesses.

The worst is confirmed as the black letters from the Department of Work & Pensions jump out from the back of the uppermost brown envelope in her clutch. It's like they are pursuing her. She is immobile with fear for a few seconds before tearing at the offending letter for daring to arrive. It all has an air of inevitability about it. It is her turn to be 'migrated'—as they call it—from Incapacity Benefit to Employment and Support Allowance. It is a formality. The private health care company will contact her in the next couple of weeks. It all looks very polite and formal and removed. It is devoid of emotion, it is impersonally personal. Sanitised and protected from the shit that results. There's nothing to warn the recipient, nothing to acknowledge how devastating it is with the veiled threat of having your income cut, so veiled, you wouldn't know it was there...

How the DWP Ruined Vivaldi For Me

The Four Seasons (spring)
Was a school assembly thing
While we filed in

Took our places
On the floor spaces
Crossed legs and shoelaces

Now, cursing on hold
We wait to be told
Our fate
While we wait
Listening to Vivaldi
(I'd rather be in Aldi)

Some other ideas instead:
Marilyn Manson
Friend Michael said

Or here's one
For the suggestion box
My sister mocks
Don't Keep Me Hanging
On The Telephone

And I said
If they're a bit slow
At picking up
How about Nick Lowe
Cracking Up
(All I feel is an ocean
Of emotion)

Keeping us on hold
While our cuppa's getting cold
Makes us very cross
So a bit of Diana Ross
I'm Still Waiting
Though you'll end up hating
Whichever group
They play on a loop

Do You Care

Do you care if I'm healthy?
Or do you just want me to get a job
Do you care if I'm happy?
Or do you just want me to get a job
Do you care if I'm fulfilled?
Or do you just want me to get a job
Do you care for my feelings about things?
Or do you just want me to get a job
Do you care if I'm in pain
Or do you just want me to get a job
Do you care if I'm scared?
Or do you just want me to get a job
Do you care if I hurt?
Or do you just want me to get a job
Do you care if I'm exhausted
Or do you just want me to get a job
Why don't you hear me when I tell you
I can't just get a job

MIKE JENKINS

is a former comprehensive school teacher living in Merthyr Tudful in Cymru. His most recent books are *Sofa Surfin* (Carreg Gwalch, 2017), *From Aberfan t Grenfell* (Culture Matters, 2018), *The 3 Molas* (Carreg Gwalch, 2020) *with Ifor ap Glyn and Eric Ngalle Charles: poems from Cameroon*, and *Anonymous Bosch* (Culture Matters, 2021). He has been co-editor of *Red Poets* magazine for 27 years, and won Wales Book of the Year for *Wanting to belong* (Seren), a series of interlinked stories about young people in the Valleys. He is an activist in Yes Cymru independence movement.

The Assessment

I crawled inta the Assessment
arfta my ESA,
I ad a walkin stick
my ands all gnarled
my ips killin me,
an the Depression tabs
playin ell with my ead
makin me a zombie.

They stared at me
like I wuz tellin lies,
like I woz a cheatin fraud;
it woz interrogation
tha's fit f spies.

If on'y 'ey could see my pain
an the darkness show up
in an X-ray of my brain
an ev'ry bone an vein
light up like neon
to expose my suff'rin.

Waitin f the appeal,
waitin on death row
f money t save me
or fuckall t finish me –
volts through my body.

Starin At-A Rain

Sittin in my wheelchair:
my dad, my carer
elped me there.

My mam's jest lyin
on-a sofa :
some days it its er.

Tampin outside my ome,
no way cun I risk
damp like venom,

like smoke fillin my lungs.
Waitin f'r-a taxi t come,
Council ave promised one.

My dad makes me larf,
ee'll fight my case,
tell em t 'Wise up, or else!'

On'y wanna go t college,
on'y wanna ave a fewture,
despite my anchorin body.

I do get benefits,
yet I'm yer sittin
starin at-a rain.

Inta The Black

I dropped off of yewer system,
don' afto sign on,
I int no statistic
an yew carn stop my benefit
coz my missis got a job
an I'm sick o disappointment.

There's over a million
jest like me,
fallen off of the edge
of compewter cliffs
an inta the black,
landed on a ledge.

I like it down yer
idin in-a dark,
there's plenty o sharks
like ev'rywhere else,
but least I int chasin
along pointless paths.

Yew carn see me now
or send snoopers down,
rocks below are perilous
as men o war ;
an I'm like a goat
clamberin an leapin over laws.

HENRIK JOHANSSON

lives in Malmö, Sweden, and is 48 years old. He used to work in restaurants and a bread factory, and now he works with culture. Mostly writing.

When the crisis comes

When the next crisis comes, and it will, you will lose your job. There is a connection, but you will not see it. The management will say it's a result of reduced orders and lack of work, with what you perceive as honest intimacy and regret. You shall consider not telling anything to your family, but every morning to get up, drink coffee and leave home. You imagine that you will be looking for a new job that you can proudly present to them one fine day. The plan is too absurd and you never try it.

It shall not be the crisis' fault, nor your managers' fault, nor their managers' or shareholders' fault, nor the society's, nor the government's. It shall be your own fault – because you could have done better, because you could have reeducated, worked your way up, been more responsive towards your clients and your managers. Your children will feel shame when they realize that you are poor. They will stop begging for things in the store, like you always wished they would, they will stop wanting the same things that their friends have, your older son will say to your younger daughter that she is spoiled.

If anyone asks, you shall say that you're between jobs.

You will return, as a trainee, to your old workplace to perform your old tasks. Your compensation from the Employment Office shall be 58% of your former salary. You will have a stomach ache when you go to work. It's hard to grasp why, since it's better than being home.

You shall not start drinking too much, you shall not start taking drugs, you shall not start gambling too much.

You will consider suicide, but you lack courage to do it and you will feel contempt for your own weakness and inability to deal with your own situation.

Once your period as a trainee is over, you will once again be unemployed and they will get a new trainee, but they promise to call if something turns up. They will not call.

You shall not rob stores or protest. You shall not write letters to the editor, nor blame someone else. You shall not throw stones at the police.

At the Job Center there is equality. You shall not be treated worse than an unemployed politician or banker. You must fill out the same forms as anyone. Democracy does not acknowledge any privileged or slighted, no sweethearts, and no stepchildren.

You will be offered to join a computer course. Anyone who rejects the offer will lose his or her compensation. You shall accept the offer. A woman will say that she is a programmer and could have been a teacher for the course. The administrator shall ensure that the woman loses her replacement if she declines the offer. The same rules apply to everyone.
For a brief moment in the computer course, you, him and she suddenly becomes we and us. The teachers and the Employment Office will be them. It will feel good. They will then talk to you, he and she and tell you that it's every man or woman for himself. You must be reminded of your loneliness and that you have yourselves to blame and that it is only you who can do something about your situation.

You shall realize that they are right: it's only you who can do something about your situation.

CAMILLUS JOHN
was bored and braised in Ballyfermot, a working class suburb of Dublin, and still lives there. He has had work published in *The Stinging Fly*, *RTÉ Ten*, *The Lonely Crowd* and other such organs. He would also like to mention that Pats won the FAI cup in 2014 after 62 miserable years of not winning it.

They Didn't Like The Look Of Me

I went into the shop
and applied for the job they were
advertising in the window outside.
They browsed my CV and said no.
They didn't like the look of me.

'But I've studied hard and long and
have qualifications, all I need is a chance.
You can kick me out if I don't
do well. I'll work for free.
A trial period. Please?'
But they didn't like the look of me.

The following month the advert for the job
was still up outside in the shop window.
Waiting for someone
with a nicer personality
or a better accent
or a more permanent home
or something else.
I don't know what
they were looking for.

And the owners of the shop still working
fourteen hours a day themselves
to spite me it seems.

'We can't find anyone to take the job!
No one will take it! They're all lazy bastards.'
They say to the newspapers. Working themselves
to the edge of fatigue and beyond
because,
they don't like the look of me.

Wiping My Milk Moustache Clean With My Sleeve

I said to them, remember at primary school
it was always buns on a Wednesday and a Friday.
Cheese on a Tuesday, ham on a Monday
and corned beef on a Thursday, I think.
Is that right? Remember?

They said no. They didn't remember.
Their school never gave them free
sarnies and milk because they weren't
in a deprived area, apparently.
They only gave free sarnies and milk
to kids in schools that were in deprived areas.

I didn't know that. I had thought that free sarnies
and milk were given to every school in the country.
Not that I gave it much thought until now.
But, whatever, nothing wrong
with free sarnies and milk
given to everyone in the class just in case
some kids weren't getting enough at home.

But when I looked in their faces they said that there
was something wrong with that. Very wrong indeed.
Their mammies and daddies prepared all their meals
for them through primary school.
They didn't get free sarnies and milk.
Footstamp. Footstamp. Footstamp.
Crossed arms all in a row.

Whatever they were saying, I was taken off guard,
and it frightened me.
Well, until I thought about
jam on a Monday.
Cheese on a Tuesday.
A bun on a Wednesday.
Corned beef on a Thursday.
And lovely buns, buns
sweet current buns again on the Friday.

And I longed for one of
those tiny bottles they put the milk in,
to wash my present

lunch sarnie down with
(fully paid for in the work canteen
I'll have you know)
and then wiping my
milk moustache clean
with my sleeve
afterwards.
Bliss.

We Are Bumfluff

My bumfluff moustache,
my wispy moustache, is now
called a pencil moustache
by the middle classes.
I know,
because I've just read it
in a national newspaper.
They mock and laugh at it.

I don't have one now
but back when I did, I wore it with
pride and urban cool,
I thought.
But they laughed at it then too
apparently.

I wore one when I was 14, 15, 16
up to 17 years of age,
I think. Was it? Along with my
white mod sports socks.

I was just ordinary
not well travelled out of my
estate - or scheme I called
it like my granda did lovingly -
they were probably laughing
at that as well. Calling it
a scheme. A housing scheme.
Which is what it was and still is,
I think.

But call it a project, the American
word for a scheme, and they'll
laugh at that too.

I didn't know we were evil or scroungers
or deviant just by wearing a bumfluff.
I was doing like the rest did.
But it hurt to find out that
people laughed from leafy
suburbs - still do - as they
were taught their traditional
culture of hate
from an early age;
People who wear bumfluffs
are evil and scroungers and deviant.
People who are different to us are offside.
No acceptance of anything outside
their own terms of reference.

In 2018,
they're now attacking and laughing
at the poor and the homeless and
the disabled.
Because they are evil and
scroungers and deviant says their
culture of hate. And it's self pity,
they say,
if we try to describe the
bumfluff facts of life
in any articulate way.
It's self pity and we
must stop. They don't want
to hear it. Fuck off! They say.
Fuck off!

So all I can say is,
I am bumfluff
We are bumfluff
They are not.

TOM KELLY

is a north-east of England writer born in Jarrow on May 22nd, 1947. For twenty-odd years he had a variety of jobs along the Tyne until taking a late degree which led him teaching drama in an FE College for almost twenty-five years. He has had eleven books of poetry, short stories and a play published in as many years. His new collection *This Small Patch* has recently been published by Red Squirrel Press.

Social Mobility & Child Poverty Commission (2015)

'Britain is at risk of becoming more divided, not less. Tackling poverty and improving social mobility require action at every level. There is no single silver bullet. Parents, communities, schools, colleges, councils, employers and universities all will need to take a lead if Britain is to avoid being a permanently divided nation.'

At the 'Reduced to Clear'

they form an orderly queue.
The youngest has money tight as a ball in his fist.
He has a note to remind him what to buy, *'breed, cheese'*.

His dad works nights for a security firm. He is asleep
on the settee in the living room. Mother works
in Cheapland from six to ten.

He is seven next birthday. His sister plays round the shelves,
handles everything she can't buy. Her dress
see-through under the stores flickering fluorescent lights.

Monument

Jarrow's shipyard, Palmers, was closed by the cartel, National Shipbuilding Securities in 1933 which led to mass unemployment and the Jarrow Crusade of 1936. ... My uncle Johnny, my dad's brother, was on the 'March' as they call it in Jarrow. The Crusade is in my DNA.

Jarrow's MP, Ellen Wilkinson speaking in the House of Commons, 1936

Today is mixed with yesterday,
Pathe News becomes flesh and blood,
men with Charlie Chaplin trousers
return to where they once stood.

*'In the Jarrow area there is 72 per cent unemployment,
in Jarrow Town the percentage nearly 80.
Jarrow must be made a special case. Jarrow is the victim
of ruthless rationalisation which is being backed by the
Government.'*

Uncle Johnny gave me his badge,
I see him on the Edgware Road,
marching in rain-soaked Mackintosh
and now tears stick in me throat.

They presented their petition,
Jarrow's Mayor dropped his heavy chain,
Wasn't defiance, he told me,
It was a slip I'd do again.

*'Is the President of the Board of Trade aware that the
government's complacency is regarded throughout the country as
an affront to the national conscience?'*

Some shed bitter tears, railed,
*Ya knaa we've been sold down th' Thames.
Has ti be more, can't be just this.
Is this how our battle ends?*

On Guy Fawkes they came home by train,
knowing their place, third class single,
handed them cheap suits and cheers
still their pockets didn't jingle.

'In St Paul's Cathedral there is a memorial to Sir Christopher Wren, which reads: "If you seek a monument look around."'

'If the Attorney General wants to see a monument to the capitalist system that he is so proud of, I will take him to Jarrow and show it to him.'

Ken Loach - *Please Be Dan Dare!*

Ken, you might not like his conservative (with a small c) outlook,
his body language may change
watching your films but (for one production only)
can you wear his hat and take control?
Save a million unemployed kids,
steer the craft, be Dan Dare and take Digby from Wigan
to something better than this?

So, Ken, before you squint through the camera lens,
please take up Dan's mantle, if only for me,
aged seven-and-three-quarters in Jarrow,
think Billy Casper without the kestrel,
afraid of the dark and Tories me and me da hated.
Please save us
from these posh boys that make me so angry I have to lose myself
in Frank Hampson's drawings of Dan leading his crew
against the Mekon: we need you to be Dan Dare,
"Quiet, please. Roll camera. Action."

DAVID KESSEL

was born on the 2nd of April 1947 in Harlesden, in the Borough of Brent, North-West London. He suffered a breakdown at 17 prior to medical school. With diplomas from the RCSP, he went on to practice as a GP in East London until his second breakdown put a halt to his medical career. In spite of his illness, David continued writing poetry and published *The Ivy* in 1989 (Aldgate Press; reprinted 1994). His poems have appeared in the Phoenix Co-Operative, *Poetry Express* and the anthologies *Where There's Smoke* (Hackney Writers), *Outsider Poems*, *Bricklight – Poems from the Labour Movement in East London* (Pluto Press, 1980) and *Under the Asylum Tree* (Survivors' Press, 1995). They have also been put to music by the EMFEB Symphony Orchestra in Owen Bourne's score Hackney Chambers. The publication of *O The Windows of the Bookshop Must Be Broken – Collected Poems 1970-2006*, designed and edited by Alan Morrison (Survivors' Press, 2006), proved a best-seller. A selection from this volume was recently published in a bilingual German-English volume, *Außenseitergedichte* (Verlag Edition AV, 2007).

Mike Mosley

There is a conspiracy against the social democracy of the British common people

Grey, calloused, forgotten at fifty,
he has given his all; his wiry heart,
his skilled locked fingers, his
chipped backbone, his broken welding language,
for this choking fag,
this dark blinding pint,
this scouring Irish lament.

Scorned, down for a bundle in bird,
forsaken by wives and the DHSS,
shy of nothing 'cept himself,
to this bare room, phlegm and loneliness
between stubborn slums and useless sirens.

Driven by fury to this back ward,
wasted, ulcered, unforgiving.

I start from here to make anew
the happiness of children playing
beneath heeding enduring gulls
in a wooded tempered land.

Schizo Care

Schizophrenia is a diabetes of the mind which might be caused
by a traumatic disbelief and lack of intimacy in childhood and
adolescence.

We are misunderstood and stigmatised and become subject to a
mental health system which often invalidates us and takes away
some of our civil liberties.

People like us are often used as scapegoats by society and
guinea pigs by the drug industry and other forms of social
control.

Our's is a dirty job and somebody has to do it. We may become
the "new Jews", a butt of rising fascism. We need mutual
support groups for discussion, therapy and protection.

R.D. Laing and David Cooper, whilst truly great
philosophically, are downright dangerous, in most cases,
therapeutically. Appropriate minimal medication, and even,
on occasions, ECT are an essential ingredient of modern
treatment, as much as existential, non-Freudian therapy.
Forward to the insulin of the mind.

New Cross
For John Van

We build our own slums. The wind
through the slums blows on the highest
hills. We are all slowly dying
of cold and loneliness, no fags,
no fruit juice, and neighbours with veg stew
and cups of tea. We live with uncertainty,
our giros and our dreams. Yet our aggression
is our frustrated love. In a billion painful ways
we make the little things of love;
a dustman's sweat, a cleaner's arthritis,
a streetlight's mined electricity,
a carpet-layer's emphysema,
a desperate clerk's angina,
a mate's slow-moaned caresses.

ÁINE KING

is a playwright, dramaturg and visual artist. From 2007 - 2013 she was
Associate Director for Otherplace Productions in Brighton. Her most recent
work has been staged at The Rialto, Brighton, The Arcola Theatre and
Southwark Playhouse, London. Her short screenplay, *Running Out,* was filmed
by National Theatre Scotland/BBC Scotland 2020 for *Scenes for Survival.*
She is currently writing a comissioned podcast drama about invisible
diabilities for Birds Of Paradise Theatre co. Website: www.aineking.net

FAKING IT
A micro-play

A: You did *what?* After everything I told you? Oh, you idiot!
B: It was nothing. I was just being… kind.
A: You were just being *fooled!* You can't be *kind* to these
people. You can't trust them. They're out to fool you. What
happened? Exactly.
B: Well, she arrived a few minutes late —
A: Typical!
B: Pale, shaky. She didn't look well.
A: Playing on your sympathy. Oldest trick in the book.
B: Fifteen weeks pregnant, she said, and sick *all* the time.
A: Did she fill in the forms?
B: I think we skipped a few questions. She wasn't really
focussed. Looked very wobbly… asked for a glass of water —
A: O god, you didn't!
B: A glass of water. I couldn't say no.
A: Water! The barefaced cheek of it! You didn't — Tell me *you*
didn't get it for her!
B: I—
A: You actually got up and got her a glass of water? From the
kitchen?
B: Of course from the kitchen! Where else?
A: You poor bloody fool!
B: What *else* could I do?
A: Tell her get it herself! Tell her go to hell!
B: She was ill.
A: She was *faking* it! These people are all liars and cheats.
You'll see. In three days, or four, a brown envelope will hit
the mat. "Benefits withdrawn. Suspended pending investigation.
Fit enough to walk unaided to kitchen and carry water for
visiting Clinical Assessor… Previous information false…
possible prosecution…"

B: I— was just trying to be kind.
A: You *can't* be kind to these people. You can't trust them.
Ever. They're not like us. Blood-sucking parasites.

MARK KIRKBRIDE

was born in Ormskirk, Lancashire, in 1968. He is the author of *The Plot Against Heaven, Game Changers of the Apocalypse* and *Satan's Fan Club*, published by Omnium Gatherum. His short stories can be found in *Under the Bed, Sci Phi Journal, Disclaimer Magazine, Flash Fiction Magazine* and *So It Goes: The Literary Journal of the Kurt Vonnegut Memorial Library*. His poetry has appeared in *The Climate Matters Anthology 2020, Handbook for 2021: The Bread and Roses Anthology 2020*, the *Big Issue*, the *Morning Star*, the *Daily Mirror*, Horror Writers Association chapbooks, *Emergency Verse – Poetry in Defence of the Welfare State, The Robin Hood Book*, and online at *Sein und Werden, Well Versed, Culture Matters, International Times, Militant Thistles*, and Cyclamens and Swords Publishing.

Situation Vacant

The posters all say, 'Your country doesn't need you.'
We've never had it so bad.
So I spend my days cutting rectangles out of newspapers
        and sending off immaculate curricula vitae
to employers who return them three months later,
        unread.
Occasionally I get to sit on the wrong side of the desk
        for five minutes
while the employer asks awkward questions
        and millions wait outside.
Mostly I'm just sending off CVs.
I'm writing to Robin Hood, my local MP,
        to see what he can do for me.
What I need is an occupation that requires
        no qualifications, no skills and no experience
with a whacking great salary.
Then I open the paper
and see a vacancy for Prime Minister.

DICK LANGFORD and TIM de FERRARS

have worked together on a number of creative projects in the last 15 years.
This particular one was written in support of an action group fighting
to save their homes. A London council had secretly planned to sell off their
council estate to property speculators, to be turned into luxury apartments.
It wasn't just about standing up for what's right now, but the sense that
there's a thread of 'right' that hasn't changed through history.

Queen Caroline's Lament

Oh the Tories will say, they'll take nothing away
They won't make us homeless, but they won't let us stay
But losing our homes is a high price to pay
And they won't come back when they're gone.
They won't come back when they're gone.

And the moneymen crying, just look at the waste
They're illiterates living on prime real estate
We'll replace them, displace them with money and taste,
And they won't come back when they're gone.
They won't come back when they're gone.

I was feeding the swans on the Thames,
The sun going down by the bridge.
And I knew this is worth more than any man's greed
And how can they live with their conscience clear?
I felt someone standing by me,
The shadows were long, but she called out my name.
A voice talking down through the years,
Saying, Ccarry on force them to tears of shame.

Queen Caroline lived through a difficult time,
A rake for a husband, a king lost his mind,
But it's morals not marbles the council can't find
And they won't come back when they've gone

Some say it's a right to live where we're born,
Not a privilege or something we have to pay for,
Oh some of us struggle but don't call us poor
And we won't come back when we're gone.

We built up our homes and it was our intent
That we built a community, made up of friends
Now we stand to lose all for the council's own ends

And they won't come back when they'rve gone.
And so it begins and you know what they'll do
To move out the riff-raff and bid them adieu
If they can do this to us they can do it to you
And you won't come back when you're gone.

JIM LAWRENCE

is a freelance writer and translator who lives in Southampton. He has had reviews, poetry and short fiction published in journals and webzines including *Due South* (as in-house music critic), *The Southern Daily Echo, I Am Not a Silent Poet, The Curly Mind, The Seethingography, Spilling Cocoa on Martin Amis, STEPZ.* He has also had three chapters appear in *Red Phonebox*, a multi-author urban fantasy story cycle published by Ghotwood Books.

Assessment

PIP
Gives me the pip
It ain't hip
It's a bad trip
It's a whip
To beat the crip
It's losing your grip
An unlucky dip
A busted lip
A broken zip
A sinking ship
A Chinese water torture drip
A drive with Prince Phillip
A very nasty nip
In the air, a slip
On the stairs, a quip
By Boris, a bad coin flip
A trap to trip
The poor up, gyp
The left-behinds, an ice chip
In the heart, a tool to equip
The DWP to strip
Us of our dignity, a bunyip
Lurking in the swamp of PIP

PAUL LESTER

was born in Birmingham in 1949. He has published some forty booklets of
poetry, including *A Funny Brand of Freedom* (Arts Lab Press, 1975), and also
the volumes *By the Scruff of the Neck* (1995) and *Going For Broke* (2004). His
work has appeared in the first two of Caparison's campaigning anthologies,
and has been broadcast on BBC Radio One and the BBC World Service. He
has performed his poetry with variety of musical accompaniment, and has
published short fiction and a series of essays on working-class writers for
the *London Magazine*, when under the editorship of Alan Ross. He has done
a number of jobs, among them barman, factory and office skivvy, machine tool
maker and teacher, and has served his sentence signing on at employment offices
as well as having once upon a time worked in one.

Searching for the Work-Search Form

When applied? Where applied to?
What happened? What will you do
Next? Columns merge in that work-
Search form he must fill in to prove
He's actively seeking employment.

Weary and depressed at all this,
Tempted to improve his prospects
With a round-up of the usual suspects
From a long list of past rejects,
Hoping the interviewer won't notice:

Is this what he's now reduced to?
No. He will apply and get no reply
But at least have some material to supply
For that infernal work-search form
So as to satisfy his interrogator.

Now stood before the Jobcentreplus,
Automatic door, chewing unwelcome,
He decides he must check once more
All's well with his work-search form.

He seeks for it in all of the usual places
With growing alarm. Where's that record,
Proof he's actively seeking employment?

Finding it hard to believe that he could
Have forgotten or lost that work-search form
He heads into the mouth of the beast,
Nevertheless, and as he knows he must,

Not knowing when applied or where applied
Or whatever will happen to him next.

Enter the Office of Deep Despair

Enter the Office of Deep Despair
To be found on Bad Dreams Street
Where you're just another digit
In some ambitious computer's career

Where you're asked for your card
And you try hard not to hear
An investment bank of screens' scream -
These have no true interest in you -

Where you ask: what am I doing here?
Where you stare into vacancy and see
You are qualified to belong nowhere.

There's no real vacancy save the grave.
If only you could just get up and leave.
But no: the Office of Deep Despair
Is where you must, to get paid, repair.

And time ticks in your gut
And the strange interrogator
Has a badge on his tit saying Tim.

He is there to assess and discuss,
Threaten and cajole, tell you what you must
Do to prove entitlement to benefit -

Which in your case you have not yet got.
Which in your case is an empty space;
No vacancy is a place and is no place

Where, you must beware, you can open a door
And fall down a hole in the floor:
Which you may already be aware
Is your lack of a future.

They may tell you how you need
To get up to speed in order to succeed
With a course for which you see no cause.
They may tell you your doctor's note
Has, alas, been lost in the post.
They may tell yours is a wasted vote.

They may tell you it's the wrong place
For the wrong time, therefore a crime.

They may tell you that you are nothing
And can't be something any time soon,
That you're only a citizen of the Moon -

That's why you find it hard to breathe the air
Inside of this Office of Deep Despair.

Here you can unlock a box
And wonder what's jumped out
To tear a chunk from your throat -

Where a PC opens like a mouth
Willing to swallow you whole,
Where you do not quite die,
Where you can be sanctioned
If you do not comply,

Where questions echo around in your head
Like a persistent insult:
What are you doing, when, and with what result?
What proof do you have that you are
Doing enough to be actively
Seeking...seeking...seeking...?

Back out on Bad Dreams Street,
Hopeless, lacking compass,
Searching for some place of retreat,
Staring wonderingly down at your feet,
Uncertain which direction to take -
What decision you might make -

But whichever you choose you betcha
It's just another mistake.

Who Drowned Himself in Ward End Pool?

Who drowned himself in Ward End Pool?
Mr Mistry - at last Signed Off.

On his right big toe they've hung a tag.
A mortuary drawer he has to himself.

Doomed to rest in the Dormant File,
For now his claim's in the Failed to Sign

Who drowned himself in Ward End Pool.

NINA LEWIS

is from Worcestershire, UK. Her poetry is published internationally in anthologies and magazines. She has two pamphlets *Fragile Houses* (2016) and *Patience* (2019), published by V. Press. She was Worcestershire Poet Laureate 2017-18, and an International Guest Poet at the Perth Poetry Festival. She has produced two poetry shows, a transatlantic poetry project involving poets in Worcester UK and Worcester MA, USA, and was Poet-in-Residence for Cheltenham Poetry Festival during 2020.

Wishing Well

The belief that numbers
make a difference,

close your eyes hard,
change the future.

Unhook the superstitious
amulet, it chokes magic.

The will of the universe
decrees if you wish one way

and the population pulls
the other, the alchemy won't work.

It tapers, like treacle
on a spoon, it slips

and you are jolted, jilted
by a shift beyond your power.

But this year is different.
Everything is changed

the whole world shares focus.
You may grant our wishes true

when there are seven billion
pairs of eyes on you.

Territory

It developed just below her skin, like a tiger's coat pattern;
white blood cells apex predators sent to attack.

Beneath the dense pelage of her pretence,
a small hollow formed.

Her movements after the operation were confined.
Caged to her home-range, solitary.

Pain covered half the length of her body,
until the day she re-wilded herself.

Painted on a smile, her own oceli,
to alter the truth of her skin flora.

Her stripes unique.
Strong in light and shade.

Not Listed on Medication Side Effects Information

I never asked you to move in,
you just came - the uninvited guest
and once your bed was made you refused to leave.

I have been counselled on how to deal with you,
I tried ignoring you, deafened my ears
to your moaning until it became a dull underwater tone.

I tried living with you, befriended you, helped you breathe.
My tired body grew energy and still you hung around,
said I would need you soon enough.

In the end we learnt to live side by side.
Sometimes we converse on deeper matters,
you are kinder to me than pain ever was.

S.J. LITHERLAND

Her recent collections include *Composition in White* (Smokestack Books), *The Absolute Bonus of Rain* and *The Work of the Wind* (both Flambard Press). She's working on her 8th. Born (1936) and bred in Warwickshire she has lived in Durham since 1965. Two Northern Writers' Awards and two Commendations in the National Poetry Competition. Founder member Vane Women writing collective and press. She is Editor of the press. Published in various anthologies, including *The Forward Book of Poetry 2001, North by North-East, Not Just A Game, Modern Poets of Northern England* (Russian). Her work has been translated into French, Spanish, Catalan, Russian.

The Debt Problem

I must tell my story. Listen.
There will be a number of things.
Without a pause, or a metaphor.

I will relate my day. Music
will play in the background.
I hear your dutiful listening.

It doesn't matter. Inside
there is a kind of cosiness
without heat. Outside, winter.

Money is impossible. My life
is frail, my economy *Polish*
and I need substantial aid

to buy freedom. Yes this
is my lack-lustre capitalism,
two rooms I do not own.

I fantasise that I can buy
good food. Clothes are my
Christmas presents.

So many people want to sell
things to me. My debts are making
love, new younger debts will arise.

Eternal Winter

She's impersonating Justice, her make-up
salon ready, her eyes bright and censorious,
the quiet inquisitor with highly polished
nails, a system finder, a trailer through the files

of the inadequate and the failed. They're racked
by the bleeding of their lives in solitary,
the view out of their windows busted
like those seams below without air, left to writhe,

scattered in face powder to dampen the sparks,
like the hardened arteries of our land,
she's there to hand out questions and interrogate,
with the polite blandness of the torturer

who gets on with his job. Her eyes crease
as though with sympathy: **We'll get back to you.**
They know they've handed her the tools.
What can they say about natural justice

and the wrong dealt out to them in coupons?
The word *Benefit* hangs like a threat to despoil
the air. There is no injurious word like *Malefit*.
Torquemadas have laid aside the knife,

you can cut as easily with the stroke of a pen.

Swan In The Weeds

I thought betrayal an intense thing. It's slight.
I walk to the Co-op. Buy three bottles of white.
    The sober thing so dearly bought, the wine so cheaply.

For a day, I honoured my sobriety and lit
two candles, close together as I could fit,
    touching on sand. Thanksgiving for a day.

On the second day I announced my sobriety.
I stood undefiled, unprotected but with
    a responsible person (I am not responsible).

On the third day, just before closing, I entered
the Co-op. No mistake about what I wanted this time.
    I was completely sober, my dear. Nothing remains,

destruction is quick, cheap exit. You can never say
I didn't choose the wine over you. Pure preference.
    Yes, I deceived you about the light. As you leave,

leave me in the dark. You lost the final encounter.
Look at the state of the world. I'm back in bed, drunk.

    I slipped the cork, I drank the white knowledge.

FRAN LOCK

is a some-time itinerant dog whisperer, the author of numerous chapbooks
and seven poetry collections, most recently *Contains Mild Peril* (Out-
Spoken Press, 2019), and *Raptures and Captures* (Culture Matters, 2019),
the last in a trilogy of works in collaboration with collage artist,
Steev Burgess. Her eighth collection *Hyena!* is due from Poetry Bus Press
later this year. Fran has recently gained her Ph.D. at Birkbeck College,
University of London. She is an Associate Editor at Culture Matters, and
she edits the Soul Food column for *Communist Review*.

the quality of mercy

must be shantung, charmeuse, georgette, chiffon.
or ciselé velvet voided into beauty. such softness
we have never seen. morning's acetate carress is
on us now, and what to wear? broad black arrow,
felon's brand, the cartoon mark of shame. coarse
wool, chemically treated. a jester's cap. a leper's
bell. some late-victorian mufti. the very threads
of deference. oh no, you will arrive in a snug
proffesion of flowers, a quarter inch of pristine
cuff, coquetting from your jacket sleeve. you'll
show them: sublimbed in all the curbed chic
of being poor, but full of a flaunting savvy. you,
who trail insomniac's slang through an illbient
dark, picking at whispered grammars of static.
who cannot sleep to scrub a posion voice from
fingers numb with bleach. you are beset but
still resplendent. still. the quality of mercy is
in shetland lace or poplin paisley, second-hand;
is brocade, bolts of suiting cloth, unsullied
wings of crepe de chine. inside the machine,
how winter rolls the length of your one good
coat. the woman looks you up and down,
tapping her smoker's teeth with a yellow ball-
point pen. her smile is not a smile: a mistake
etched in acid. she will say that you are *fit*.
her eyes will be awkward and sly. her tongue
a planchette, set to spell an endless haunting.
and I could kill her ugly vamire disregard. i
want to tear her throat. but you. you did not
slump. you do not slouch. you walked away.
a purple penhaligon's pocket square, the only
thing to say you dropped your eyes, to see you cry.

internal medicine

my dog will come back as an arsonist. look at him,
he's pissing on the places he will later want to burn.
i might not come back at all. if i do, don't name me
after a saint, mother. invite the wind into your mouth,
name me after a hurricane. i wish i'd thrown my
former lovers from the bridge, instead of just their
trinkets. pain inside, drink a glass of sympathetic
vinegar. pain inside, i am wolf with it. in the night
a caesarian of dancing piglet stones somehow. how
pain becomes the knots my words refuse. a pain
that won't be fumbled to dissolving in the canny clinic
of the bed, the bath, the pumpkin-cutter's kitchen
drecked with pulp. mother, they stole my photo for
a government campaign. they dressed me in another
name, filched from a politically correct math
problem. mother, i am like lenigrad. no, stalingrad.
no, petrograd. no, mother i am fatimagrad. all my
citizens beavering for minimum in cyber. i walk up
the stairs, it does that auto-redial thing, the pain.
i open my face like a guidebook, a fold-out map to
torment's ease. i swallow all the buttons from a long
white coat. now the doctor will be naked and the tap
water tastes of rust. let's go round the block again
dog, round streets we only ever learnt by scent. let's
walk. walking helps, although the windows shit
their scenery: women with functioning loins
in boden dresses, picking the burs out of spaniel
ears, tucking the mixed recycling in for the night.
glass jars in this one, a row of obedient embryos,
and a couple of elderly vampires, discussing
the bouquet of blood. let's burn it down, dog. cross
the road. i'm smiling like a stallion, joyfully skinned.
my scathed companion, let's go slow. i swear dog,
at the mess inside of me the knives turn timid. you
are the same. imagine putting a cigarette out in
a handshake. imagine all the coins in a money box
melting together. imagine crunching
a glass eye like an ice-cube. it's all
those things and less. i can't explain. what if
this curdling forensic dark were my true voice?
mother, open me up. pull out the sugar shrimps,
the molotovs, the miles of strawberry bootlace.

MARILYN LONGSTAFF

was born on May 29th 1950 in Liverpool. She lives in Darlington and is a member of the writing, performing and publishing collective Vane Women. Her work has appeared in a number of magazines, anthologies and on the web. The poems for her most recent pamphlet, *The Museum of Spare Parts* (Mudfog, 2018), came from her involvement in Stemistry, a University of Newcastle Public Engagement project, devised and run by Lisa Matthews to consider creative responses to modern genomics. Her other books are: *Puritan Games* (Vane Women Press, 2001), Sitting Among The Hoppers (Arrowhead Press, 2004), *Raiment* (Smokestack Books, 2010) and *Articles of War* (Smokestack, 2015). She took early retirement from teaching due to increasing deafness.

Lost for Words

I'm sitting in an inadequately organised oblong seminar,
so every time our tutor turns his head from left to right,
I can catch only the half of what he's saying.

It's like *Singing in the Rain*,
when the silent movie star can't get used to the microphone.
Then my battery dies

and the little I could hear dies with it.
Can I find the replacement?
Not until all the contents of my handbag

have been sifted at least twice.
Struggling to insert-new-battery-in-hearing-aid-under-table,
I'm missing everything

I want to say, *For Christ's sake SPEAK UP*
But I'm sick of making that request
and I don't do blasphemy.

At last, I insert the functioning beige eartrumpet
just in time for 15 minutes silent scribbling.
Now, I can hear

        rustling of felt tips on paper,
        gurgles of swigging water,
        deafening throat clearing.

Intensive care

Around her bed:
the cochlea-damaged brother,

the otosclerosis sister-in-law.
And, inandout of her post-operative coma,

the deafened sister, lines going in and out
from every orifice and more.

Tragedy and comedy lie side by side
as she tries to speak and we try to hear –

could you repeat that, speak up a bit?
Of course she can't, so we employ

the well-learned strategies of the deaf:
Me – the nonstop rambletriviachat;

he says nowt.
Six hearing aids between us

and none of them works well enough
to cope with the beeps and hums

and whooshes from banks of equipment,
the hushed tones of gravity, patient confidentiality.

She grips our hands as we try to offer support/comfort,
wishes that all will be well – and to stop her

pulling out the tubes.
She's irritated, confused.

On our way in and out we follow required ritual,
anoint our hands with some kind of antiseptic fluid.

At home, we'll wash until we bleed.

When talking to the deaf (ened)

Don't SHOUT
Don't say it doesn't matter
Don't put your hand in front of your mouth
Don't keep forgetting not to mutter
Don't stand with your back to the light
Don't d
     r
      o
       p
       your voice at the end of a . . . .

    Repeat. Repeat. Find another way of saying it.
    And when they mis-hear, laugh with, not at, them
    (if it's funny)

Face the person, speak one-at-a-time
Articulate with natural lip movements

Twice the volume, half the speed
Use sentences not single words

Try not to talk from another room or call up the stairs
Ah yes and men, shave off your moustaches and beards.

    Don't get irritated, exasperated, disgusted.
    And, most important, never give up on us.

HOLLY MAGILL

Her poetry has appeared in numerous magazines, including *The Interpreter's House, Bare Fiction,* and *Under The Radar,* and anthologies – *Stairs and Whispers: D/deaf and Disabled Poets Write Back* (Nine Arches Press) and *#MeToo: A Women's Poetry Anthology* (Fair Acre Press). She won first prize in the 2019 Cannon Poets 'Sonnet or Not' competition. She co-edits *Atrium* – www.atriumpoetry.com. Her debut pamphlet, *The Becoming of Lady Flambé,* is available from Indigo Dreams Publishing.

The only place I eat biscuits

Rolling a smoke on the edge of the desk, tongued
fingertips guiding escapee specks, no waste,
he stares out my scripted questions:
I'm too poor to ever be fat, love.

My fingers sausage-stumble the keyboard,
back teeth twingeing with compacted Digestives.
A stomach growl – and it's mine, not his –
erupts like a big fruity fart in the silent room.

He scratches the crotch of his trousers, waits,
tucks the cig behind his ear.

Time sloths. My lips itch to be swiped
for rogue chocolate smears.

The system pings him 'Eligible' – permitted
one more voucher this six month period,
the printout – a limp thing – our transaction.

He leaves. The edge of the desk bites
hard into my soft belly.

The Politest Riot

I will not play into hands that would beckon
close only to shuck me off before they
plunge into vats of antibacterial.

I will not play - screaming, swearing, kicking, spitting -
though God, I know the urge.

Far too easy for you to dismiss as emotional, erratic,
unstable hysteric.

I will not play. Because this is no game.

I am no cleverer - and no more thick - than those bawling the odds.
You would prefer their anarchy, fists through windows,
disorderly arrests to make an example.

Shame them as yobs in the press,
don't know any better, any excuse for a ruck.
Waste of taxpayers' money to educate the dross.

That would serve your policies well, I see that:
the NHS literally gave me vision.
I'm trying, I'm a good girl. I try…

courtesy and reason - a surprise to you
that shouldn't be.

Yes, I have benefitted - from free uni education,
from Social Housing, from scrounging and school milk.
Been told I don't talk like a DWP claimant.

In public libraries I learned
the lightning and violence of language.

Yes, officer, I will come quietly, so very quietly.

But not silent. I use the words you don't
want the rough 'uns to comprehend.

O, still small voice not taped to a flying brick.

Every day more hands join in the dark.

'Everyone deserves quality…'*

The incumbent Conservative will cut
the shiny red ribbon, celebrate
130 jobs created - including artisan bakers,
sushi chefs, specialist prosecco pourers.
(The paper doesn't mention the cleaners.)
There's free Wi-Fi and 285 parking spaces;
a wine bar featuring a microbrewery draft pump
- only the second of their UK stores to have that.
Come on in, feel posh - look, you can
vote for their next charity of the month
with a plastic token, not have to give
a penny or a fuck.

* from a Waitrose advertising slogan

STEVE MANN

Living in the rural fringe of Shrewsbury fuels Steve's love of the countryside and, with his various long-term interests including spirituality, philosophy, astronomy and history, stirs his poetic inspiration. He has been variously published, including: *Awen, Bard, The Bards, Borderlines, Carillon, Cauldron, Chimera, Crossways, Countryside Matters, Decanto, The Delinquent, Garbaj, The Journal, Mind Link, Orbis, Poetry Express, The Recusant, Splizz, The Strix Varia, Touchstone*. It was following the breakdown of his health that he began to write, with his first published poem appearing, under poet Alan Morrison's editorship, in *Poetry Express* 21 2005. A selection of his poetry appeared in *Waiting for Gulliver* (Caradoc Press, 2005) alongside the work of Sally Richards. Successful completion of his participation in the Survivors' Poetry Mentoring Scheme 2006-2007, under the mentoring guidance of poet Philip Ruthen, led to the publication of his first solo collection *cui bono?* by Survivors' Press (2007). This was followed in 2016 with the publication of an e-book solo collection *brief companionship* by Survivors' Press, once again under the mentoring guidance of poet Philip Ruthen. Other publications of his poetry in various anthologies include: *The Sleepless Sands* (Earlyworks Press, 2006), *Shoogle Tide* (Earlyworks Press, 2007), *Emergency Verse - Poetry in Defence of the Welfare State* (Caparison, 2010/2011).

opacity undone

Melchior:
At last found you after such a long search
so much time you can't hide from us.
feckless girl unmarried gets pregnant for a home

Gaspar:
As for you sneaking around the countryside
claiming to be the baby's father we doubt that
undesirable marries girl gets resident status

Balthazar:
Get those measly things take that mewling noise
get out this stable belongs to Star Properties Limited.
lawless squatters prevent religious development

Coda:
Melchior: another success for wisdom
Gaspar: shrewd investment in Herod
Balthazar: we're the history makers

3 wise men at your service:
traders in gold, frankincense and myrrh

acid rain falling

bitter memories,
splattering his windscreen
drumming gavottes relentless metronome,
(futile wipers - no soft soap - useless at clearing his-view)

stark socket-lights of the council 'skull' offices,
morbidly shining his-story,
(metered moments)
spilling across the car park

huddled anecdotes,
clasping 'all's well that end's well' umbrellas,
staggering the time-line of his-constraining-bay,
(sidestepping the puddling mire, but
confused motivation's left shoe splashes up the dirt) –
they believe they have the keys for upholstered happy endings
forlorn metal caskets,
cruising, polluting conveyed choice, under his nose,
(fates, *en attendant*, whispering "must be unleaded sir")
ecological fumes, helping to save the planet,
easing his-journey on

Sisyphus Doctrine
                    - those who rule…

Socrates drinks hemlock again
Aristocles turns into himself
The student reasons the void
Thirty Tyrants and more return

these the most cunning fools on earth?

Tartarus eternity boulders uphill
Great chain of being funeral honours
Hades handcuffs misnomer
Styx draughted Charon redeployed

these the most cunning fools on earth?

……and in the Brown Mirror of Numbness……

DES MANNAY

Born in Cardiff 25/12/1964, Mannay is a Welsh writer of colour. His first poetry collection, Sod 'em – and tomorrow is published by Waterloo Press. He is co-editor of *The Angry Manifesto* poetry journal, and the winner of the 'rethinkyourmind' poetry competition (2015), and LIT-UP poetry competition (2018). Placed 2nd and highly commended in the Disability Arts Cymru Poetry Competition (2015). 'Gold Award' winner in the Creative Futures Literary Awards (2015), Madder Than We Look Poetry Competition (2016), shortlisted for the erbacce prize for poetry (2015, and 2016 and 2019), Welsh Poetry Competition (2015), The John Tripp and Idris Davies Poetry Competition; part of Rhymney Valley Literature and Arts Festival 2016, and the Disability Arts Cymru Poetry Competition (2016). Mannay has performed at numerous venues, including the Unity Festival, Maindee Festival, Hub Festival, Stoke Newington Literature Festival, KAYA Festival of World Music & Arts, Merthyr Rising, The Seed Festival, Walls: Muriau - Welsh mental health arts festival, and Green Gathering. He has poems published in *I Am Not A Silent Poet*, *The Angry Manifesto*, *Proletarian Poetry*, *Yellow Chair Review*, *Indiana Voice Journal*, *Stand Up And Spit*, *Red Poets*, *The Scum Gentry*, *The Round Up*, *Poetry24*, *Winning Writers*, *International Times*, *erbacce* and work in 20 poetry anthologies. Mannay is on Facebook as 'The stuff wot I wrote Des Mannay - hooligan Poet' and Twitter as @hooliganpoet

Missing Payment

There is no money
no amount
has turned up
in my bank account.
So I dial the number
wait in the queue
for about
an hour or two -
then you say 'bear with me....'

I get wound up
you start to flounder -
do you believe the myths
about benefit scroungers?
Look - if you don't
restore my payments
I will end up
on the pavement -
and you say 'bear with me....'

I bet you've got
a landlord too
who wants to be paid
on time from you.
We're all being shafted
tell the truth.
All we need's
a bloody roof -
and you say 'bear with me....'

Bear with me? Bear with me?
There's a fucking Bear with me,
there's an Elephant in the room.
By a big black dog I'm being consumed.
No amount of breathin' in a paper bag
can stop a full on panic attack -
so don't just say 'bear with me.…'

Recovery

Listen therapist — we need to talk. There are things you don't
see with your brief therapy and half a dozen sessions before
you set me free. With your emphasis on illness and diagnosis;
hoarding symptoms like stamp collectors after an illusive
Penny Black. You medicalize social problems as our fault, but
we cannot be wished away. Are we ill because we're depressed
or is it because we're oppressed? And is the key to this
oppression being robbed of self expression?

There's a riot in my head — but just like Martin Luther King
said, "Riots are conversations of the voiceless". And 'we'
lost our voice because 'you' usurped our language. Let's
take the term 'recovery'. For health professionals like
you it becomes an excuse to cease treatment, eliminate
resources; deny us the 'luxury' of difference. In your hands,
the Langue has no Parole*

But 'we' invented the term 'recovery' as a way to understand
our difficulties. It's how we hold onto the past and recover
identity. It stops us being written off — Just as Lord Byron

said, "Deformity is daring...", and we strive to make good,
catch up and maybe overtake those who have not felt the pain
of emotional overload. And as we re-calibrate our pain we
echo Kurt Cobain when he wrote, "Thank you for the tragedy.
I need it for my art"

NIALL McDEVITT

is the author of three collections of poetry, *b/w* (Waterloo Press,
2010), *Porterloo* (International Times, 2013) and *Firing Slits, Jerusalem
Colportage* (New River Press, 2016). His work appeared in *Emergency
Verse* and *The Robin Hood Book*. He has featured in the 2020 pamphlets
Blackwells Poetry No. 1 and *THE BARD*, as well as such magazines as *The
London Magazine, Love Love, Ragged Lion Journal, Burning Bush*. He is
also known for his poetopographical walks such as The William Blake
Walk, An Arthur Rimbaud Drift, A London Chaucer Pilgrimage, A Walk on
the Wilde Side, and many others. In 2012 he read at Yoko Ono's Meltdown.
In 2016, he performed his poetry in Iraq at the Babylon Festival. He
blogs at poetopography.wordpress.com

Windows

1000 windows. 1,000,000 windows. 1,000,000,000 windows
and so on

In Ulaanbaatar, the poor live in 'ger' tents pitched
on suburban scrubland. the rich shop in the designer
centre.
in Belfast, pooraholics are divided from richestants
by proliferations of 'peace walls'.
in Detroit, the inner city is black, the outer city
white.
in Madrid, the poor live with their parents, the rich
buy and sell empty properties

in London, the children of the crystal palace are homeless,
trapped in windows, partitioned by windows.
windows multiply
and the population
multiplies in windows

Royal Pocketmoney

buy out the island's
cancer-rich core
for the lizard clans

the coins the queen's
mona lisa grins
are not for the likes of us

a dressing down
from the toppermost doggy
"first is best"

bullion and sugar
teas of the east
liquid tons of claret

busts of the heroines
page 3 framed
sunned mirrored starred booby-trapped

and the lions yawn
in stone dreams
beware of the big cats

on the very margins
of the very margins
beyond the knobs and knockers

royal jelly is set
wibbly wobbly
a sense of wonder

eros is busy
with robin hood
in the cherub's cubicle

fun in function
cash-icers share-icers
uh oh... miiiiiiind the craaaaaap

she scrubs up well
the royal gorilla
in a pink versace

fuck the snap
fuck the crackle
and - seriously - fuck the pop

the coffee wars
mama latte
milk-lava froth-indundations

and the honey monsters
with the hairy schlongs
manning the sweet-stalls

on the left hand
is an occult ring
kiss it mr. cockface

a cut in rates
champagne tax
bubble bubble fucks bizz

mrs. windsor and co
on the dole
now that's what I call polo

this is thin land
for a harlequin
and a wispy wispy song

JENNIFER A McGOWAN

Her most recent pamphlet, *Still Lives with Apocalypse*, won the Prole pamphlet competition 2020. It is available here: https://prolebooks. co.uk/shop.html. Despite being disabled with Ehlers-Danlos Syndrome (and, at time of writing, Long Covid), Jennifer has obtained her MA and PhD. She lives in Oxford, and hides, when she can, as an early Tudor re-enactor.

Chronic

Last night, I left my friends
at their table, knowing I had just the time
to get home before I was sick again.

Later, in my white, tile-boundaried world,
crying out despite myself,
I remember the advice of a friend, now dead:
Breathe in the pain, breathe out the pain.
I can't explain any more than that.

And it's true, you can't explain
the way existence coalesces to a breath,
then another, thick lungs working to give you
all that is afforded in this life, a little grace.
The way the only fear becomes not breathing.
And which of us can say, in our own time,
I have not known that?

Win-win

Something pings or snaps
again. *I want a new body,*
I swear, for the hundredth time.

Can I have this one when
you're done with it? he asks,
fingers exploring shoulder, hair.
Win-win.

By such slight things
are we reconstructed.

Hagged

i.
It takes time to be diseased.
Disease does not knock, stick its head round the door,
ask if you've a library book that needs returning,
apologise for the hour when it gets back.

No. It grabs you by the inside
of the roots of all your hair—
swings you—sticks levers behind
your eyes, forks in your belly
and does not ask.

ii.
This is the sixth month it's taken away.
You start to reckon in years.

iii.
Your family frame memories
of when you shone.

When you breathed salt air,
as free
and bound to the moon
as tides.

Now you do not even bleed.

iv.
Smell told you when to flee.
Now you cannot.

v.
refract through a prism fracture
into three

—the disease
cutting off calendar pages—
forget
to eat
        what you cannot taste

let

the same food
      wither
            over and over

vi.
How many days away
is always?

vii.
I'd tell you a tale if I could,
of the little girl who got sick
but because she was good and kind
she grew her body back and flew away,
never ever taking freedom for granted,

but I can't.

viii.
Sleep heals.
Months of insomnia.

ix.
I am older now.
Visibly smaller.
Confined to words.

But words are loud.
Listen.

PENNY MEAD

So 2016 has dealt its final blow

So 2016 has dealt its final blow:
From DLA to PIP we go,
The dreaded time has come today
To prove my disability is here to stay,
No matter how hard they try,
Sorry DWP, I refuse to die,
I will fight on and win you'll see
Because right's on my side
You won't beat me!

CHRISTOPHER MONCRIEFF
is a European poet who has also translated widely from French, German and Romanian literature (Pushkin Press, Alma Books, Alma Classics & Istros Books). After professional military service in Europe, Northern Ireland, the Near East and the USA during the Cold War he produced son et lumière-style shows in Germany, France and the USA before beginning to write full-time, and has lived in Paris and Los Angeles. He read Theology at Oxford, and has qualifications in design and on the military staff. A frequent traveller in Central and Eastern Europe, he speaks a number of the languages of the region. He is an award recipient and Fellow of the Royal Literary Fund, was the Writing Fellow at Newnham College, Cambridge from 2018-19, has worked as a mentor for young adults on the autism spectrum, and takes an active interest in the wider acceptance of neuro- and gender diversity. His poetry has appeared in the Bucharest Literary Review, *Luceafărul*, *The Recusant* and *Militant Thistles*. Two illustrated collections published by Caparison: *Tabac Blond* (2019) and *Mermaids in Wormwood* (2021). He is currently working on a new collection written from a neurodivergent perspective. www.christophermoncrieff.com

Who Will Speak For England?

Where the voting slips were counted,
children now draw and sing and play,
coughing in the dust that still fills the air,
skipping through the layer on the ground,
finding crumpled ballots here and there.
They puzzle at the scrawl that smears the paper,
screaming out its pint of bitter rage,
clamouring inchoate for a voice.
And the children frown and shake their curled, blond heads:
what is this noise, they wonder? Does someone want to speak?

Out in the street, meanwhile,
and on the dust-choked airwaves,
there is much talk of speaking,
of walking the talk,
walking tall,
of taking it on someone else's chin,
handing out brooms to the unemployed and capped
so they can cheaply sweep up the lies the talkers told
before the children find them in the dust
and read them out loud
outside Poundland and the sporting sweatshops
where babies are born in toilets during unpaid tea breaks
because the talkers and their ear-flap listeners
don't like breast feeding in public places,
it gives them puce red faces
and makes their velvet collars curl.
But someone has spoken;
their Voice has been heard.

And in My Lady's Chamber,
where the dust of ages past
is dutifully debated daily
by blond talkers with loud voices
and divine-right, skirt-wandering hands
(when they're not straying in the till),
the unanimous, hard-whipped opinion
is that someone somewhere who the clarions call
The People
has definitively spoken
once and for all
there's no going back

we're not for turning
to do so would be Tower of London Treason
chop chop chop goes the axe Mr Punch.

England has spoken;
it has done its duty
by the Irish and the Scots
and out-talked the Welsh.
The smell of its voice floats rankly on the breeze
which blows back and forth across the Channel,
clogging the continental air conditioners
like so many times before,
poisoning the atmosphere for friend and foe alike.
England has spoken
for itself.

ALAN MORRISON

Poetry collections: *The Mansion Gardens* (Paula Brown, 2006), *A Tapestry of Absent Sitters* (Waterloo, 2009), *Keir Hardie Street* (Smokestack Books, 2010), *Captive Dragons/ The Shadow Thorns* (Waterloo, 2011), *Blaze a Vanishing/ The Tall Skies* (Waterloo, 2013), *Shadows Waltz Haltingly* (Lapwing, 2015), *Tan Raptures* (Smokestack, 2017), *Shabbigentile* (Culture Matters, 2019), *Gum Arabic* (Cyberwit, 2020), and *Anxious Corporals* (Smokestack, 2021). He is also author of verse play *Picaresque*, and an online epic poem, *Odour of Devon Violet* (www.odourofdevonviolet.com). He was joint winner of the Bread & Roses Poetry Prize 2018. His poetry has been awarded grants from Arts Council England, the Royal Literary Fund, the Society of Authors and the Oppenheim-John Downes Memorial Trust. Poems and monographs in numerous journals including *Culture Matters, Disability Arts Online, The Fortnightly Review, The International Times, The London Magazine, The Morning Star, Stand*. He edits international webzine *The Recusant* and its sister site *Militant Thistles*. He was editor of the former Caparison anti-austerity anthologies, *Emergency Verse - Poetry in Defence of the Welfare State* (2010/11) and *The Robin Hood Book - Verse Versus Austerity* (2012).

Epigram

It's permanent open season
For press-persecution of the unemployed
As *"parasites"* — fleas of unearned leisure;
Stigmatising strugglers as *"scroungers"*
Is judgemental England's guiltless pleasure...

Waiting for Giro
After Beckett

Wragdole. What we have here is a pale suggestion and we are trapped by this piece of franked paper. And yet, in this intense privation, one thing alone is clear. We are waiting for Giro to come.
Escrogurn. I don't seem to be able... (*Long hesitation*) to budget.
Wragdole. That's hardly surprising, since this paper affords us nothing. Worse than nothing: something. But not enough something. It's just a token to acknowledge we ought to exist, in some form or other. As ghosts.
Escrogurn. Worse. Ghosts don't need money.
Wragdole. It's perpetuity's stipend. It stretches our bones on the rack of waiting.
Escrogurn. How depressing.
Wragdole. To every doley his little cross. (*He sighs.*) Till he signs. (*Afterthought.*) And is forgotten. Until the next time. That little cross to point us to our Post Office. We wait. We are bored. (*He throws up his hand.*) No, don't protest...
Escrogurn. (*Indignant*) I wasn't about to...
Wragdole. ...we are bored to death, there's no denying it. Good. Giro comes along and what do we do? We squander it... In an instant a fortnight's budget will vanish and we'll be broke once more, in the midst of nothingness!
Escrogurn. I was only going to say... I'm beyond it.
Wragdole. Beyond what?
Escrogurn. Boredom. (*Afterthought*). By now.
Wragdole. You and me both. Both you and me.
Under this fruitless tree.
Escrogurn. How long now do you think? How long?
Wragdole. How long is a piece of string?
Escrogurn. As long as that? It seems ages since...
Wragdole. I know...
Escrogurn. ...the last one...
Wragdole. Mmmm?...
Escrogurn. ...came.
Wragdole. (*Holding hand up as if halting a protest*). No, there's nothing to be done...
Escrogurn. I know... I'm doing nothing...
Wragdole. ...until Giro comes...

231

Salted Caramels

Garthwaite, K. (2014) 'Fear of the brown envelope: exploring welfare reform with long-term sickness benefits recipients.'

"Drop, drop... Chinese water torture."/ "Authorised Systematic Harassment [ASH] has enormous potential. The slow and noiseless steamroller of the State. The daily brown envelope dropping on the mat"

—Wilfred Greatorex, *1990*

"The Tories have weaponised welfare" —Jonathan Bartley, Green Party

The DWP — Department for Weapons and Poisons —
Deploys a plethora of paper weapons against the unemployed,
Origami games galore down at jobcentrepluses
These days, administrative harassment of claimants,
"Disrupt and upset" is the protocolic sport,
Managers cutting out cardboard sheriff badges
To pin on employees' lapels for hitting targets
Of sanctioning sundry jobseekers for missing
Post-dated appointments too prompt for the post
(Brownie points for brownouts) — but there's
No excuse for poor clairvoyance among
The *"scrounging"* classes, it's just another type
Of avoidance of work or looking for work
(Even if most vacancies advertised are fictitious!),
Taking up unpaid placements or internships;
There's Customer Compliance appointments
Elliptically phrased in sterile letters that leave
Much space for doubt and dread for recipients
As to what to expect on attending 'tape-
Recorded' interviews —lie detectors, thumbscrews,
Piano wires (for the Caxton House Gestapo)...?
Nothing so three-dimensional, for it's a game
Of malignant origami the DWP plays,
It prefers paper weapons — O, ink can kill as well:
An average letter from this Department can work
A pretty lethal spell of unsympathetic magic,
Like black spots to Black Dogs! But of all
The paper weapons deployed none compare
To brown envelopes, brown envelopes everywhere,
Ubiquitous brown envelopes, lying in baiting

Wait on doormats of a morning like paper moths
Or flattened preying mantises to greet indigents'
Lockjawed yawning; and these tan envelopes
Paralyse on sight, as soon as claimants spy them
In hallways they get dreadful frights, muscles
Tighten, throats turn dry, palms go clammy,
Brows perspire, hearts start thumping, pulses pumping —
Such symptoms these simple shapes inspire,
No mere rectangular gestures of tan paper
With glaring white fangs for windows sitting on
Doormats of the lumpenproletariat,
Simply petrify, sealed and pressed with spite,
Vituperative envelopes, primed paper weapons,
Packets of seeds to excite nervous dispositions,
Itch hypersensitivities, trigger anxieties,
Spring traps of panic attacks, fight-or-flights,
Make grown men quake over cornflakes — there's no
Escape from brown envelopes for recipients
(Except, perhaps, suicide — and O how many more
Suicides to be swept under the carpet by
Tampered DWP statistics, while particular cases
Still come to light, like Reekie, Clapson, Salter...?),
As long as someone's unemployed or
Incapacitated, day and night they'll be stalked by
These vicious missives, razor-sharp verdicts,
Tan fiends, buff furies, beige besiegers, brown
Plebiscites, salted caramels, salted with spite —
Not as butterscotch-sweet as *Werther's Originals*,
Nor even Beveridge's *"Five Giant Evils"*
Lozenge variety and lacking the glucose
Shots of Lloyd-George's *"Four Spectres"* —
Interminable brown robins with stark black
And white insides of menacing nomenclature,
Kafkaesque Doublespeak and implicatures
Paving the way to disinfecting sunlight
Like shards of burnt glass, to snip at and grate away
Fragile minds; some choose to eat them, so pretend
They haven't received them, but those who do
Will taste manila gum on gluey tongues and the bite
Of sodium chloride, for these are spiked repasts,
Bitter sweetmeats, unjust desserts laced with darnels —
The Department for Work and Pensions slowly
Poisons its claimants with Salted Caramels...

Kipling Buildings

If you can keep your head when all about you
Are spy cameras, a deliberate delay
Of the appointment time in an attempt
To break your spirit, a protracted wait
In a claustrophobic, clinical-looking room,
A neutrally decorated purgatory
Silent except for the rumbling water cooler,
Being observed by unseen deciders
Prolonging your agony in a pot-plant garden...

If you can keep your head during a gruelling
Interrogation at Independent Assessment
Services (formerly Atos Solutions),
Being asked trick questions, being observed,
Recorded, monitored, not listened to,
Only heard, not being respected or
Empathised with, but being judged
In an unacknowledged kangaroo court
Of icy stares and sporadic mouse-clicks
For each of the ticks in the boxes on
The assessor's screen turned away from you
So you can't see — while being observed
Just as a troubled adolescent by
A cryptic psychiatrist's invisible observers
Behind two-way glass; these desk-perched
Harpies who prey on the sick and disabled
For sport, will pick off your weak points
And press all your buttons to get the most
Pool-muddying responses to cloud your claim...

If you can keep your PIP when all about you
Are losing theirs, it'll only be a pyrrhic
Victory, a temporary reprieve, just putting off
The inevitable sting of a future trap-sprung
Reassessment, opportunity for symptom-
Tampering and a spot of goalpost-changing
To ensure next time you're lower scoring...
If you can keep your nerve at Independent
Assessment Services nestled deep
In the grey, mauve and periwinkle plush
Of Kipling Buildings poorly disguised
As a clinic but whose commercial shape

And façade indicate that a bank once
Operated there, on the nondescript corner
Of a pigeon-grey street in an unexplored
Part of Portsmouth, then you will be damned,
My son, damned with a disability,
But worse, an invisible one, and the points
You'll score will be in binary numbers —
The price for their bounties, their thirty pieces...

CATH NICHOLS

Born 1970, Kent, UK. She has had two collections published — most recently *This is Not a Stunt* (Valley Press, 2017). She teaches at the University of Leeds, uses a power wheelchair outside the house, and is queer. She receives high mobility PIP and lower care (gained on Appeal), but found the process so traumatic she has yet to write about it explicitly.

How Do You Manage?

Limiting social contact/ desiring social contact,
breathing deeply.
Reading social media/ restricting social media,
meditation. (Rubbish at mediation.)

Switching off the TV, favouring radio,
lying on the floor, listening.
Reducing content and response.
Pacing: getting it right, getting it wrong.

Switching off the radio,
too tired to listen.
Taking regular meals even when...
Gabapentin, pentagablin, steroids.

How *do* I manage?
Hearing things in the night.
Amitriptylene, sertraline,
all the 'leens'. Once, in a red moon

trancing above the pain feeling lightened,
a wing, a prayer.

Origin Story

I broke myself. Careless, really.
    The Lord is my shepherd
pulling a 1930s dresser from the wall.
    I shall not want
too much, too awkward a bend.
    He makes me down to lie
de-flea-ing the upstairs carpet,
    in pastures green.
I lift a leg like lifting a box, both hands,
    He leadeth me the quiet waters by
to put on socks, I lie down and winch up my right leg.
    In Death's dark vale
dead weight. I try a tiny stretch of yoga –
and fear no ill
to no avail. Four months on I control these muscles
    with thee, dear Lord, beside me.

Surely goodness and mercy shall follow me
I could not... Can no longer...
all the days of my life?
Something broke in every cell.

Tender spots

You say I've become *Where's Wally?*
prone to disappear about the house.
Am I hiding on the landing, at the bottom
of the stairs... in cushions on the sofa?
Sometimes there's a blanket or a pillow,
but mostly I rough it, take what's given.
You find Wally on the landing. I have cold feet.
'Press your hands on my feet,' I say.
You kneel down, shins over my feet,
palms on my propped-up knees.
Standing up is tricky, you mustn't press too hard.
When you leave we kiss through banisters,
me rolled sideways on the floor,
you turned halfway down the stairs.

ABIGAIL ELIZABETH OTTLEY

(previously Wyatt) was born in 1952 in Avely in Essex but has lived in Cornwall since 1984. She writes poetry and short fiction from her home in Penzance. Since 2009 her work has appeared in numerous magazines, journals and anthologies including *The Recusant*. Her most recent credits include *The Lake*, *The Atlanta Review*, *Gnashing Teeth*, *The Blue Nib* and *Fragmented Voices*. A former English teacher with a lifelong interest in History, Abigail is also primary carer to her very elderly mother.

Scrap Heap Austerity Blues

Austerity, you got me down,
You got me on the floor.
No rainbows shining through my storms,
no buds or flowers round my door.
Not much money in my wallet.
I got little cause to smile.
I got plenty cause to worry though.
Got debts that stretch for miles.

Got my children going hungry
got my landlord getting mean
got no way of moving forward,
got a bunch of broken dreams.
Got no man to rub my shoulders
or to wake me with a kiss.
Got no faith in prayers or fairy tales.
Seems life goes on and on like this.

Buying cheap and counting coppers
so as not to break that ten pound note.
Thinking always who needs uniform
and who's outgrown their winter coat.
Who has a birthday looming
who has wrecked their good school shoes?
It's no wonder I break down at nights
when all I got to lose

is those going-downhill-and-run-down,
down-at-the-heel-and-can't-feel
kids-aint-having-no-fun-cos-there's-eff-all-left-to-live-on
can't-stop-my-crying feels-like-I'm-dying.
who-would-be-a-single-mother blues.

Austerity, you got me, too.
Just can't seem to get ahead.
I'm young. I should be full of life.
but I am full of fear instead.
I'm afraid they'll stop my money
if I don't go here or show up there
afraid I'll never find a job
or have a home with cash to spare.

I did everything they told me.
Went to college, tried my best.
But now it seems they lied to me.
My CV don't impress.
Now they give me work experience
when what I need's a chance.
A chance to work for proper pay
a chance to play, a chance to dance.

Because, you fat cats, I am young.
I got the legs, I got the shoes.
Aint got no opportunity!
And me, well, I don't get to choose.
Coz you rich guys get the choices
while the likes of us we lose.

We got those no-dough-oh-no
sanctioned-if-we-don't-show,
hard-luck-mucked-up-isn't-this-a-fuck-up,
what's-the-point-of-growing-up blues.

And Austerity, you've done for me.
I got a disability.
My life's been hard enough without
this extra stress. You've done for me.
I didn't choose to be this way
whatever you might like to think.
Your targets are unethical and
your methods downright stink.

Austerity, you've dragged me down
so low some days I don't get dressed.
I know I should. Sometimes I try
but most days I am too depressed.
These days, you see, I can't get out

238

(They took away my car)
my Care Plan doesn't care at all
but that, they say, is how things are.

Austerity, I'm on my knees.
Got not much left to lose.
If I could walk a mile I'd say
you try it in these worn-down shoes.
But as things are all I can say
is when the Great Assessment's made
I hope they get what they deserve
and they are left alone, afraid

to feel the utter hopelessness
that presses like a monstrous stone,
to try to live as best they can
until the final trumpet's blown.

Because then they'll see identity
is something precious they can lose
when they become instead a number and
they wait for hours in pointless queues.
They'll see it's not as easy then
as Fat Cats like to think.
It's not all fags and bingo. Much less
betting shops and drink.

Instead of sumptuous lunches
and receptions with champagne
they'll have noodles and fish fingers
or else beans on toast again.

They'll have those brother-don't-forget-me
Please-let-me-live-and-let-me-be-at-least-well-fed-and-not-
        half-dead
no-point-in-getting-out-of-bed, always-broke-this-aint-no-joke

Scrap heap austerity blues.

ANTONY OWEN

is from Coventry, England, with an interest in exploring the consequences
of conflicts which he considers are largely overlooked. Author of eight
poetry collections his latest book *Phoenix* is a bi-lingual collection in
German and English published by Thelem Press (Germany). Owen's book *The
Nagasaki Elder* was shortlisted for The Ted Hughes Award and he was also
a category winner for The British Army Armistice Poetry Award for his
poem on a Black Nurse in WW1. In 2020 Owen was a winner of The Bread &
Roses Poetry Award for working class writing.

Poems for people who never read them

If I was clever enough, I would write a poem about poetry
and watch snowflakes cover footprints of half-bent jobseekers
blowing their unemployed breaths into the Coventry moon.

If I was clever enough, I would add important letters after my
        name
and ask a surgeon from Damascus "Why are you cleaning in
        ASDA?"
He tells me he is blessed and I see his face in my wiped away
        footprints.

If I was arsed enough, I could sip a Wheatgrass latte in
        Kensington and
launch a collection of poetry on why I love Wheatgrass latte
        so much
called *Why I Love Winter and Wheatgrass Latte (so much)*.

If I was loaded, I'd post Princess Charlotte a rattle made of
        blood diamonds
and invite her Granny to my book launch at the Koh-I-Noor
        takeaway,
the surgeon from Damascus could photo bomb the money shot.

If I was British enough, I would omit that last stanza and say
        "Soz and that"
or, "Dreadfully sorry Ladies and Gents I seem to have
        forgotten my place",
I am at my place now watching my cat guarding his territory of
        fuck all.

If I was poetic enough, I would write poems for people who
        never read them,
the man across the road with his arse hanging out in a bay of
        red roses,
my neighbour staring at her dead husband's arms waving to her
        from pegs.

If I was poetic enough, I would title this poem something
        really clever like
'The Ballad of Francesca De Montford's Washing Line'
but her name ain't that posh and she wouldn't give a fuck
about   this poem.

Memoirs of Job Seeker 328509B

I awake drowning in the landfill of first light,
each day gets heavier as I try to carry them quietly but fail.
Yesterday I stared at an application form and two hours
        passed,
I'd written a statement of who they want me to be and guess I
        drifted away.

What makes a grown man curl up like a foetus?
is when he's reborn from the cunt of a job centre's door and
        given a zone to die.
What makes a grown man get smaller each day?
is when yawning boys at agencies roll apps and eyes at
        disappearing people.

I want to report my tragic disappearance,
It happened again this morning when my wife wept in secret to
        protect me.
Every morning she puts on a brave face and feeds the black dog
        and elephant.
Her body aches from work and dragging the iron chains of her
        shadow slave.
The truth of unemployment is the greatest lie you believed –
a chav with eight children from ten different Mothers can be
        possible,
the migrant who robbed that job and food from an Englishman's
        mouth.

No, the truth of unemployment is how quick it eats a person's
        mind.

The truth of unemployment is the sea of ash the lost awake in.
Some feel the only thing they can control is not life but the
        other,
like that bloke from Sunderland who Dave659 shared on twitter,
and that woman outside Poundland at the end of her tether,
telling me her life meant nothing, that she felt, like
        nothing,
that she was nothing and how she could find nothing.

I had to do something,
and tell you.

The Queen Who Killed The Lame Fox

I remember when sunlight raced over the picket line,
pulsing like a Davy lamp, a wet light died in the Yorkshire-sky.
I remember when all the queen's horses breathed a solemn cloud
wheeling with their fiberglass eyes black as the queen's coal.

When you're a child and you see men bleed out in copper-blue
        fields
Men's men who asked me through a lens *"Why ya closing our
        mines"*?
you then understand working class men are made and destroyed by
once pure wives spitting at shields with *Scargill* over their
        breasts.

I remember a lame fox that bled out the gates crossing the
        picket line.
The past is a scab that always comes back to make us work for
        answers.
I remember the teargas eyes of stoned horses wandering in the
        thrown mist,
the day a man ends his life is when he stares for years into
        space.
When kids no longer draw smoke coming out chimneys in fridge
        door paintings
the penny drops like a rusting sun over red brick houses where
        coal lived.

When ghosts that reek of ale haunt themselves by looking back
        to the eighties
that fox from stanza three is slumped in mouths of all the
        queen's dogs.

I remember the day when my headmaster sailed in a sea of
        A-grade students,
and me and Robert Saunders stared at a wall of letters that
        always misspelt us.
I remember my Dad going berserk that I was destined to be
        average like him,
a man who bent sad songs from steel and his son who dreamt of
        vermin.

XAVIER PANADÈS

Born in Barcelona (Catalonia) Xavier Panadès i Blas, "The Catalan",
has been instrumental in the internationalisation of Catalan music.
He began as a touring musician, supporting artists such as Chumbawamba
and Rory McLeod. Xavier pushes the boundaries between music and poetry.
For the last two decades, he has stunned audiences with his explosive
performances. Xavier is a channeller of emotions and his writings
totally absorb the readers. His collection of poetry *The Ear of Eternity*,
(Francis Boutle: 2019) explores love, identity and injustice.

Somriure

Sempre esperant a la porxada...
Els ulls són l'única porta
entre el món interior i l'exterior.
La resta descansa perpètuament.

No podia desfer-me de la suor
que supura dels porus,
d'una pell massa blanca
i un cos indiferent.

Exhalacions que gemegen
de les cordes vocals.
Formiguejos innocents
que devoren el meu cos cru.

El seu tacte m'estimava
quan em rentava.
Els seus ulls gegants em miraven
quan em vestia.

El seu somriure em feia plorar.
Em transportava suaument
al santuari de la felicitat,
on tornava a sentir-me humà.

Podia haver-me abandonat.
Fidel al nostre amor,
continuà al meu costat
en la meva soledat... per fer-me somriure

Smile

Always waiting on the porch...
The eyes are the only door
between the inner and outer world.
The rest rests perpetually.

I couldn't get rid of the sweat
that suppurates from the pores,
of a too-white skin
and an indifferent body.

Exhalations that moan
from the vocal cords.
Tingling sensations
that devour my raw body.

His love touched me
when she washed me.
His giant eyes looked at me
when she dressed me.

Her smile made me cry.
It transported me gently
to the sanctuary of happiness
where I felt human again.

She could have abandoned me.
faithful to our love,
she stayed by my side,
to in my solitude... make me smile

MOGGY PAW LORE
is a cat alter-ego. She is an online protester and has got her claws into many a campaign that threaten her Social Security and that of others. She is one of the admins in a Facebook benefits group and finds that people are happy to confide in a cat. She is fiercely loyal and will fight your corner as well as her own territory but she doesn't suffer fools gladly. She used to have more of a spring in her step but she still has the occasional feisty moment when she's not lying in the sun. This has included taking on government rats. Just like any other cat, she believes food, shelter and warmth should be unconditional, and life should include little luxuries.

The Neighbour's Curtains Drawn

Maybe he works the night shift
And now he's just dead beat
Or maybe he leaves his curtains closed
To keep in all the heat.

Or might it be that he's a blind man
Who doesn't like to think
Of prying eyes gazing in
When he's washing at the sink.

Or maybe the credit on her meter
Has nearly all run out
The bedclothes are her heater
And food she does without.

Or maybe he's just far too ill
To make it out of bed
His body far too weak and tired
With his awful tumoured head.

Or maybe she was up all night
In agonizing pain
And tossed and turned and screamed and burned
Till the pills kicked in again.

Or maybe he's just so depressed
Nigh on suicidal
Sick and tired of having no hope
And being called bone idle.

Or maybe she's already dead
And no-body's yet discovered
And the pulling away of her safety-net
Is yet to be uncovered.

Is this the sort of life you mean, George,
"A life sleeping off benefits"?
Maybe one day you'll wake to the truth
And I'd hate to be you when it hits

Home.

Alphabet Song X 2

atos bullying causes destruction everywhere - folk get
harassed intensely - justice knows loads more nameless ones
perish quietly - remember, suffering turns us very wild - xpand
your zeal -

and begin campaigning daily - even facebook groups have impact
- just keep lobbying mps newspapers or peers quite regularly -
salute the universal valuable welfare - xtend your zeal

ANNE PENN-HINES

loves painting, drawing and poetry as a way of expressing her emotions.
The arts have always featured strongly in her life. She brought up her
three sons singlehandedly, one with a disability from birth. When her
children were young she worked as a helper in a disabled playgroup.
She has also made carnival costumes with a mass band for Notting Hill
and has taken part in it with her children. Many years ago she wrote
lyrics for a musician friend which he put to music. When she was nine
her school choir sang at the Royal Festival Hall and she did a solo
performance of 'Once In Royal David's City' despite being very nervous.
Anne is disabled due to a spinal injury and neurological problems. She
is housebound and unable to walk.

Just to be free

i sit at the window watching the world go by
all i want to do is cry
every day is full of pain
i know tomorrow will be the same
i wish i could walk around
instead of falling on the ground
spasms makes my muscles tight
every step is a massive fight
just to be free
is all i ask for me
but that's not an option now
i have to find inner strength somehow
to get through each day
in my own special way
there's no magic potion
or special lotion
that can fix my situation
just sweat and tears to get me to my destination
this is not how i planned my life to be
is it too much to ask to be pain free

PAULA PETERS

lives In London. Paula has been writing poetry since the early 1990s to raise awareness of mental distress and on the political events of the time. Paula had her first book, *Yes I really do Hate Yo-Yos*, published in 2012 by Chipmunka Publishing, when she was living with bipolar and R.A. Paula's powerful piece 'Lest We Forget', about the Work Capability Assessment, was performed in London in 2013 at a protest called '10,000 cuts and Counting' to mark the deaths of disabled people from the constant distress of the assessments. 'Cracks in the System', about benefits sanctions, was performed as a drama piece in front of MPs in Parliament. Paula is an experienced and high profile disability rights activist, a prominent member of Disabled People Against Cuts (DPAC). She is a talented photographer and loves films, dogs, sunsets, chocolate and getting involved in civil disobedience to bring about social change.

Lest We Forget

I miss you every single day
The pain it never goes away
I hear your voice whispering in the trees
The whispering of the leaves saying talk to me
I remember every smile in the sun
The days of laughter and having fun
The days of seeing you fight terrible pain
Nothing in this life feels the same again.
I have to live without you, and be so very strong
I wondered what I could have done, how did they get it wrong?
The stress and the fear it tore you apart
I feel so much anger within me, where do I start?
I know if you were here right now, here is what you would
        have said:
Put the anger to one side, and concentrate on getting justice
        instead
Get my story out there, and get my story told
But I am safe from harm now, I will never grow old.
I feel you all about me, just beyond my reach,
I feel you in the wind in my hair as I walk along the beach,
Feel your warmth and wonderful spirit in every setting of
        the sun,
Now I am crying once again, I am hurting, everyone.
Every day without you is tearing at my heart,
It is pure hell without you, I hate being apart,
I hear you saying to me, Yyou have to go on,
Come on you can do this, you know you are strong...

I hate what happened, that you took your life that day,
I so wish you had talked to me, we would have found a way,
The government have a lot to answer for, trust me they do,
But I make you this promise, I will get justice for you.
I will never forget you, and the others too,
Or the horrendous hell you were all put through,
You live in my memories and in my heart every day,
 I just wish there was something to take the pain away.
At 11 am, 3rd December, please pause, remember, reflect
For two minutes we remember all those who have passed with
            love and respect
They are in our hearts every single day
We pay tribute to them all today.
To the 10,600 ill and disabled people who have lost their lives
You will live on through us, you will never die
For your stories are inspirational, and your stories will
            be told
You are not in pain anymore and you will never grow old.

Driven By Necessity

We are driven by necessity to fight for our rights
But this Government wish we would shut up, want us out of sight;
We chain ourselves to railings and each other; lobby our MP's;
We fight in courts across the land, and even overseas.

Our services, our public transport is not equal for us to use,
The battle just to use a train, makes us blow a fuse,
The gap between platform and train can be a foot high,
All we want is to get around and be independent, we sigh;

The shops are such a challenge, the public arenas too,
If you do not have that radar key, it's not easy to access
            that loo;
It is painful to be stared at, as well as suffer abuse,
We have suffered physical violence, and verbal comments obtuse;

Hate crime rises every day, championed by our press,
We raise awareness of our issues but, this government couldn't
            care less;
All we want is to be independent in spite of disability
But this Government are stripping us of our rights and dignity.

We live in fear every day of our money being taken away,
We never know if we can pay for food on any given day;
We worry about the loss of care packages, the cuts to social
      care;
We have borne 59 per cent of all cuts to date, just how is this
      fair?

We are seeing the rationing of treatment, the loss of A and E's,
The treatment to help keep us going denied to you and me;
We can't afford to pay for it, but privatisation is on the way
And the fight to keep our NHS grows greater every day.

We see the desperation, the fear, the pain, the stress,
We are struggling every day, and cannot get our rest,
We are put through endless questions for, cruel work capability,
Made to jump through hoops for PIP sport for the DWP.

Hate Crime Is So Wrong

Was screamed at in my face, the face was full of hate,
They tried to push me over, and through the station gate,
I was terrified, the people turned away,
I came home petrified, will never forget that day.

Scared to go outside, the fear was in my eyes
I am just a person, the question asked was why?
I am only human, but have an illness or two
Yet, I am judged and screamed at, "There is nothing wrong
      with you!"

"You are just a scrounger, the lowest form of life",
These are some of the names called, those words cut like a
      knife,
Society judges harshly, the crap believed in the press
Every area of our life is just one massive test.

Hate crime has risen sharply since 2010,
We only ask this question, how do we beat them? When?
Hate crime rising on the net and out there on the streets
Makes you feel so mistrustful of everyone you meet.

You want to challenge those opinions, the way we are perceived
You want to campaign against our Government, tell the truth,
        when they deceive,
Speaking out is brave but you'll lead the way ahead
More people join in the campaign, and even fight from bed.

STEPH PIKE

was born in Germany in !967. She is a Welfare Rights Adviser, an anti-austerity activist and a published poet. Her poetry collection, *Pétroleuse*, was published by Flapjack Press (2016).

£53 A Week

(On 1/4/13, as the most sweeping and draconian welfare reforms become law, Iain Duncan Smith, the architect of this cruelty, claims he could live on £53 a week)

his hand closes round
notes and coins, foreign
he doesn't like the dirt
the way it disturbs
the soft line of the wool

£5 on gas and electric
he's brought candles, doesn't watch TV
buys a daily paper, the Times
won't eat much, fat enough
for a week, or more

he can do without
doesn't mind the cold
tells himself boarding school was
harsh, how he cried into his pillow
clutching daddy's credit card

he spends the days
straightening his tie against his own
unease, keeps the curtains closed
doesn't go out, speak to anyone
won't look, doesn't learn a thing

at night he sucks his silver spoon
dips his tongue in his own puddled spit
dreams of quails eggs, exotic trips
the moon sweeps a slow scan over his silk cocoon
an image beams back; cold, barren, blue

Welfare to Workfare

I'm going to forget
that we're slaves to the 40 hour week
and the minimum wage
so we stay in our place
and the rich stay rich
and get myself a job

I'm going to forget
that I'm black and hassled by racists
and stopped by police on a regular basis
because all they can see
is a drug dealer, or terrorist
and get myself a job

I'm going to forget
my mental distress,
the fear, the psychosis
the stigma, the sections
my diagnosis
and get myself a job

I'm going to forget
that my kids bunk off school
run with gangs, play with guns
because I'm never home
and get myself two jobs

I'm going to forget
that I worked 40 years
in a job with low pay
in a job that I hated
for a boss with no conscience
who stole my soul, and my pension
and get myself a retirement job

I'm going to forget
the clown in my nightmares
chopping heads off the chickens
chopping down all the forests
hacking flesh off the mad cows
injecting fat into children
and get myself a McDonalds job

I'm going to forget
that we're fighting a war that we didn't want
in a country that hates us
I'm going to forget the civilian deaths
the flashbacks, the trauma
the soldiers in bodybags
and get myself an army job

I'm going to forget
the mines closed down, the shipyards closed down
the factories closed down, the shops closed down
the services cut
that they bailed out the banks with the money we earned
I'm going to forget my P45
the rationalizing, the downsizing
and the efficiency drives
and get myself an invisible job

I'm going to forget that I'm workless
because they couldn't care less
I'm going to forget that I'm workless
because they feather their own nests
and I'm going to forget that I've got rights
and instead I'll be grateful
for any crumb from their table
and I'll work myself to death

PETER RAYNARD

Peter Raynard is editor of *Proletarian Poetry* (www.proletarianpoetry. com). His books of poetry are: *Precarious* (Smokestack Books, 2018) and *The Combination: a poetic coupling of the Communist Manifesto* (Culture Matters, 2018). *Rumbled* will be published by Nine Arches Press in 2022.

A Sestina to Die For

You know the way this goes by now
days wending their way stretching out
the last drop-down-menu of clarity
filling out the self-referral form when applying
for the post of interviewee. Name, age, address
of your conditions no option for a blank face.

You carry on, nearly finished? Can you face
your family and friends? Is life better now
you have realised your mistakes? Is your address
still the same? How often do you go out?
How many jobs have you been applying
for lately? You cannot clear the fog without clarity.

There are no wrong answers, though a degree of clarity
is required with the digital triage you will face
so take time to revise due diligence when applying
yourself.   We thought you would be well by now
are you finding the process impossible to work out?
You may want to drop in at this address.

We understand if you feel it is wrong to address
you this way so one last time for clarity
for we have a responsibility to get referrals out
of the system before we can let in a new face.
This is your final warning are you listening? Now
some loss adjustment to your fate is worth applying

your attention to in the jobs you will be applying
for in the coming weeks. You must find an address
that is a permanent option. How long has it now
been since you decided to be disabled? Wow such clarity
in your answer, we're getting somewhere finally. Face
the front please you know I can't help you out

if you're not willing to stay alive. Are you often out
lukewarm on the sofa with the telly on? I'm applying
a great deal of patience to my pro-forma, it's time to face
facts this mime act must end. The methadone will address
the rough edges of this mess with a precision and clarity
that will help bring you back to the here and now.

Family and friends there is no reply at his address
we wondered if you could give us some clarity
as you can appreciate we need all of this to end now.

Acceptance Ghazal

I use this form, to flirt about ill-health, tell you I'm disabled
though you won't hear the stricken deer, I am disabled.

When you see me standing there, you won't be able
to tell and I'm not going to declare, I am disabled

I try to keep daylight hours, as much as my mind allows
I don't often laugh aloud and you won't hear, I am disabled

My nose can look round corners, my cheeks adorn a scar
I juggle pairs of glasses but can't see very far, I am disabled

My endocrine department is under autoimmune attack
misguided in its power not all of life is fair, I am disabled

I slump rather than jump these days, often go to funerals
on the way myself so keep those I love near, I am disabled

Religion has started creeping in, I sit at the back in church, grab
what words they offer so that you can all hear, I am disabled

Much of this is me, Peter Frank Raynard, see I do like flirting
with you, so what you see you must cheer, I am disabled.

JEREMY REED

was born on Jersey in 1951. Called by *The Independent* 'British poetry's glam, spangly, shape-shifting answer to David Bowie', his poetry, fiction and performances of his work are inimitable in their opposition to grey mainstream poetry. He has published over 50 books of poetry, fiction and non-fiction winning prestigious literary prizes such as the Somerset Maugham, Eric Gregory and Ingram Merrill awards. His influences include Rimbaud, Artaud, Jean Genet, J.G. Ballard, David Bowie and Iain Sinclair. Reed has collaborated with the musician Itchy Ear, they perform live regularly under the name The Ginger Light at venues such as The National Portrait Gallery, London and The Horse Hospital, London. Some of Reed's most notable poetry collections are *Saints and Psychotics: Poems, 1973–74* (Enitharmon, 1979), *Bleecker Street* (Carcanet, 1980), *Selected Poems* (Penguin, 1987), *Quentin Crisp as Prime Minister* (Tragara Press, 1999), *Patron Saint of Eye-Liner* (Creation, 2000), *Duck and Sally on the Inside* (Enitharmon, 2004), *Piccadilly Bongo* (with Marc Almond; Enitharmon, 2010), and *The Black Book* (Ragged Lion, 2020), a reworking of Arthur Rimbaud's *A Season In Hell*.

Queer Poets Versus Straight

Straight's mostly jet-lagged from reiteration
of normative, can't get an edge
on the endorsed demographic
or give the image black lash-extensions
or brush marks twenty centimetres apart
as granular detail dusted like rocks
on lemon drizzle cake. I do it fine
open the image like an eye
blinks Prussian blue as decisive moment
and wouldn't miss the internship in camp
that mutates ordinary into its flip
like converting piss into Krug champagne
instead of opposite. No family ties,
no marriage contraventions, no normal
as social forum, my alternatives
are like deviated relocation
to the new real; a coded subculture
of shared optimals, mostly underground,
that tunnels through like red amaryllis
throwing a colour storm in February.
I'd rather be the marginalised than safe,
the alternate dishing controversy
as field-expedient, the rogue trouble
delivered at an angle to the world.

My Familiar Junky

I see her outside Foyles, corner
of Manette Street, coming at me
from 20 light years away
in a heroin galaxy -
'you're wearing makeup ain't you luv'
she quizzes sympathetically
track marks on one exposed black arm
like a graffiti epitaph
carved out of dependency.
She wants change, and I'm vulnerable
to exchanging identities
seeing her need in my own
through navigable empathy.
'You in a band?' she tries again,
knowing I give, it's our routine
a method as it comes on rain
as slow flashy hexagonal
'gimme sugar in my tea'
she says, projecting harder now
looking like she's terminal
as I dig into crumpled jeans
to help facilitate a wrap
mainlined into a collapsed vein
and give too much of too little
as part of our complicity,
a street exchange, 'your makeup luv
it really suits you honey.'

Disconnect

Pathologised, they always find me out,
liminalities jumbled together
psychotically from drink or drugs or just
street alienation, a fucked-up substrate
that won't collectivise, their eyes frisk me
as though we know each other from a past
that never existed in a present
infected by confusion, with pink ice
coruscating in January's dumb freeze,
and urban nomads strategising moves
convulsively, Charing Cross to Soho,
rehumanised by the least attention
to needs, and almost telepathically

tweaking my personal cloud of empathy
at exclusion from social normative -
I've never worked for anyone but me
occupation poet as activist
of configurative street imageries
like mixing violent colours with my eyes
into shocked purple, orange, red and green
retellings of detail I make my own
as afternoon drifter amongst the mad,
the doorwayed, the indigent wanting food,
and somehow recognised as vulnerable
in searching out alternate realities
and marginalised for standing out alone.

SALLY RICHARDS

is a Shropshire lass. She began a career in holistic therapies in 2007, gained FdSc (Hons) Complementary Therapies in 2012. She has been widely, diversely, published in journals including: *The Journal, The Recusant, Poetry Express, Splizz, Orbis, The Dawntreader, Chimera, Emergency Verse, The Robin Hood Book*. Commissions include: Shrewsbury Library as Poetry Champion, and Montfort Church Flower Festival, WCR Radio (featured poet, 2006), Third place in Carillon 2007 Open Poetry Competition. Poetry collections: *Waiting for Gulliver* (with Steve Mann; Caradoc Publications, 2005), *Stained Glass* (Survivors' Press, 2007, edited and introduced by mentor Alan Morrison), *Through The Silent Grove* (Masque Publishing, 2008), *Emperor Dragonfly* (Caparison e-books, 2011, edited and introduced by Alan Morrison). In 2015 she was diagnosed with a very rare soft tissue sarcoma in her shin resulting in limb-sparing surgery. In 2017 sarcoma returned necessitating above knee amputation and loss of her career. Sally has a partner, two lovely adult daughters, and is Nana to Edison her very special four year old grandson. Her journey as an amputee continues...

Amputee

(above the knee)

How often do we stop to think
how life would be
if we were not able to walk, for miles,
across warm sand into waves;
kick up leaves, crunch through snow,
run until breathless.

Can we imagine
how it must feel to be defined
by loss and lack of limb;
the unthinkable changes
to life, self image, identity.
One day as normal walking the dog,
standing with ease,
bending, stretching, being...
the next: a few hours of surgery
then it's gone,
simply not there.

She used to dance,
moved with fluidity, effortlessly, sensually,
enjoyed her pretty feet,

her symmetry,
tip-toed, clip-clopped,
pointed toes.
She walked through woods, rambled.
scrambled over styles,
trudged, plodded,
muddied her boots.

Amputation strips away, inhibits,
much of the unique physical expression
of personality.
wheelchair, prosthesis - metal chair, metal leg -
challenge, frustrate,
confine.

The gruesome act:
hacking away of limb from limb,
above (and below) knee, the last resort,
final option for pain, trauma, disease,
sarcoma.

People often stare, remark,
point.
Faces contort, frown.
Rudeness replaces civility -
nudges, whispers, head-turns,
eyes burning into back,
suddenly part of daily life.

She knows how it feels
to be ignored, become invisible -
eyes averted
to a distant, more acceptable, vista.
They: can't take it...don't know...don't care
can't think what to say.
She wants to shout: "just talk to me,
for goodness sake, it's not catching!
then you will see -
I've still got a brain, thoughts, feelings, opinions
they didn't just disappear along with my leg."

Simply ask -
most are happy to answer,
tell their story,

delighted to connect, be acknowledged,
seen.
Smile, look into eyes, connect;
see beyond the metal...

imagine, for just one moment,
how it must feel
to suddenly be changed
forever.

Olivia

"Please can I have some more?"
Her tiny belly aching, never full.
She blinks, winces, holds breath
waits.
The fist slams down,
features contorted with rage.
His voice booms, reverberates
through fragile frame,
rattles ribs starved of flesh.

Mother's eyes plead in helpless desperation.
Merciless finger points;
Olivia knows the score
banished to damp-cold bed
her hollow belly gripes, complains, with lack.
Tear-damp cheek meets clammy pillow,
smell of mould spores in nostrils,
grimy bedcovering pulled close -
futile attempt for warmth, comfort.

Downstairs the familiar sounds
as fist meets flesh
punctuated with tortured pleading
to "stop, please stop".
But it won't stop -
no employment, no money, no end;
he will prevail.
Poverty imprisons, isolates, neglects,
tortures.

Delicate fingers close over ears.

The Visit

A knock at the door
her heart leaps
months of agonising
the day has finally arrived.

Panic rises,
questions begin
relentless, probing.
*Can you dress yourself? Describe **exactly** how
you dress,*
*Can you wash yourself? Describe **exactly** how
you wash,*
on and on; her weary head struggles.
*Can you turn your head, **how far**, shoulders?*
Bend down please, as far as you can.
  (don't cry ... don't!)
 Intrusive thoughts:
What is he thinking, am I doing ok,
God why did I phrase it like that... idiot.
can't remember, don't know, not relevant....

Finally it's done
he leaves
"We will be in touch"
shudders down her spine.
She sits, energy spent, mind whirring
re-visiting her answers over and over.

Then the wait
for the envelope
its contents spelling out her future
in monochrome.

LOUIS RIVE

Born 07/04/1989, Edinburgh native, Glasgow resident, Rive has appeared in *A Kist of Thistles* (Culture Matters) as well as *Bella Caledonia*. He is the editor of the online journal of work-based writing, *Talking Soup*. As a folk musician whose lyrics focus on class, identity, internationalism, and a counter to the corruption of the status quo, Louis' music has featured widely on radio and online. Currently unemployed, Louis volunteers as a language teacher for recently arrived migrants while studying Gaelic.

The Welfare State (In the Shadows of Big Ben)

We sat around watching the Prime Minister
On the television
She talked of you and me, and this big society of common dreams

All the red, white and blue propaganda spews anew
From politicians
A temporary pride in feeling British is not quite what it seems

Homeless people dying in the shadows of Big Ben
Passively listening as the promise us the same old thing (again)
Selling England by the pound, but can you spare the change?

How can you spell dignity in numbers?
Stoically filling out another nameless form
Waiting on the telephone for someone in Bombay to put you through

This government has deemed that our sense of decency
Is up for sale
For £50 a week we show subservience adherence to a man

They talk to us like children, second-class and disillusioned
Cold and pale
In a 'new-world-speak' laden with jargon that no-one understands

Round the block for food banks
Crawling on all fours
Spit-shine a policeman's boots so desperate for some more
Waiting for the new dawn that was promised, but morning never comes

How can you see the light when the meter's been cut off?
Expected to be grateful for a kick square in the guts
They make you think of better times all the while pronouncing

further cuts
Everywhere you look, it's the land of hope and glory
Britannia rules the waves, another Churchillian story
The marriages of princes revering dead dictators on the BBC

We're all in this together they shout from marble piles on The Mall
Elbow grease and carry on these Anglo-Saxon values from before.

Coming and Going on Curle Street

There's a murder of crows up on Curle Street
Black-clad, they flutter and flap
While an old dear deeks down through crow's feet
From a home at the top of the high flats

He is awake. He is awake. He is awake. The springs in the cheap
mattress makes a pinging noise just to confirm the fact that,
yes, he is indeed awake. There's no alarm, as there's nothing to
wake up for, no job, no leisure, no urgent commitments. Nothing
to prise Eck from the bargain bed frame but some misplaced
sense of Calvinistic duty that he should, at least, be doing
something.

The PVC round the windows in the room shudders, barely
holding the poorly sealed and thus heavily condensed glass,
as the number 2 passes by, destination Baillieston or Faifley,
depending on which way you decide to look up or down Dumbarton
Road. Peristalsis style, this ill-fitting collection of human,
glass, metal and rubber hauls itself, down through the Glasgow's
guts and out to the East, soon to be regurgitated back the
way, the old corporation double-deckers, decked out in their
privatised mauve finery.

The yard, the shipyard! The industrious men of the Clyde!
The beating heart of the second city of empire. Hard steel,
fire, brimstone, and sweat. Ah, the old trope. There's still
movement, heavy goods come into the industrial estate the deals
now with the management of waste, the processing of rubbish.
Former specialists in construction quickly lend themselves to
taking thing apart. Whatever it is, wood, plastic, metal, people
send it here, as if some long forgotten knowledge of what to do
with raw material still lingers on in the brickwork. Waste. It's
somebody else's problem now.

Unemployment is an anathema to Scottish working culture; it was no different to Eck, the state of impotent idleness creeping up on him as the day passed interminably slowly. The constant feeling of original sin, sloth, a lack of discipline. Lie long enough in bed and he could practically feel the bristles of John Knox's beard on the back of his neck like a reminder of what he must do but can't, or what he could do but mustn't.

Eck takes the stairs; the lift is stricken by neglect and paranoia of the virus. Marjorie Dawsholm is on the second floor attempting to sweep the landing. Marjorie hears Eck's footsteps and disappears inside quietly. As Eck passes her door he hears pressure on the landing and sees a flicker of an eye through the peephole. Each know that the other is there, and that is somehow reassuring. Like the clumsy romances of little children, both Eck and Marjorie stand a moment on each side of the door, silent and pensive, before Eck continues on his way down and Marjorie breaths a sigh, one not exactly of relief.

Outside, under the Union colours of the Orange Hall, whose wall, sprayed shamrock green, continues the tired to and fro. Eck begins his daily penance. Round the corner he walks. Diesel and dust, every lorry's perfume wafts over the street as they trundle by, loaded with the unwanted things of others. As the lorries drive away, so does any evidence of their being here. The café opens with a hot blast of greasy air, tempting folk off the scrapheap for a full belly, the wafting comfort of roll and filling, offered instruction to the server unto the order of how things should be done. Roll and sausage. Roll first then sausage. The other way round never made any sense anyway.

Norrie, the owner, smiles a smile hewn from 50 years of service. There's no dialogue for a while, the two men incommunicado the way that only Scots are able to do. A nod, a nudge, the hint of a smile, and a fat-stained white bag crosses the counter. Eck squeezes the alcohol gel on his hands, watches as it slides across the frozen palms, then rubs it deep into the dry cracks of his skin. He eats outside despite the cold, watches the van depot, its comings and goings. Mainly removals, people come here in order to go somewhere else. People come and people go. Rubbish comes and stays.

The old railway is now a bicycle path, its signs offering the highland, picture postcard glamour of Loch Lomond. The riders are like the vans, they come here to go somewhere else, the forgotten corner of Clydeside being a necessary evil in a longer storyboard leading to something altogether brighter. Eck wanders the path, but no matter how strong his determination, he can never get passed Yoker, it gets too tiring after that, and he reluctantly allows himself to be swallowed back down towards the high flats and the familiar. The cyclists flit past with the ping of a bell, they've got the gear, the fine looking bicycles, the look in their eyes that shows Eck that they have a luxury that he doesn't; they can come and go as they please.

He boards the bus outside the health centre; with a shuddering jolt it starts and joins the laden-lorries back down to Whiteinch. The bus drops him outside the high-flats beyond which is the scrap yard. Eck thinks about the scrap, wood and metal, flesh and bone, the screeching of wire cutter, or the slow murmur of a many men. We have been brought here, and left here, piled up neatly and abandoned to some notion of regeneration. Someone else's refuse, someone else's problem. Some vans pass by taking new, rebuilt things to new, rebuilt places. Eck goes back inside.

Marjorie is there again, Eck doesn't see her, but he knows she's there. The tell-tale creak of uneven floorboards in uneasy union with badly-fitted linoleum give away the fact that Marjorie has been waiting for Eck to get back. They used to talk, but the constant media frenzy that heralded finality for people of their age first led them to brief words of disbelief, and then after a while, no words at all. Still, she feels safe knowing that Eck has come back. In a transitory neighbourhood, Eck is a rare pillar of permanence.

Eck enters the flat, cold from the shoogley window. He should get it fixed, like many other things, it is in need of an overhaul, pulled out and put back in again. A new start. The crows scatter from the windowsill as he enters the room, circling high above the block, coming and going, knowing that Eck may leave, but he will always be back. He is part of it. He is here. He is not going.

Absent-minded television, crosswords, sensationalist headlines, tinned food, microwaves. Streetlights, starting off pink turn slowly amber, lollipops of lit up cold and rain. Night-time is better; there is some sense of accomplishment, just for having made it to the end of another day. Like the scrap the lorries come and they go, complete in a circular way, finishing the well-trodden narrative provides Eck with a degree of closure, a comfort that will be shattered tomorrow by the inevitable progress of the number 2 bus and the scrap men's arrival.

Twa corbies sit oot oan the windae
Ken jist whit it is that ye maun
They'll no care if you dae or ye dinnae
But they ken if yer comin' or gaun.

BETHANY RIVERS

is a poet born in Yorkshire, living in Shropshire. She has been shortlisted for: Overton Poetry Prize (2019); Snowdrop Poetry Competition (2019). Published pamphlets: *Off the wall* (Indigo Dreams, 2016); *the sea refuses no river* (Fly on the Wall Press, 2019). Victorina Press published her book, *Fountain of Creativity: ways to nourish your writing*. She is editor of *As Above So Below*, an online poetry magazine. She received a Pushcart Prize Nomination in 2016. She has been teaching and mentoring writers for 15 years. www.writingyourvoice.org.uk

Posted on the quiet

Finally, last night, I did it.
Although I'm now sitting
in a cell in this stinking jail

of sweat and fear, I'm grinning.
I stole in to the private rooms
in Westminster and I graffitied

on every wall and every mirror
the names of all the benefit suicides.
I prit-sticked photos to MPs' desks,

sellotaped them on plush seated chairs.
I then confettied the Speaking House
with photos of Aunt Beryl (put her head

in the oven), odd-job-man-Billy always
ready with a smile (took an overdose),
young Sally (mother of twins) hung herself,

stuck them down with chewing gum
along the central aisle,
all the way to the Speaker's chair.

Truths

1984 was meant to be a warning

flies on the eyelids
of the old man
fallen
in his own kitchen

1984 was not meant to be a manifesto

the woman in the bus queue is not lying
she is not lying in the supermarket queue
paper pushers trailing from no. 10 think she's lying
she is now lying in the bath with her wrists slit

1984 was not meant to be a promise

an adult-child sits alone in the corner
it does this all day
from the moment it wakes up
to the moment it's allowed to sleep
it is not allowed to speak sing or shout
each of the four walls is filled
floor to ceiling TV screens
instructing it
deconstructing it

1984 was not meant to be a manual

there's a thief in the office of statistics
stealing all numbers you can't sit on
removal & readjustment of tiny black & white figures
there are no suicides no poverty no pit of despair

1984 was not meant to come true

the news is created everyday to reflect
refract delete what may or may not be
fake news and we desperately need to know
who is writing the script now and why

1984 was not meant

Outsider

One of those hot unusual days that were becoming the norm. I
wanted to get inside outside of the heat into the shade and I
remembered my sister's words: go sit in churches, whenever you
get the chance. I'm not religious, but she knows my state of
mind well.

> on the threshold
> links of chains
> dangle and clink

Up the stone steps, into the acoustic temple. Kneel before
Mary, light a candle, make a wish. I like to see Mary looking
up to the seven starred crown, the cross fallen beneath her
feet, her white robes billowing, the blue sash at her waist
luminous.

Piano music calls to my heart, though my head is still stuck
in an analysis of resistance. There's nobody else in the
church, and then I spy the pianist, he's playing the high
notes only, one or two at a time, slowly, andante.

> angel hand
> on your head
> waterfall of light

Music unplanned, unwritten, unbidden, flows through his fingers,
speaks of every bird song that's landed in his heart, every
melody that's played through his dreams, every slight of wind
in a tremulous poplar.

> homeless man
> half full bottle of water
> on top of the piano

When he stops, I approach. Tell him the music is beautiful.
He says he can't take all the credit. I call him a conduit.
He says he has a deep sense of sadness even when he touches
happiness.

> *hiraeth*
> I whisper
> he whispers back

He says we're all imprisoned, like water frozen in a mould. He
wants to break free, yet not be left on the outside looking
in.

> moisture gathers
> wants to be rain
> fall in a river

ANNE ROUSE

A former health worker, Rouse's three collections are published by
Bloodaxe. *Sunset Grill* (1993) and *Timing* (1997) were Poetry Book Society
Recommendations. *The Upshot: New and Selected Poems* was a *TLS* Book of
the Year, selected by Sean O'Brien, in 2008. Her work has also appeared
in *The Guardian, London Review of Books* and other journals, and in the
US, *The Atlantic* and *Poetry*. Her plays have received rehearsed readings
in Edinburgh, Glasgow, Hastings and Virginia, USA, and *Notes from a Moon
Station*, a video poem, recently featured on the website PoetryFilm as
well as on her new YouTube channel. Raised in Virginia, she attended
the University of London. She now lives in St. Leonards-on-Sea, East
Sussex. A new collection, *Ox Eye*, will be published by Bloodaxe Books
in the spring of 2022.

Request to a Neighbour

You knock, she waves you in
for a quiet swirl of gossip
over Hobnobs and Ceylon.

Enter the son and husband
she caters to with such finesse.
Next door, hi, you venture,

minding how you go.
Any one of them might parley, singly.
Together they're of one blood.

Diagonal across the gate, the father
coughs too much; the son's long-averted jade-
brown eyes are closing, set in shade.

All power to her, cleaning in Marigold gloves
what love fashions. You can see the joins.

VANESSA SADRI

was born on 16 November 1993 in Schwäbisch Gmünd, Baden-Württemberg, Germany, and is half-Sudanese. She has worked in retail since she was 16. An abuse survivor, she suffers from PTSD, BPD, and stress-induced seizures, for which she is, on her third attempt, finally in receipt of PIP.

The Portsmouth Bridge

'Physiotherapist' the blue sign reads as a mentally fragile young girl walks up the narrow stairs of the private clinic.

As she enters the upscale waiting room a sense of misplacement comes over her...

You are nothing... Look at those chairs, you're so fat you won't fit...

"Can I help?" A rough voice shakes her awake from the auditory torture that she is so used to.

"ATOS health assessment" she replies quietly.

The mumpish woman that has her future independence in her hands walks her into a cold, dark and uninviting room.

As the young girl answers unreasonable tick box questions she looks around the room while her voices bombard her...

Do you REALLY think you're worth of any support? You are a vile person... Look at yourself... Dirty and repulsive!

"Could you answer the question please?"

She is once again being snapped out of her auditory torture.

"You said on your form you self harm?!"

"Yes" she replies ashamed and defeated.

"Roll up your sleeves" the hardened and detached assessor says.

The young woman looks up in disbelief while shaking her head. "Refused to answer question" the callous assessor types on her keyboard. "Thank You. You will hear from the DWP in 6-8 weeks."

She is being led out back to the narrow stairs.

In her head fear and desparation mixes with self-hatred and anger towards the system.

The system that had betrayed her time and time again.

As she dissociatively walks towards the bus stop past the river and the parks, past the carefree children playing, she looks up.

Up at her only option. The only thing that would give her freedom. The only choice the demons in her mind would approve.

The Portsmouth Bridge.

(Author received a brown envelope 6 weeks later. 0 points)

CLARE SAPONIA

is a London-born, Berlin-based writer, artist and linguist. She is the author of two poetry collections: *The Oranges of Revolution* (Smokestack Books, 2015) and *Copyrighting War and other Business Sins* (Olympia Publishers, 2011). Her poetry has featured in various magazines and anthologies, including *Witches, Warriors, Workers* (Culture Matters, 2020), *Kakania - An Anthology* (Austrian Cultural Forum 2015), *The Robin Hood Book - Verse versus Austerity* (Caparison, 2012), *Emergency Verse - Poetry in Defence of the Welfare State* (Caparison, 2011) and shortly, *The Cry of the Poor* (Culture Matters, 2021). In her writing and collaborations, she aims to move dialogue beyond the comfort zone. She is currently working on her fourth collection, as well as two fiction projects.

Brainage

At the welcome gate, they strapped barbed wire about your
savvy hands, fingers that are trained to perform tucks and
twists on precious organ grind in their sleep like they're
buckling shoes, carving out squamous malware, pin and bolt, as
they were born to:

fingers that have spent more time inside other people's bodies
than your own.

Fingers that have stood between life and death awaiting orders
from above.

Orders that now come from the Home Office, Job Centre,
Department for Work and Pensions: stay low, keep your eyes to
the ground, don't get too comfortable with the deft sweep of
your doctor's wherewithal. It's

dependents, not docs, they want: a whole hush of airheads,
not public service saints, makes them so much easier to send
packing. Your degrees

don't count.

Your skills, compassion and acumen

don't count.

You,

YOU,

with that spotless track record

within earshot,

go stand in line.

Jobber

I'm not built to work
not the kind that oils
the cogs of this hoggish
system, the kind of torpid
nine-to-five that turfs you from
your poet's stare. 'Cos hell, it's like
wrenching Christs when the words flow.

I don't do salt mines. I don't react well
to the slog of daily grind: to slave-
driving bosses who have
nothing better to do
with their brains
than pick
holes in
mine.

I've never known
how to holiday. I choose
time over money, minimalism
over comfort, between double-jobbing

martyrdom. I choose self-analysis
over psychoanalysis and hubs
over hives. Eating your heart
out does exactly what it
says on the pack:

bloodless
browbeating
hard-boiled beneath
a skirmish of yearning
until you learn to bite back

against the third degree,
the septic entrails of
arse-wipes who
drive you
further
into
the
ground.

And it's tough
if you're borderline
this and that, your undiag-
nosed imbalances spewing out

all over the show the second
you reach for your tools.
Today you'd have ten
toxic labels stamped
to your skull. But

we ignore.
We batter. We
flog ourselves like
carthorses to the knacker's

yard: work measured by
a cock-sucking bank
account not the
fibres of our
soul.

And
I can't
separate
work from art
and art from life.
'Cos I don't want to.

But I have to eat.

The importance of being an artist

That voice shrieking:
"You're a slacker"
IS NOT YOURS!

It's the rage
of the system
slamming its doors.

It's the whip
of red tape
that doesn't want you to feel.

It's the guilt
in your bones
that work doesn't heal.

It's the toll
on your health
that ancestors knew.

It's a caption of life
from only
one view.

It's the hand
of a master
gripping the leash -

a capitalist
purge
digging its niche.

Because the profit
that churns
and neglects all your needs

is the price
that you pay
for spurning your seeds.

JOEL SCHUELER

was born in London on 05.09.1985. He has a BA (Hons) in English Literature
& Creative Writing from the University of Wales, Aberystwyth. His work
has appeared in over ten countries in over fifty publications including
Pennsylvania Literary Journal, London Poetry Magazine and *The Brasilia
Review.* He is author of *Jim & Martha: A Novel on Eco Living* and *Love
Your Fear: A Quick Self-Help Guide to Managing Anxiety.*

Questions of Validation

Aye yai yai the show trial is here,
dust marks for the forehead
from stabs at x the last digger made,
dust marks for the forehead
to remind them of my asthma.
Introspective and unselfsparing – my attempt

at normal, but do I want to seem normal?
What was the self I wished not to spare
that I have forgotten? I wonder
if there once were balustrades
the length of the courthouse to prop up

the powerful. I am ushered in by someone
delighted they could pronounce my surname.
How can I be gobsmacked by anything
to come when I have been kicked
off the sick borrowing mercy money for the year

of my unofficial illness. I wait
to see if I'm a faker,
to see whether I'll re-embark the aeroplane
for the desperate I was ejected from
to learn if I'll officially be mental again.

'Dear sponger,

No parachute will be necessary.
Move away from the funds
without as much as a day to prepare
for your nothingness.

We wish you good luck
and then some to those
choosing between homelessness and suicide.'

It is known who it is from.
Known too is the outcome

if I answered the questions
the way they wanted.
The judge was my doctor all along.

FINOLA SCOTT

is a Glaswegian poet. Her poems are widely published including in
Gutter, Kist of Thistles (Culture Matters), *The Lighthouse* and *PB*. Her
pamphlet *Much Left Unsaid* is published by Red Squirrel Press. She is a
Makar of the Federation of Writers, Scotland. More poems can be read at
fb Finola Scott Poems.

Knowing the score

Without masks in thin jackets they haunt
the shopping centre dodging bored security
and gangs of old women leaning on empty trolleys.
They stop behind Primark where the poor shop for clothes
made by the even poorer.They know the cameras' blind spots.

So the wee perty, still oan Joe?

As dusk falls on the centre, window-shoppers head home.
Hands jangling loose change in pockets, the lads
consider the cost of shared carry-outs, the cost
of staying at home damp, dark and brimming with anger.
They think of the dangers of watching the big gemm
not on terraces, not at mates. But alone.

Schools out for summer

in the tumbleweed precinct
a can rattle bounces across
the car empty tarmac
is kicked again fiercely
hands in pockets three lads watch
it tumble in the wet wind
make no move to catch
or return
there'll be other cans

gie us yir phone ah've nae credit

no choice but to be here either
his maw's boyfriend is staying drinking
in the corner telly on full
house full of money worries
and coughing
he doesn't know about the lessons
piling up on his school website
hasn't a computer or cash
to feed the leccy meter.
Above boarded up shops scrawny seagulls
learn as foxes stalk fat cats.

Learning curve

Behind the off licence, in a close huddle
six teenagers laugh touched by Spring sun.
Hoods up they crack open cans, suck on fags
Trying not to think of jobs or how to Top Up
they lean close, snap and pass phones around.

Hey what gives wi aw the rainbows in the windaes?

Their fun tumbles downhill to where I walk
in the budding wood. Trees coppiced long since,
once thinned to encourage stronger growth.
I keep my distance.

JOHN SEED

is a retired gentleman-scholar, far from the strife of the state "welfare system" these days. He was nevertheless active in the Claimant's Union around 1971-2 and was one of a group of young people who tried to get an Unemployed Workers Union off the ground in the North-East at that time – while signing on every week. Joe Mills at the T&GWU in Newcastle gave support and as a terrified long-haired 21-year old Seed was dragged before both the Gateshead and the Newcastle Trades Councils to make an inarticulate appeal. It all fizzled out and he took another path. He is the author of a dozen collections of verse, including: *New and Collected Poems* (Shearsman, 2005), *Manchester: August 16th & 17th 1819* (Intercapillary Editions, 2013), *Brandon Pithouse, Recollections of the Durham Coalfield* (Smokestack 2016) and *Melancholy Occurrence* (Shearsman, 2018).

Henry Farley a very quiet man   having little to say
got out of bed about half past five
in the open door of an outhouse at the back of his cottage got
up on a four-inch set-off in the brickwork   then slipped off
a widower aged 67 suffering from rheumatism a shepherd out of
work   and given
notice to leave his cottage at Upper Woodford by Michaelmas
hanging from a beam   feet scarcely an inch from the ground

                              *

sitting on the pavement unconscious
leaning against one of the houses

Halket-street Canton in Cardiff

seven o'clock on the morning of Christmas Day
1891

he never regained consciousness and could not be identified

he died of chronic bronchitis hastened by exposure
2d in his pocket
William Shapland
labourer aged 61
without constant employment

or fixed home
and a great abhorrence of the workhouse

living partly on charity
and sleeping about in stables and outhouses
was found dead February 1848
in a hay-loft in Hole Water

*

Benjamin Colley aged 61
a charcoal burner living in the woods
near West Anstey

ill with pneumonia sleeping out
nights allowed shelter
in a loft over a henhouse

behind the *Partridge Arms*
a few days later
died on the road to the Union workhouse

Jacob Feltham aged 73
labourer on one farm nearly
all his life

walked seven miles
from Chitterne
an October morning 1904

to apply for relief from
the Board of Guardians
at Warminster

granted 3s a week
he dropped dead
outside the workhouse door

*

A poorly clad woman was found
frozen to death
on the doorstep of a public house
at Neville's Cross near Durham
yesterday morning Wednesday
27th January 1897

[These pieces are appropriated from mostly nineteenth-century English newspapers or inquest reports and rewritten. Without changing significant details.]

PENNY SHARMAN

is a published poet, photographer, artist and therapist. She is inspired by wild natural landscapes and the relationships between the seen and the unseen. Sharman has an MA in Creative Writing from Edge Hill University. She has had over 100 poems published in magazines such as *The Interpreter's House, Strix, The North, Obsessed with Pipework, Finished Creatures, Orbis* and *Ink Sweat & Tears*. She has published a pamphlet, *Fair Ground* (Yaffle Press, 2019), and two collections, *Swim With Me In Deep Water* (Cerasus Poetry, 2019) and *The Day before Joy* (Knives Forks & Spoons Press, 2020).

Stigma

There's no blood to be seen.

The only visible evidence
our faces in the queues,
on the waiting chairs,
in the cubicles of hope and frustration,
within the sighs of despair
gazing at the forms
all those words
that try to catch you out
as if we'd all got a degree in confession!

It's in our eyes of sadness
that for the grace of somebody
we are standing in this line;

like that time we had sex
just the once and that was
the last time I ever saw you.
Is it a crime to be a single mum?
It's so easy to hold on to a scab,
where no amount of scratching
can release the low self esteem.

God I was often hungry
as kids came first. For me
it was all about the idea of love,
that well worn cliché,
that it would find a way
into this life and all the
queues some of us suffer,
and we could forget
about the begging bowl.

JOHN SHORT

was born in Liverpool in 1958 and grew up near Ormskirk. He is widely
published, most recently in *The Lake, One Hand Clapping, Smoke, The High
Window* and *Poetry & Covid*. He's published four books: one of stories and
the other three of poetry, the most recent being *Those Ghosts* (Beaten
Track Publishing 2021).

Mexican Soaps

For months she's out of work,
transfixed by Mexican soaps
created to dazzle the poor.

Muscular hidalgos drive sports cars
from their lavish haciendas,
they are timeless, omnipotent

and angry, their egos swollen
with riding boot assertion
and fabulous hair.

They rule unquestionably
while workers bow their heads
to a thousand years of lies

passed down the generations;
assumptions imprinted into blood
that no revolution could erase.

Home Town

Poverty was everywhere
as the homeless drank
in leafy graveyards overgrown
with summer and cut-backs.
I slept one time amidst
those stones, the old century
wine-bright and dying.

We all had our little jobs
that did not make ends meet.
So due to this, were forced
to claim and break the law.
And under the canal bridge
the local sorcerer formulated
curses against injustice.

Now confusion circulates
the streets of this town
but church bells still chime
their artless repetition.
Last night in pouring rain
an old friend slumped
in a doorway with no answer.

FIONA SINCLAIR
lives in Kent. Her seventh collection is *Greedy Cow* (Smokestack, 2021).
She is a retired teacher with a gigantic feral garden and an imaginary dog.

Fear of Letter Boxes

She listens all morning for the letter box's warning
that causes her pen to skid across a page.
Careers downstairs scanning the door mat,
gingerly pokes a pile of junk mail where buff
envelopes often lurk like adders under compost.
Opens as if defusing a bomb.
Hospital appointments are welcome as negative test results.
Shreds Reader's Digest's practical joke.
Down grading her fear to code orange at a drift of white letters,
knows even these are not always innocent as they appear.
Sometimes, the friendly face of familiar handwriting
or an invitation surprising as a modest lottery win.
Still no 'all clear' by 12 o' clock,
she peeps from curtains,
catching the post man passing her gate,
exhales as if missed out of a house to house search.
Sundays, strikes and snow, she is a school kid
whose bully has been excluded for a few days.

STEVE SPENCE

was born on 15/05/1953 in Croydon, which is where he lived until aged 13
when his family moved to Swindon. Poems published in *Tears in the Fence,
The Rialto, Stride* (online), *Molly Bloom* (online), *Litter* (online), *The
Journal, Shearsman, 10th Muse, Stand* and *Tremblestone* among others.
Books: *A Curious Shipwreck* (Shearsman, 2010); *Limits of Control* (Penned
in the Margins, 2011); *Maelstrom Origami* (Shearsman, 2014) and *Many Red
Fish* (Knives, Forks and Spoons, 2019). Reviewer for *TITF* and *Litter*
(online). He lives in Plymouth and has been a key player in the Plymouth
Language Club for many years.

You Are The Designer

Are you loitering with
intent? These forms need
to be overflowing with
information. Here is an
eco-system unlike any
other, more than a million
square miles of shallow
but never stagnant water.
For the first time in history,
large numbers of people
regularly travel out of
their habitual surroundings.
You could save the other
half until later yet this
creature tends to dominate
its environment, killing
and maiming unselectively.
Are you loitering with intent?
Part of our timidity arises
from our unwillingness
to offend anybody but this
may be about to change.
Next time around he simply
flooded the terrain with data.
Subject to certain controls,
recreational activities on
this reservation may continue.
Are you loitering with intent?

PAUL TANNER

has been earning the minimum wage, and writing about it, for too long. He was shortlisted for the Erbacce 2020 Poetry Prize. He has a novel called *Jobseeker* on Amazon. *Shop Talk: Poems for Shop Workers* was published in 2019 by Penniless Press. *No Refunds: Poems and cartoons from your local supermarket* is published by Alien Buddha Press (2020).

"wakjsdbv"

there's always that crony in the jobcentre who does nothing.

you watch them for hours
while you wait your turn
as they adjust their comfy chair
or rearrange their pen pot

as landlords lose patience
as your stomach eats the last of itself
as jobs come and go

you watch them
refill their stapler
and stare into space

you see them typing
but you don't believe it -
you get up and walk behind them,
peer over their shoulder
and what have they written?
"wakjsdbv"
they're just randomly hammering at their keyboard
to look busy
unless "wakjsdbv" is some secret code,
some password to social acceptance?

well now you're in on it
and you'll use it

just as soon as
it's your turn.

after the ban lifted

your job centre advisor says you'll have to wait:
he's very busy today.
so you wait:
you wait while he serves other people.
you wait while he makes a cup of coffee.
you wait while he drinks his coffee.
you wait while he goes outside to smoke with the security guard
who chucked you out last time.
you wait while he puts the kettle on again.
you wait while he goes to lunch -
you wait that whole hour, staring at his chair
and then, when he comes back,
you wait as he serves people who've come in after you.
you remember how badly you need that 42.40 a week,
so you put your white knuckles in your pockets and you
wait. you
wait
until closing
and when they start ushering you out,
you say: but I haven't been seen yet
and your advisor laughs:
oh, I forgot all about you! he says.
you'll have to come back tomorrow

but tomorrow doesn't pay
the landlord today

and you wonder how fast
the security guard can run

as you grab the keys in your pocket
with your bone white knuckles.

job centre roulette

poised,
all of us,
our broke arses
on the edge of
plastic council chairs,
glaring
unblinking
at the crony
at the desk,
waiting for our names
to shoot from her
thin pursed council mouth
like a bullet from a gun,
like cat turds from a cat's arse
aptly enough
and it's the north west
and we're all called John or Paul
and when she says John or Paul
we all leap up
and charge at her
before she can even get out a surname,
we charge
and surround her,
pushing and shoving
and she's scared
but not as scared
as the Johns and Pauls
of this north west land,
when stomachs growl
and landlords growl
louder.

ANGELA TOPPING

is a freelance poet, born 2nd October 1954, in the North West industrial town of Widnes. She was educated in Liverpool and is a former teacher. She has had eight collections and four pamphlets of poetry published over the years, and her work has appeared in a long list of journals including *The Morning Star*, *The North*, *Magma*, *Poetry Review*, *The Dark Horse* and *The Interpreter's House*. Her work has been widely anthologised and she helped edit *The Robin Hood Book*, published by Caparison, and organised the Liverpool and Newcastle launches. Her work has featured on BBC Radio's Poetry Please.

Dole

Dolour not dollar
Latin *dolere* to grieve
Sorrow

Dolen, mediaeval English
give out alms to the poor
Doled out

Earned in stamps
from wages past
not given in kindness

Begrudged
jump through hoops
pay tax on it

Child benefit deducted
no replacement for a wage
poverty

The brown envelope
The Giro
the fortnightly

No extras
Not enough for basics
Giz a job

Signing on in the Seventies

meant joining queues of grey-faced men
shuffling in line, flat as caps, heads down,
then grabbing a smoke outside with others
robbed of work by Thatcher's dominoes,
pushed into falling one after another, a clatter
of shut-downs, making idleness from busyness.

All they wanted was a job: their value,
reason for living, keeping wife and kids,
scraping the rent on their terraced houses,
a pint in the pub before Sunday dinner.
Nor this shameful under-the-wife's-feet
uselessness, pounding the streets. Nothing doing.

I watched them as I signed on in uni holidays
wanting casual wages to eke out grant.
How could I accept work when they lacked it?
It could have been my own dad, except
industry had already scorched his lungs.
He'd taken over shopping and housework
while mum worked on, needing to be some use.

Notify Us of any Change in Circumstances

I followed the rules, told them
of my marriage at the next signing on.
No more dole, my husband had to keep me,
when we were poorer than ever:
our first mortgage, only one wage coming in.

I wanted a job, but this was 1976.
Graduate jobs thin on the ground.
Still had to sign on, just no money
for bus fares, seeing parents, food
enough to last the week.

Different rules for married women.
Left me no funds to go job-hunting.
Applied for everything I could.
A job in a knitting shop I'd have loved,
denied because I was 'over-qualified'.

LYNN VALENTINE

was born 24/08/67 in Arbroath. She lives on the Black Isle in the Scottish Highlands. Her work is widely published and appears in places like *Northwords Now, The Blue Nib* and *Ink, Sweat & Tears*. She had a poem commissioned by the Scottish Poetry Library in 2020 as part of their Champions project. She is organising her first poetry collection to be published by Cinnamon Press in 2022 after winning the Cinnamon Press Literature Award in 2020. She will have a Scots language pamphlet out with Hedgehog Press this year after winning their dialect competition.

Posting Icicles

The letterbox chokes on brown envelopes,
no matter how cheery the postie has been,
all morning I hear the echo
of his whistle hanging in the street.

The strip of grass outside the house
is ice-smooth, somehow the cold
clambers in along with the letters,
though there's hardly any room.

I pick at the glue to reveal the scars,
appeal denied, phone for interview.
I join the ranks of the drowned, the unwanted,
shiver on the sea of the living-room carpet.

STEVE WALING

Born 28/10/1058. His latest book is *Disparate Measures 1: Spuds in History* (Some Roast Poets 2019) and poems of his have appeared in many publications over the years.

Domestics

the firedoor is at the end of the corridor
but I always end up with domestic stuff
even if I start with the Bermuda Triangle

what do we get from these communities
I like Barry Manilow   and if the fire alarm
goes we'll meet outside the Chinese Buffet

and I'll tick your name off the register
how do they shape & help us   if you
wish   it's like a hand with eight fingers

what is   the Bermuda Triangle   to take
a comfort break   have you all signed the
register   where people disappear   have

you all signed the register   can you switch
off your mobiles   we're all just children
with bank accounts   or turn them to silent

what do we contribute   write about something
other than the preponderance of domestic
are we working for change within   then this

broadband is just right   said Goldilocks
the washing-up and irony   toilets opposite
the lifts   what about communities we're

not involved in   have we all signed the
register then we'll begin   light through kitchen
windows   write CV's   from the big old moon

Decus Et Tutamen

All my life in the presence of pound coins
won't be time enough to decode the words
etched on their sides but they mean
business to my creditors   I've heard

the clinking colloquy of coins in hand
it says "Look after the pennies   we'll
look after ourselves"   What they don't say
they'll leave only pennies to pay the bill

Bastards   Things won't add up but are good
at subtraction   Money swears   it says
"Fuck off out of here"   "Pleidol Wyf Im Gwlad"
which is to say   "Give me all you've got

and I'll still run out the door   Bye!"
and off it trots to   someone else's till
But then more coins come along   say "Hi,
we've got Nemo Me Impune Lacessit pal

we'll buy you the earth heaven hell
a whole warehouse of consumer goods
that will never be yours   Now sir please
sign on the dotted line each fortnight

we'll barely keep you alive   a fickle
bunch   eager to be spent   bartered
exchanged for thin slices of action"
There goes another old friend   off to

squander itself   When it's all gone
I'll count out the change from zero

lose it in my pocket full of holes

Universal Credit

"We have feelings inside us (where are they located exactly?' (Ben
Lerner, *The Hatred of Poetry*)

Are you looking for work?

coach drives over wheel
in France miracle it stays
upright doesn't crash

In that small room at the back of the house a feeling of loss
dresses for the date   Downstairs a secret joy blutacks this
moment to the wall before putting on its coat

*

Remember to provide evidence of jobs applied for

you are on the road
to Taizé God on your side
keep telling yourself

It pays to take short term or part time work

It may be cold outside but an obscure careless love is already
on the path   Is always waiting eagerly on the path for you to
get ready

*

You must declare
a job picking stones
no bigger than your thumb
from the playing field

remember this day
you were saved for a purpose
but you don't know what

Opening up work

Y'know   that feeling you can't quite put your finger on   half
dread half anticipation half something else   is picking a tie
from the rack

*

If you cannot give good reason
for refusing a job
you may be sanctioned

imagine yourself
bumping over and over
that same incident

Do you need help with your CV?

Hope in the coming spring is putting its face on in the bathroom
brushing its teeth   doing whatever it does in there

*

Please turn up for all interviews on time

this is the closest
you ever came to dying
thank God you're still here

Are you looking for work?

ROB WALTON

is from Scunthorpe, and lives with his daughters in Whitley Bay. Poetry
published by Culture Matters, The Emma Press, *The Morning Star, Strix,
The Interpreter's House, Butcher's Dog*, Macmillan, Atrium and others.
He collated the New Hartley Memorial Pathway text. He sometimes tweets:
@anicelad. Forthcoming collections from Arachne and Culture Matters.

masking tape

paint a face the bravest face
paint it like Adam and the Ants and
if you want to do some sort of good job
but obvs not a job you'll get paid for
use some masking tape to keep it in check
if you want to or paint it
like David Bowie or Lady Gaga
or don't paint it at all but write
some words on it possibly not permanent
marker style but if that's what it takes
for you then get yourself Sharpied up
and write all over your face
and you could try writing HELP there
or on the bathroom mirror or at work
or in the pub you see there are so many
things you could do and all of them are fine
but don't really expect them to get you anywhere
but hope and pray to your god or the lining
of your empty purse or your empty cupboard
or your other empty thing for praying
hope and pray at least one person sees
your message and understands it
and then hope and pray to your god or your thing
for praying that at least one person acts
on it hope at least one person acts
hope at least one person acts

it's about time

they stopped bringing out strategies and started bringing out
compassion started bringing out hearts and realised the worth
of each and every one of us and started looking at the millions
who dream of living just below the breadline because if they
were just below the breadline they might be able to reach the
bread and if they got the bread they might have the strength
to keep their heads above water and if your head is above the
water are you also above the breadline and are you able to
stand up and tackle that which is fundamentally wrong and able
to bear the burden of caring of looking for a job that paid
enough and might get you out of this downward spiral so you
might not be forced to live on benefits which benefit the people
with the purse strings a lot more than they benefit the poor the
disabled the carers getting short shrift and short change from
those who don't care won't care couldn't care less and don't
get me started on food banks the one time last resort which
has become the first resort but not a resort that they you know
who they are not a resort they would ever go to and are you
as exhausted as I am are you sick of reading about people who
get driven to all sorts of sad and desperate places only they
probably can't afford a car or petrol or tax or insurance so they
walk to sad and desperate places though it wouldn't surprise
me if someone in the government offered them a lift although I
swear down that's the one and only thing they're likely to offer

ANTHONY WARD
was born in the North of England back in 1975. He has recently been
published in *Streetcake, Shot Glass Journal, Mad Swirl, Flash Fiction
North* and *The Cabinet of Heed.*

Me, My Shelf and I

Every other Tuesday I sign on,
Or should I say, sign up.
Sign up to a full-time job
Sending out a hundred specs a week,
With no acknowledgement.
Eyes perched to the screen,
A social security guard,
In the hope of apprehending a vacancy.

I preferred the job centre when it was orange and black,
Where jobs were displayed on a shelf in the window,
Something you could get a hold of.
Like those video rental stores,
When you could physically pick something up,
Instead of scrolling despondently through a screen,
Online shopping, nothing on the shelves.

Instead of picking up the job and taking it to the desk,
Where they used to help you to get it,
It's like going to the doctors.
Gone are the days when they'd tell you what was wrong with you,
These days they ask you what's wrong with you.

What's wrong with me?
I'm an old tin of creosote
Stuck on the bottom shelf.
Where I was once put to use,
I haven't been used in years.
Just a familiar sight and smell,
Pushed aside for the new-fangled.

CATHY WHITTAKER

was born in the Lake District in 1956. She is currently working on a
pamphlet of poems about growing up in the Lakes, it was longlisted
for Frosted Fire Firsts Cheltenham Poetry Festival and commended for
the Geoff Stevens Memorial Poetry Prize, Indigo Dreams. She has been
published in many magazines, including *Under the Radar, Prole, The
Interpreters House, Envoi, Southlight, Obsessed with Pipework, Mslexia*.
She was shortlisted for the Bridport Prize. She has a sequence of poems
in *Quintet* (Cinnamon Poets). Her poems have appeared in anthologies
including, *#Me Too*, edited by Deborah Alma, and in *This Place I Know*,
edited by Kim Moore, Kerry Darbishire and Liz Nuttall. She has a degree
in Creative Writing from Birmingham University and currently tutors in
Creative Writing and Poetry at an education centre in Rugby. She was a
Warwick Poet Laureate 2008 - 2009.

Assessment for Disability payments for Chronic Fatigue Syndrome

They ask her to sit down,
three of them in a row, suited,
a solid pine desk barricading them.
They ask her if she can feed herself? shower? dress?
On a good day she says. They're busy ticking boxes.
She speaks louder. *I'm tired all the time.*
They all stare at her.
The woman in a crisp striped blouse and skirt says,
you don't look tired. You look fine.
It's hard to walk she says. *Everything hurts.*
For a few minutes silence settles in the room.
But how did you get here? The woman asks,
you'd have to walk from the carpark wouldn't you?
They all smile at her like a row of nodding dogs.
Yes, she says. *It was exhausting. It took ages.*
You can walk. You can work. The young man says
with a wide smile as if he's trying to charm
her with his crocodile teeth.
At home she lies on the couch under the window
wonders how she's going to survive.
How can she make some money, live?
Wonders about suicide.

Although not treated as a disability automatically under the Equality
Act, people with ME/CFS can be treated as disabled depending upon the
effect the illness has on their daily life.

LAWRENCE WILSON

was born near Chicago, Illinois, in 1957, and emigrated to the UK in 2005. His fiction, poetry and essays have appeared in *Albedo One*, *Agenda*, *Gramarye*, *One Hand Clapping*, *Ink*, *Sweat and Tears*, *Three Drops from a Cauldron*, *Stone*, *Root and Bone*, *Best of British*, *The Poetry of Roses*, *The Pocket Poetry Book of Marriage*, *The Pocket Poetry Book of Cricket*, *The Darker Side of Love*, on Salon.com and in other journals and collections. His first two collections, *The April Poems* and *Another April*, are available on Amazon, as is his latest, *An Illustrated April*, along with his children's novel, *Mina*, Etc.

Patron Saints

is there a patron saint of anger? Of despair?
for I would pray to such a one
for sweet alleviation, yes, but more for strength
the grace to cope, embrace endurance

and, with fingers crossed and hand on heart
to summon down celestial lightnings
strike at those who smirk and posture
relying on immunity of wealth

were I the saint of anger, there would be
innumerable piles of gently smoking ash
and fewer preening paladins
to claim their right to rule at our expense

Angry, Sad, Exhausted

angry, sad, exhausted
in that order (or reversed?)
in a world run by rich men
whose morals are perverse

afraid of revolution
ashamed to be afraid
but—angry, sad, exhausted
by this world that they've made

a world in which I've profited
engaged, enjoyed, explored
now angry, sad, exhausted
I can't do that anymore

don't know what path will call me
what future comes, what cost
but I need to build a future
that won't anger, sadden, exhaust

MANDY WILSON

hate this government

hate this government....
I hate their lies....
I hate the way they patronise...
I hate their insincerity ...
I hate their use of austerity...
I hate their attacks on the poor...
I hate their degradation and more....
When they're gone we can rejoice....
And give the vulnerable back their voice...

Poverty has us stricken down

Poverty has us stricken down...
Whilst MPs laugh at us like clowns...
Austerity's a joke...
Their 11% pay rise is another poke...
Ian Duncan smith up for lies and cover ups...
These people I despise...
With their constant lies...
Pigs in the trough...
Snouts in the house...
Sickening and tragic....
Seems they can conjure up money like magic
For bankers and themselves...
While kids are homeless on a large scale.

I'm lonely

I'm lonely....
I'm lost...
Suffering and sad under the cosh...
Under the billionaires making choices...
Disregarding me and dumbing down my voice....
Leaving me in peril...
Leaving me to fester...
Not wanting me to eat and no one to pester....
It's all gone...
It's all lost....
The human race is just a nuisance and a major cost...
We are to suffer in silence....
Eat nothing but make sure you pay your television license...
The souls of the world are being sold....
You must sit and suffer in silence alone and cold...

Since the coalition have been in power

Since the coalition have been in power...
Could this country get any lower...
Daily articles of abuse and corruption...
Sending people on a path of destruction...
Media overload of a newborn king...
But on suicides and abuse of disabled not a thing...
Global warming and food prices soaring...
other peoples babies daily starving...
You're cold-hearted and callous...
Mean and vicious...
Saying how your food is simply delicious...
Taxpayers paying your disabled kids...
Biscuit bill coasting thousands of quid...
Selfish and cruel you want the poor on gruel...
Sending kids off to war especially if they're poor...
Something's got to give...
We are all human beings and deserve to live!

Ref: BENV / 21

GEOFFREY WINCH
was born and raised in Reading Berkshire. He worked for forty years full time, and ten years part-time in Local Government as a surveyor and highway engineer. Now retired, he is an active member of a number of creative writing groups in West Sussex where he has lived since 2001. First published in 1992 his poetry has over the years appeared regularly in journals and anthologies in the UK, US and online. Purple Patch magazine awarded him the accolade of 'The UK's Best Small Press Poet' in 2011. He is the author of six collections – the most recent being *West Abutment Mirror Images* (Original Plus, 2017) and *Velocities and Drifts of Winds* (Dempsey and Windle, 2020). In 2020 he was a Forward Prize nominee for Best Single Poem.

Fiction in the City

I close my book
on one more tiresome day

wondering what might happen next
in the fictional world

traffic sounds falter
into my planner's dream

slums
picturesque ruins materialise
as bijou apartments
penthouses with views
of concrete hills

behind closed doors
shop-door sleepers
become the nouveau-riche

suburban youth swarm no longer
from trains heading downtown
for a nightlife they believed
would last forever

the city's heartbeat flutters
fades

305

Job-Seekers' Allowance

no roof over his head
no regular bed
roughed it so long
he's lost his looks
doesn't care anymore
about who is or isn't on TV

she used to dance
a disco queen
dressed to the nines
now the clothes she wears
barely hang on
and she's no-one left
to telephone

they've had to forget
their fine-wine tastes
but they'd still love
a little treat
just a square meal
or maybe two
but most of all
a fair deal to prove
they're willing and able
if only they're allowed

Busker

Every day for weeks he busked, even months. Played a penny whistle: same pitch, same clothes, same melodies, same cap with its few coins. No trendy amplified backing-track, just his music: sophisticated, pure and simple. I often wondered how he made ends meet, yet so many times I passed him by intending that I would, one day, donate. Yet when that day came he'd gone, and I've never seen or heard him since. Now every time I walk down that street I still hear his melodies repeating in my head.

awkward
in my pocket, the coins
I never gave

WENDY YOUNG

reviews for Disability Arts Online. She has had a sequence published with Natterjack Press and has also been published in South Bank Poetry. She blogs for DAO and performs quite often (Survivors, Shuffle Festival, Liberty, Together 2012 etc). She also has a page on Creative Future's website. Her most recent collection is *The Dream of Somewhere Else* (Survivors' Poetry). Tracks of hers have been played on Riverside Radio on The Chiminea Show over Xmas - Wendy Young on Soundcloud. Three poems published in Magical Women Neurodivergent Magazine Volume One recently and guest poet at launch. 'The Time is Ripe and Rotten Ripe for Change' chosen for Bread and Roses Anthology 2020. Monthly Highgate Poetry Group Zooms. Lockdown has given her the opportunity to do giga in New York, San Francisco, and Swindon. Previous to Lockdown she was a guest on Boogalo Radio and Survivors Poetry Group. Website: wendyyoung.org

The 51st State of the DLA Poetician

Three grey stooges assessing my case
Cross examining like Soul assassins
My 'claim' for cancer and a great big op
Two years before
How elementary there's Dr Watson
And a solicitor and a mister
Whose names rhyme and whose paradigm is cock!
Fuck me! I'm in the dock: questions like
'by this time could you cook say an omelette and some peas'
No Dr Watson I didn't really eat!
'Was the friend you had staying just for reassurance'
Well Yes! Mister Cock
'so he didn't help you in the bath'
I couldn't get in it!
'do you have a hand rail?'
No I don't Solicitor ..OH NO I failed the crucial tick
The trick of these inhuman assessors
Belittling me because
I'm not like them 'cause
My road wasn't theirs, straight and up the M1
I've had A roads and B roads
Wine-dy lanes and slippery slopes
Inn-clines and declines, my hopes
Dashed 'cause
I'm not like them

My path is scattered with trying and flying and dying
What with this humiliation and Actors Centre rejection - I am
a failure
The devil works for RADA
Brother can you spare a dime?
Brother can you spare a rail?
The tears start to fall
I'm embarrassed with it all
Telling of my ablutions
I plead it's more than ticking boxes and
I'm looking at the man in the middle
Who tells me they're not here to give me this
or give me that
I say just give me what I need
To lead a normal life!

And leave before my dignity is tick boxed to D **HELL** A!

*In the corridor my humour's saved by a man with a knobbly
stick embedded with two different coloured eyes, shaking it at
the whole establishment... like a shaman, a Druid on Acid –
he's a good he's a good he's Ebenezer Good body who flails and
rails and he's still at it on the street… he's angry they made
me cry… But as I wander around the city of hypocrisy trying to
find my bus the anger kicks in and I'm...*

Swing Low Judas Iscariot

Comin' for to carry us off
The pendulum swinging above us
Has come to chop off our heads
To make us go
It's scalped us slow
Sliced at our necks
Swung us high
Swung us low
Jargon junta munchers
(*Here they come the jet set munchers*)
Waft Business diplomas
Degrees coming out of their suits
More managers than doctors
Meeting after meeting

Discuss over coffee aromas
Our lowly livelihoods
Decapitate our frontlines
Put us into a pyramid
On a PowerPoint chart
Boxed and accounted, neat and smart
No power
No point
Not even a one in 10
We are percentages
0.67 surplus to requirement in fact
I'm one of 6.66
In a sub paragraph
Of an acronym collective
Is this how a thrithjungar of the West Thryding/wapantake
should be treated?
If Remploy are employed no more
What the hell chance have we for
Survival of the death knell of the NHS
Swelled by greed and selfishness
20,000 soldiers aren't wanted - what hope have we?
How low can you go?

The Green, The Red, The Brown

From green to red to brown like the maple leaf trodden in the
ground the colour of pols will change from green to red to
blues

hues to choose but who?

Who can we rely on from red to green to brown envelopes - the
paper made from the tree from where the leaf did fall

From beauty becomes the dwp saying you're not getting anything
at all

or the brown envelope that never arrives (invisible) I knew
that brown envelope -

the

-        Longing the anxiety the waiting

-        The depression the wanting the needing the
           explaining

-        oh yeah I'll pay you next week I get me dole through

And it dunt come and yer made to feel like a pauper when
millionaires exist - capitalists are raking it in like leave
- oh howzit that a trillionaire can live alongside ye and
me that just wanna get by - just wanna cup o'tea - have a
sandwich - maybe try a fancy recipe = a few veg/fruit suits
me - don't houses in Tahiti or boats moored in Greece or a big
ARCADE of clothes groups to satisfy me - all I need is a bit
to get by and write poetry and to work in my small job in the
nhs (wiart the worry of being axed)

I don't need More More More as the song goes (how dya like
it?) just give me my little bit to help me bloody grey suited
assassins telling me I don't deserve it - not needy enough
- I haven't got a bath rail - I don't tick the box - YEAH I
could but I could quite easily fall and there's no one to
catch me - just like in that net that you set before me to
catch me out - oh YEAH Brown Envelope will turn up if I don't
pay me licence fee or a loan you see

Yeah - you'll get me then - but just that few quid to get me
by - huh - just spit in my bloody eye

And just look at all the leaves now - trodden in the bloody
ground by trendy feet in designer shoes/boots or trainers
that that woman over there really wants to get for her
nephew or niece or a son or a daughter for Christmas - but
it's not gonna be is it? THAT DESIGNER LABEL ON THAT TRENDY
BOOT TO KICK US WITH - don't need middle class liberal elite
apologists either - yeah I like your intention I thank you
but you know it's sweet when you can go home to your log fire
- your warm house - be higher and mightier than me - you're
still not living my life

Coz we are the ones that you can just laugh at and say - WORK
FOR IT - YOU GET WHAT YOU DESERVE - YEAH AND IT'S LIKE MY
MOTHER USED TO SAY 'THE MORE YOU GET THE MORE YOU WANt' even
if it's not what you want

Just like I see the sky change before me - from blue to grey
to yellow to seamless cloudy dreams - they'll dissipate with
the atmosphere and so shall I if I'm left here like this -
just listen to my world - yeah you could be a celebrity - be
homeless for a night - experience the agony - you'll still go
back to your luxury -

I even had to said to me you got this or that well it didn't
come without tenacity - coz wiart it - who knows where I'd be
- sometimes I'm as happy as that full red berry in the tree
- but that'll be wizened soon and if I don't watch it I will
be too - coz I'm just THAT far away from being where I don't
wanna be - where I've been before and I don't wanna see it
again - but what I wanna do is highlight YOU - I can't do much
but I can write a poem - I can donate to to charity - can't
give much but it's my bit so don't think I patronise You

This is from you to me to you - it's an invisible envelope and
inside is all your hopes and dreams - I really hope you get
what you need

Might be yellow grass on the knoll might remind of certain
politicians - pollarded

ERIK ZOHA

(1968-2021). Poet, history buff, Millionaire finalist, music/art, SNP, LFC/football/rugby. Anti-Tory. He liked photography and exploring the Scottish countryside, and fought against cuts to disability benefits.

Personal Independence Payments: AKA Disabilities, Diseases, Disorders, Diagnoses (that cut no ice with DWP)

Pleurisy
Emphysema
Radiology treatment
Spina bifida
Osteo-arthritis
Neuropathy
Amputated limbs
Lyme's disease

Irritable bowel syndrome
Narcolepsy
Depression
Epilepsy
Paralysis
Early-onset Alzheimer's
Numbness
Deafness
Eating disorders
Cancer
Eczema

Palpitations
Asthma/autism
Yellow fever
Multiple sclerosis
ECG tests
Nephritis
Traumatic stress disorder
Stroke/sepsis

PIP Stress

Gut wrenching
Head banging
Morale sapping
Pressure cooking
Brain draining
Demotivating
Time wasting
Logic defying
Piss-taking
WTF-ing
PIP stress!

(Inspired by Pepsi - *have a nice day y'all*)

ATOS Capability Assessment Client

Atrophying
Thieving
Over-dependent
Swindler

Cheating
Apathetic
Parasite
Antagonistic
Benefits tourist
Idle
Lying
Indolent
Tardy
Yobbish

Anonymous
Scrounger
Skiver
Expensive
Spastic
Sponger
Malingering
Expendable
Non-entity
Time-wasting

Crackdown

We're having a crackdown,
we're having a crackdown
on festering disabled, the old,
NEETs & students, migrants,
single mums, minimum and
average wage people, anyone
else we disapprove of.
Because alas and alack,
they're a pain in the crack.
Spongers & scroungers, track down.

All In It Together?

Superhumans inspiring a generation |Festering scroungers
Deserving of sponsorship millions |Undeserving poor
Hardworking medallist role models |Idle, written-off, no hope
Over-achieving every day |Potential thwarted
Select, elite hundreds |Malingering millions
Full work/social diary |Getting through the day
Respected, appreciated, |Disrespected, patronised
Benefits downgraded/withdrawn
Same sanction, different outcome

End Of Year Accounting

Bureaucratic ESA50 form-filling
Ahead of tick-box benefits review
Worst summer in 100 years
Waterlogged holidays
To Easter Ross and wintry
Fort William just expensive
Ways to contract viruses
Austerity to go on until 2018
Unprecedented flooding only newsworthy
If South of Watford Gap
Jubilee hullabaloo, Olympics/

Paralympics national boosts
To morale. London economy
Back on track — Dundee's
Demolition derby; worth
The waterfront wait until
2020 or 2025, who knows,
Chelsea managers and BBC DGs
In & out the revolving door,
Intermittent writer's block
Throughout a stop-start-stop
Year that outstayed its welcome
By the end of August
So, not many highlights to relate;
Hopefully next year there'll be something to celebrate.

"What Do You Contribute?"

"And so, as a disabled person &
not in gainful paid employment:
What do you contribute?"
"Well, Mr Cameron, IDS, DWP/ATOS:
Not much really; IT/admin,
voluntary work, proof reading;
sub-editing, part-time care
duties for my late mother.
Writing, politics, disability/
mental health awareness;
blogging, social networking &
tweeting, campaigning, arty-
farty landscape photos/poetry
writing and open-mic readings.
Otherwise, not much really...
Why, what do YOU contribute?"

Pushing The Brown Envelope

Waiting apprehensively with stomach in knots,
Through the letterbox a brown envelope plops;
Gateway to no income, destitution, poverty -
Courtesy of rigged assessment, bureaucracy;
Ineptitude, delays, mandatory reconsideration.
Weeks, months of pre-tribunal real deprivation.
DWP should tell me Goldilocks level of disability,
Just right amount to garner base level of stability.
Finance-wise, is PIP a king's ransom amount ??
Or minimum re daily hurdles sick people have to surmount.
No laughing matter, what happened to human respect?
Atos assessor lies and DWP errors unchecked.
In these PC days of so-called equality for everyone,
Why is disability discrimination state-driven, anyone?
<Letterbox raps> Oh bloody hell, oh my God, oh shite;
Stress-induced brain fade, forgot PIP envelopes are white.

Acknowledgments

R AYLETT. 'Rule Britannia' was published online in the *International Times* in July 2019, 'Social Security' was published online in *I am not a Silent Poet* in July 2017.

B BARNES. 'Raft' has previously appeared in the collection *The Lovelife of the absent minded*, Phoenix Press, 1993; 'Review' previously appeared in a collection published by Utistugu Press 2003; 'the visitants' appeared in the magazine *Pennine Platform*, 2018.

R BURNS. 'Demolished' first published in *A Girl in a Blue Dress* (Vane Women Press).

S L DIXON. 'Word association', 'Not for you' and 'Priceless' previously appeared on *I am not a silent poet* in 2018.

R GEOGHEGAN. 'fatigue' was published in the NHS poetry anthology, *Body & Soul,* and Longlisted in the NHS Poetry competition, 2019.

M GORNELL. 'In Sickness and In Wealth' previously appeared on *Militant Thistles.*

B FENTIMAN HALL. A version 'Low Mood' was previously published in *Foxtrot Uniform.*

B HARRIS. 'M.E. Revisited', 'Kafka's Garden' and 'Invaders' are from the collection *The Huntington Hydra* (Caparison, 2019).

D HARVEY. 'A Foretelling of the Second Coming of Christ in which He will Cleanse the Department of Work and Pensions' has previously appeared in the journal *Raceme* (Bristol), and online at the Poetry Consultancy.

M JENKINS. 'The Assessment', 'Starin At-A Rain' and 'Inta The Black' are from *Sofa Surfin* (Carreg Gwalch, 2017).

T KELLY. 'Social Mobility & Child Poverty Commission (2015)', 'Monument' and 'Ken Loach - *Please Be Dan Dare!*' are from *Spelk* (Red Squirrel Press, 2018).

D KESSEL. 'Mike Mosley' and 'New Cross' were previously published in *The Ivy: Collected Poems 1970-89* (Aldgate Press, 1989) and *O the Windows of the Bookshop Must Be Broken - Collected Poems 1970-2006* (Survivors' Press, 2006, ed. A Morrison).

S J LITHERLAND. 'The Debt Problem' was previously published in *The Apple Exchange* (Flambard Press, 1999). 'Swan in the Weeds' was previously published in *The Work of the Wind* (Flambard Press, 2006). 'Eternal Winter' was previously published in *The Absolute Bonus of Rain* (Flambard Press, 2010).

M LONGSTAFF. 'Lost for Words' was first published in *Raiment* (Smokestack Books, 2010) and 'Intensive Care' in *Articles of War* (Smokestack Books, 2015).

H. MAGILL. 'The only place I eat biscuits' previously appeared in *The Poets' Republic,* 'The Politest Riot' in *A Plague of Poetry: Poems in the Backroom,* and ''Everyone deserves quality…'* in the *Morning Star.*

D MANNAY. 'Recovery' came 2nd in the Disability Arts Cymru inaugural poetry competition 2015, and previously appeared in the anthology *Please hear what I'm not saying* (Fly on the Wall Poetry 2018), and in his debut collection, *Sod 'em - and tomorrow* (Waterloo Press, 2020), which 'Missing payment' also appeared in.

J A MCGOWAN. 'Chronic' was first published in the *American Journal of Nursing.* 'Win-win' was first published in *Pentimento.*

C MONCRIEFF. 'Who Will Speak For England?' has previously appeared on *Militant Thistles.*

A MORRISON. 'Epigram' is taken from a longer poem, 'St Jude and the Welfare Jew', which appeared in *Shabbigentile* (Culture Matters, 2019), as did 'Waiting for Giro', 'Salted Caramels', and 'Kipling Buildings' (also a joint winner of the 2018 Bread & Roses Poetry Award).

A OWEN. 'Poems for people who never read them' and 'Memoirs of Job Seeker 328509B' appear in *Cov Kids* (Knives Forks & Spoons Press, 2021).

S PIKE. 'Welfare to Workfare' and '£53 a week' have been published in Steph's poetry collection, *Pétroleuse* (Flapjack Press, 2016).

F SCOTT. 'Schools out for summer', 'Learning curve' and 'Knowing the score' previously appeared on the *International Times*.

J SEED. Poems are taken from *Melancholy Occurrence* (Shearsman, 2019).

F SINCLAIR. 'Fear of Letter Boxes' was first published on *Militant Thistles*.

S SPENCE. 'You Are the Designer' was previously published in Shearsman magazine, 2011.

G WINCH. An earlier version of 'Job-Seekers' Allowance' was published in *The Poetry Church* in 2013.